ON THE OTHER SIDE OF THE
RAINBOW

A Sojourn Toward the Light

LONNY DARGAVEL

BALBOA.
PRESS

A DIVISION OF HAY HOUSE

Balboa Press books may be ordered through booksellers or by contacting:

Balboa Press
A Division of Hay House
1663 Liberty Drive
Bloomington, IN 47403
www.balboapress.com
1 (877) 407-4847

Because of the dynamic nature of the Internet, any web addresses or links contained in this book may have changed since publication and may no longer be valid. The views expressed in this work are solely those of the author and do not necessarily reflect the views of the publisher, and the publisher hereby disclaims any responsibility for them.

The author of this book does not dispense medical advice or prescribe the use of any technique as a form of treatment for physical, emotional, or medical problems without the advice of a physician, either directly or indirectly. The intent of the author is only to offer information of a general nature to help you in your quest for emotional and spiritual well-being. In the event you use any of the information in this book for yourself, which is your constitutional right, the author and the publisher assume no responsibility for your actions.

Any people depicted in stock imagery provided by Getty Images are models,
and such images are being used for illustrative purposes only.
Certain stock imagery © Getty Images.

Print information available on the last page.

ISBN: 978-1-9822-0718-2 (sc)
ISBN: 978-1-9822-0719-9 (e)

Balboa Press rev. date: 06/27/2018

Contents

Dedication vii

On The Other Side Of The Rainbow 1

Cassino's To Cardinals Part 1 61

Cassino's To Cardinals Part 2 89

Lesson's From The Light Part 1 105

Lesson's From The Light Part 2 145

Bibliography 165

About The Author 167

Dedication

To Mother Mary who protected me in my time of need. To Jesus for teaching me and allowing me to witness life on the 'Other Side.' For Christ commanding Evil to leave time and time again. To Archangel Michael for his help in need. For my loved ones whom i adore now and forever, Thomas and Maude Dargavel for the blessing of a great and wonderful life. As well to my teachers, in the physical who i learned so much from, especially Jean Toward and to those in spirit like Grandfather, Stalking Wolf, also to my other spirit guides and Angels, including my Grandparents. To Many Horses my kind mentor, friend and brother. And to lots of friends who i know were sent from above to help defend me and guide in times of despair and need. To OUR CREATOR for his mercy and peace and for telling me to believe and trust what i witness and to follow my own path and guiding me along each step of the way. God Bless

I HAVE TO TRY TO TURN THESE RECENT EVENTS into a positive thing. I have to use them as a catalyst that propels me to heal myself in a real and permanent way. The horoscope said that this year, remove pain; don't just continue to numb it. The only way to heal on a deep level is to understand your behaviour. Just saying stop doing destructive things that destroy your self-worth doesn't seem to be enough. You have to take a good hard look at what is going on and why. What's beneath it, what is the need that is being met? When i do this, i think i can move past the self-loathing and shame and actually find some good. We are all human and want to be loved. Love those parts of ourselves that we're ashamed of by realizing the motives behind the actions or behaviour. Our real heartfelt human needs and desires. One of my favourite readings states it well by saying....

... "we don't take on an attitude of perfection, rather, we draw closer to those things we feel are imperfect and let them be the openings through which the potentiality of the soul enters into life."

Care of the Soul - Thomas Moore

The underlying motivation may be good but the ways we attempt to meet these needs can often be self-destructive. We have to have compassion for ourselves. When we connect with the underlying reason, we will connect with our true selves. I suspect you will find a gentleness and innocence there. Rediscover and reclaim that innocence. By doing this, we can be reborn or purified; like the natives have their sweat lodges for purification. The sweat lodge is supposed to represent the womb of mother earth. We too, can purify ourselves by rediscovering our inner child. The one that wants to be loved. In a sense, we can be reborn as gentle, innocent souls who wanted to love and be loved. We now can choose things that honour and bring into life to this part of ourselves. I once had a dream that i talked with a deer and after so, i realized that the power in this wonderful animal. There is a lot of power in gentleness and innocence. I feel that power comes from the love we have for ourselves when we operate in 'good ways.' By doing things that make us feel good about ourselves we reward ourselves with love. We like who we are and this is the best feeling there is. You also see that the love that we seek externally can be provided by ourselves. Providing for ourselves may be seen as a lonely thing but i believe it is a necessary thing and is alignment with the ultimate reality of life.

First I want to state that having a loving relationship with a partner and good friends is something that we should all strive for and cherish if we have them. But even if we have them, we need to be self- providing. You cannot spend your life waiting for someone else to come along and make you happy and fulfilled. You are responsible for your own happiness. You are capable of meeting your own needs give carrying towards yourself instead of looking for someone to get it for you. Love yourself and you will not be so needy in relationships and will be a stronger partner. You will not need a relationship as much and be able to make wiser decisions in regards to whether a relationship is good or bad for you.

I read a wonderful book once called, How to be your Own Best Friend, by Mildred Newman, Bernard Berkowitz and JeanOwen. And what i got from this was to treat yourself like you would treat your best friend. Enjoy your own company as much as that of others; even more so i think. Buddhists believe that suffering is caused by attachment to people and things external to ourselves that we feel brings us happiness. In the book, Entering the Stream, by Samuel Bercholz, it talks about how we suffer when we don't have these things. We suffer when we have them because we are afraid we will lose them. We suffer when we lose them, while at some point we have to because everything is impermanent. You must think detachment. Attachment implies needing, possessing, ownership and control. Detachment does not mean not loving. Simply it is the grasping mind that causes suffering. Another wonderful book is Wayne Dyer's, Your Sacred Self, where he talks about our need to "stop looking outside of ourselves but to turn our eyes around and look inward." A Confucius quote from that book i believe states...

"What the undeveloped man seeks is outside. What the advanced man seeks is within himself."

I wrote after a breakup that you'll never be lonely once you realize you are always alone. Life is a constant separation. Life is like a journey. A journey of self-discovery. You begin it alone and you end it alone. No one travels the whole way with you. Different people come into your life and travel part of the path with you, side by side but eventually you separate from them. Your destinies, fate, the will of the Gods, place a fork in the road. There is a reason they were part of your life and there is a reason that they stop being part of your life. Even though someone who once was an important part of your life has taken a different path. You are still connected; they are still a part of you and you of them. I believe you are still connected in your souls and will probably be together once again in the after life or another lifetime, if there is still Karma or true love between you. I will share some insights and personal experiences about the continuity of life and past connections with significant individuals at a later time.

Going back, it is our inward connection that is the most important and needs to be nurtured. Talk to yourself, be honest with yourself. Forgive yourself. We must be able to forgive ourselves and to have understanding and compassion for the things that we have done that were ashamed about. Understanding should bring awareness that our intentions, if we look deep enough, were pure and we have to love those intentions but realize the ways we went about meeting those needs resulted in us having bad feelings about ourselves. We have to heal this by making a choice to stop making those bad decisions. When we make bad choices, we do major damage to our self-love. While positive choices encourage self-love which brings us strength and power and further motivates us to continue on this path.

I attended a workshop by a Native American elder. One of his teachings was called 'Eagle Feather' teachings. Just like the eagle feather has two sides, one of the sides being good while the other not so good, we have choices in every moment and we have to try to make the positive choice. Feeling good about who we are is a wonderful thing and encourages us to embrace life and to share our love with the world. I feel that many times, our bad choices may be subtle at first but they become like a slippery slope that lead to worse and worse choices. I feel i need to be very aware of these initial choices and know where they will lead, stopping them at an early stage is important to my success. I have to keep bringing myself back to that gentle innocent nature that i want to develop again. I made a list of some of the positive activities that i used to do and want to rediscover because they were healthy activities that did not cause any damage to my psyche or to my life. I want to become that innocent person again.

... "You will find yourself again only in the simple and forgotten things..."

Jung

I suggest you make a list for yourself and put it on your fridge or in your room and plan to follow through on your choices in your free time. I also make a list of chores or errands or issues i need to address and meeting these makes me feel good about myself as well. I need to find a good balance between my two lists. I need to make sure i reward myself by taking some fun time. My positive activity list is mostly about individual alone time that helps to build and nurture my relationship with myself. This i feel is essential in connecting to our inner selves. I myself am currently not involved with anyone and want to purify myself and get back to the person i used to be and liked. I would like to have the right person in my life to share some of these activities but i also feel excited about doing things on my own. Another personal note is that i just recently lost both of my parents and they were a big part of my life. I would frequently take my parents on outings alone or together and to me, these were the best things i ever did. These are sacred moments to me that i will cherish forever. Again, i do feel spending time with friends who genuinely care about you is important. Especially ones you can talk and share your feelings with and only ones that encourage your positive choices and behaviours. But i am talking about providing activities for ourselves. Developing a positive relationship with all aspects of ourselves. Truly loving the person we are, connecting to our souls and then allowing that love to radiate outward into the world. By doing this, we will also become better friends and better spouses, better children and better parents.

My personal activity list that i am just making up now because i am in the process of trying to transform myself and go back to being the person i used to be before i got caught up in gambling and other undesirable past times.

- Buy something for yourself; it feels a lot better than giving your money away to a casino.

- Read a book especially about transformation, healing, spirit or a feel good book. Some of my favourites are - To Kill a Mockingbird (Harper Lee), Never Cry Wolf (Farley Mowat). Some spiritual books i thought were great were Care of the Soul by Thomas Moore, Your Sacred Self by Wayne Dyer. I found that when i was first going on a spiritual path, the books seemed to come along at the right time. Another fun thing was going to used bookstores or thrift stores. It was like a treasure hunt.

- Go for a walk, somewhere around water. Ask that the water be blessed, put some tobacco in or near the water. A native friend of mine, Many Horses, says that tobacco is sacred and its felt 'big time' on the other side. You bless it and offer it as a gift.

- Go for a long car ride. Plan special outings for yourself, i.e., i am going to go to Toronto one day and take the trolley car along Queen Street. My Dad and i did that one time and our trolley car broke down.

- Join a meditation group or meditate on your own.

- Do something for someone else; give away some clothes or items. Give some money or food to a homeless person.

- Take Tai Chi or try to remember it myself from when i used to do it.

- Write down your thoughts and feelings.

- Go for a hike in nature even in the wintertime (don't forget the tobacco). While there, try to identify the plants and trees. Notice what animals you see. Try to find a nice sunny spot to sit in for a while and absorb that much needed wonderful sun energy.

- Ride a bike. You can take your bike to various places on the back of your car for interesting outings.

- Go to church. Try different ones to see if you can find the one you like. Personally i like spiritualist churches. Prayer is very healing.

- Send energy to the earth. I like to picture the earth between my hands. I will then fill it with wonderful golden energy like the morning sun. I remember how good the earth feels when it is warmed by the sun in the early morning. Sometimes, i will fill and surround the earth with a rainbow or sometimes i imagine i am holding a ball of bright white light over and around the earth in my mind. This light is so bright it burns off anything negative; feel the earth and all the creation - thank you.

- Watch a feel good or inspirational or funny movie. A few of my favourite movies are Hearts in Atlantis, Little Buddha, Defending Your Life.

- Go jogging or walking.

- Go to various beaches, camping

- Listen to your inner self about activities or places you should go or pay attention to signs that seem to speak to you.

- Go to various groups i.e., Buddhist teachings, Native American circles, meditation groups, nature groups, to meet new people and feel the excitement in trying new things.

If you have parents or children, take them on outings. It was the best thing i ever did and it gave them something to look forward to. It added excitement and life to their lives and it gave me wonderful memories.

Since their passing, i have taken some trips and i imagine that they're along for the ride and i actually think they are as i frequently can feel their energy and love with me and i will tell them how much they meant to me. I will pass on some more things that i have learned that have helped me deal with my grief at a later point.

There are some of the positive things that i have found were beneficial to me and i need to explore again. I felt good about myself when i chose healing activities and i was proud of myself for not doing things that were harmful to me in some way. I was also proud of myself for being courageous and trying new things and meeting new people. It was exciting because you never knew where it would lead. Of course, there's a part of me that goes oh ya, that's real exciting going for a hike in the middle of winter involved in a program that offered an 'owl prowl', hearing someone doing owl calls to see if she can get a response. Not quite the same as playing a slot machine and having a beer but i didn't lose thousands of dollars doing that other stuff so i have to remind myself of what's important and healthy and know that those exciting things are very dangerous, at least these other activities also allow me to connect to my inner-self to build a dialogue with myself to connect with nature. They also allow me to meet people who are on similar paths and to open myself to new experiences, learning and spiritual awareness and growth. They are healthy for the mind, body and soul. I used to do these things and i slipped for quite a while. So now, it's time to bring myself back although i know it won't be easy. Those vices have a lot of pull so i have to constantly watch myself and continue to try to make good choices in the moment. Knowing that often, choices are a slippery slope and knowing the pain there is when bad choices are made versus the reward of good choices. I have to always have a dialogue with myself and i have to be very honest with myself. There's no sense trying to fool yourself. Transformation seems to take constant work. Like i said before, you have to examine the motivation behind certain behaviours that you're not very proud of. For me, a big problem is that I recently got into was gambling. I have to look at why i went this way and i know that the motivation behind it was good and full of light. I wanted to have some abundance in my life and to share this abundance with my parents. I wanted them to feel like winners in life and i wanted to have good times with them and celebrations.

Spirit gave me this and initially it was working very well. I asked why this was happening and i saw that it was a gift from the spirit for the good work that i was selflessly undertaking. I took my parents to a casino that none of us had come to before. It was one of those days where i could tell was being orchestrated by spirit. Everything was great. We had a wonderful time and i took them out for dinner with the winnings. A short while later, i took my Mothers'car into be repaired because it wasn't fixed right after an accident. My Mother was in a car accident and it happened at the exact time that i was trying to depossess an individual who was causing me trouble through a dowsing technique. The demon went after my Mother. I immediately called a teacher of mine to tell her and she at the time was watching t.v. and on the news they were reporting how Mother Mary's face appeared on a grilled cheese sandwich. I recognize now the significance for me and my family, that our desperate situation was not ignored. After my mothers car was repaired there was still some damage to the undercarriage that the garage refused to repair,so i took it to another garage to get an estimate. On that day both my parents were busy and i had to kill some time to wait for the repair so i went to a casino (i was on vacation) and i won $300.00. When i called the garage the repair was going to be $300.00. I took the day off work to spend time with my parents and when i went to their house they both had plans for the day. On the table was a newspaper facing up with an ad for another local casino. So i went and i won $1500.00.

I asked spirit why this was happening and i saw two hands handing me a silver platter. Then i was shown a specific machine at one of the casinos and i saw two trees filled with crows. These to me represented future gifts or wins. I felt spirit was rewarding me for my good energy work. Mostly this involved sending energy to earth but also included good acts like donating money to charities like World Vision and World Wildlife Fund and giving money to street people. Also i was growing and sending sage to a Shaman. The problem started when i blew a big gift from spirit and the subsequent celebration i was supposed to have with my family. Shortly after the vision i mentioned i saw a hawk sitting in a tree and it reminded me of the crows. After getting finished work i decided to go to the casino. I decided to stop somewhere on the way. I had a strong clenching feeling in my stomach but i ignored it and stopped anyway. When i got of to the casino, that machine was occupied so i went to another. Within five minutes that machine that i missed, that i saw in the vision, went off. I didn't know what it paid but it was a dollar machine and the maximum was either 7 or 10 thousand dollars. I blew the gift from spirit. I kept going to try to make up for it. Without saying how, i felt that others were somehow able to attach to my energy and steal my karma from me while interfering with my ability to collect it. I went frequently to try to collect on these wins before they were all gone. I had a dream of two zombies sitting there eating all these rabbits which to me, represented fertility. I began losing and it just spiralled into a terrible mess. I lost the light. I was angry at spirit and at myself and sick that i couldn't share something wonderful with my parents. Another aspect of me began to emerge, one that i am not proud of. A part of me was being allowed to express itself through this manner, a lustful side. Maybe it is my shadow- self, but in the midst of gambling it didn't seem to care about anything else of course, except for my parents. This part of me has surfaced in the past with drinking and smoking, drugs and flirtatious behaviour. It all seemed to be connected. That part of me may be a part of myself or it may be a negative spirit that attached itself to me. In any event, i know that my initial involvement in going to casinos were pure and that i wanted so much to share abundance, fertility and good times with my family whom i loved more than anything. I have recently lost both of them within one day of each other and missing that big win still hurts me very much because i screwed up a wonderful memory.

I have to forgive myself and know that my intention and love for my parents was the underlying cause and for that, i feel very good about. There are other things that i have struggled with since their leaving not knowing whether some choices i made or didn't make would have kept them healthy and prolonged their life. I being a healer had to face some difficult decisions and i had to do it mostly alone because i did not have a clear enough connection with spirit to follow its guidance. I am trying very hard to forgive myself and the only thing i can do is to know i am not perfect but what was perfect was my desire to help my parents and for loving them more than anything in the world. So i ask them for forgiveness and constantly tell them how much they meant and still mean to me. Forgiving ourselves is very hard but it is the most important thing. We have to love ourselves, even though we make mistakes.

Again, knowing my intentions were pure helps me to come to better terms with events. Love is everlasting. I can still feel their love and their presence. I feel that i have gotten off topic a little but i needed to deal with these feelings right now and i am using this writing to heal my grief as well as trying to transform myself into becoming a person i can be proud of again because feeling good about yourself is the most important thing. When you don't feel good about yourself you hate the world and are easily led to negative and destructive behaviours and activities, which reinforce your negative self-image.

Going back to the gambling, i realized there is an aspect of myself that wants to be expressed and it loves the environment of casinos and to me has a sexual element in a lustful way. It is also connected to smoking and drinking coffee. This part of myself i thought in the past was my feminine side wanting expression. Maybe it is what Jung refers to as the shadow self or maybe my own dark side. I've seen how destructive it can be to allow this side to get too carried away. I also know that a negative spirit or energy becomes attracted to me encouraging me and keeping me involved in that space. In the past, i found that i had to honour that part of me that needed expression but i had to find healthy ways to express it and what seemed to work was taking on activities that were away from the mundane part of life and were adventurous and exciting. To me, this was done through attaching my bike to my car and going out of town to tour other places like Toronto. Another way was to try going to places and join groups or classes where i didn't know anyone. Seeking out these types of activities and adventures seemed to appeal to this side of myself and was much healthier. I feel that it is important to have compassion and understanding to all aspects of ourselves. Especially our own dark sides. I think we also have to understand that addictions have spirits or energies that attach themselves to us and to keep us feeding that addition. This may not be the case for all people that go to casinos but is definitely the case for me. I need to understand and accept that as well in having compassion for my past behaviour to help forgive myself and deal with the guilt.

Now as i try to transcend my grief over the loss of both of my parents i am focussing on trying to keep myself from going on the wrong path. I'm trying to use this experience in my life to rise above any negative or destructive behaviours to keep myself in the light and doing things that would make my parents proud. I also want to honour them and honour myself, doing things that make me proud of myself as well. I want to come again into my own power instead of doing things that are powerless or giving my power and energy away to unhealthy things that try to control me. Take control of my own life, feel the power gained in making positive choices.

Forgiving myself for falling is necessary because i can't keep carrying around the guilt, anger and self- hatred. Using the negative experiences of the past learning experiences and making a new start today is what my current attitude has to be. I need to plan positive and exciting outings for myself. Also a big part of keeping me on the good path is focussing my energy on taking care of my brother who has some difficulties. Mostly this involves keeping him fed so i need to keep thinking about what to make for suppers and what groceries i need to get. Some may see having to care for him as a burden but i realize that it is a blessing to me that will help me to transform myself. I have to be healthy and strong to make sure he is okay. This is something i promised to my parents i would do. Preparing decent meals is a real challenge for me and does take quite a bit of energy.

In realizing that i am also dealing with a powerful energy or spirit i need to focus on my spiritual health. I may need to seek spiritual help in dealing with these matters through prayer and through attending church to help sustain healthy living. I may have to acknowledge that in having trouble controlling the gambling and ask for assistance from God. In this manner, this addiction is much like the alcoholics pledge to God to admit they were powerless to their behaviour and ask for God's strength to help them to manage. It is important not to be too stubborn or in denial if you can't control it. Admit it, to be honest with yourself. Talk to God about what is going on in your life. Keep an open dialogue with God. Presently i have a lot of anger and resentment for God or the powers that be and i need to work through this and i can only do it by expressing my feelings and asking for help in coming to terms with my relationship with the universe. Having an unhealthy relationship with God and yourself will only encourage negative and destructive behaviour. It's okay to express negative feelings to God. Keep talking keep expressing your deepest feelings and thoughts. Confusion and anger are among mine at present. I asked that God, the universe and the powers that be please help me to understand why and accept the events that have unfolded. Maybe i never will understand them but i am asking for guidance as to what direction i need to go next to be aligned with the will of God. Faith that is shaken needs to be renewed. And that renewal may be constant life-long thing in attempts to bring about a peaceful and harmonious life, keeping trying to build on this connection.

I'm very upset with myself for i feel that i may have been given some guidance spiritually over ways to help my parents and i chose not to take it. I know that i tried this one thing in particular but changed my mind because i wasn't sure if it would be helpful or harmful. I wonder if things would be different now if i saw it through. Then i look back at what happened and say that must have been guidance. But everything that happens isn't guidance. It's hard to tell what is God's will, what is guidance from spirit and what isn't. I'm sick about it. What i am talking about is those magnetic bracelets. So i am beating myself up again. How can i possibly forgive myself? I have to remind myself that i love my parents more than anything in this world and i would do anything to help them. I simply did not know whether or not those things would have hurt them or helped them. I don't know when something is from spirit and when it isn't, i have also had some doubts about spiritual guidance. Obviously, it's easy now that they're not here to say i wish i would have tried this or that. Maybe it would have made a difference. Again, in trying to heal i confirm my love for my parents and ask them for forgiveness for not knowing who was best and ask God for forgiveness for the same. I was afraid to hurt them, so how do you follow God's will when you don't know what that will is?

I also feel i have situations happen when i feel that the spiritual guidance i was receiving was not for my highest and best good. For example, with various women that i have been led to i felt i needed something more from a relationship than they were offering and the timing may not have been right. I'm trying to come to terms with some of the bad decisions i made. Especially the ones that affected my parents. I don't know if i can ever forgive myself. I feel that my parents trusted in me and i let them down. I feel they would still be alive today if i had just kept those bracelets on them. I wore one and i took it off because I didn't like the feel of it. It hurt my wrists so that's why i took them back off my parents. I should have left them on my parents and observed how they did. I think i did with my Dad for a bit. I don't think his walking improved any. As you can tell this is critical that i come to terms with this. I just had another insight into why i wanted to gamble. It provided me with an escape for the nightmares that i have been burdened with. My Mother liked the bracelet and i took it from her because i was afraid it might be harmful. I think i made a large mistake. I once bought these magnetic insoles for my parents. They cost me a lot of money but i threw them out because someone told me they screw up the polarities in a person's body. This negative experience with magnetic therapy affected me as well. I should have researched it. I wonder if the magnets could have drawn arthritis and cancer from their bodies. Even through the magnet may provide immediate relief.

What are the long-term effects? It just isn't a natural feeling. Remember two things you don't know what the long term effects might be and i tried it myself and didn't like the way it felt. It hurt my wrist. I asked my teacher if i can and she said they were good for short periods. So when beating yourself up remember all the facts. In order to heal i have to get everything out. I need to purge myself of everything. Even though it is very painful i must deal with all my feelings. I know that i have to be strong in order to care for my brother. I have to heal myself first. One thing i have to remind myself of is what Sylvia Brown says in her book about transcending grief. "Know that they are in bliss my friend", Many Horses says "it's like going from skid row to paradise". I promised my parents that i would take care of my brother and i will keep this promise. It will be the most important thing i do for them. I will not hurt them by failing. Mostly this means keeping him fed and keeping the house in order and keeping him company and not being too hard on him about things, just get him to clean up after himself.

This will help me to heal and stay focussed. Caring for others is healing and i know they will be happy and i know they will help me. After my Mother died, my friend and mentor Many Horses told me "think about the love you have between you and share it with the world. That was her gift to you and you honour her when you do that. He also said when you stay in this energy or in the light she will be able to see you when you don't you disappear to her. Stay on the good path and she will be able to help you big time from the other side." My Father passed away the next day and i know he will help me as well. I have felt their energy around me, my Brother and the house quite a bit. I find it helpful to talk to them. Play some of their favourite music, take some drives and ask them to come along. I also try to look at things this way. If you care about your parents you don't want to hurt them by letting yourself suffer too much or by digressing into unhealthy behaviour or states of mind. Do you want to hurt them or do you love them? Another friend Raymon Grace told me i should feel proud of yourself for what you have done for your parents, he said i did everything right.I can only hope that its true now.

One reading that i have helped me to see things in a good way. It was something my Mother liked as well. I think it helped her in dealing with the many losses of her Brothers and Sisters and friends. I feel the poem by Henry Van Dyke, entitled Standing Upon The Seashore explains death in a very easy way and tells how they're not really gone just "out of our sight", it begins "I am standing on the seashore..." (It goes on to state), "Gone from my sight that is all."

It's very beautiful and i recommend that everyone takes the time to look it up who has lost someone. It soothes better than any therapy can. I think about how happy it would have made them to see everyone again. People that they thought they lost forever and this makes my loss lighter, my Father kept all the obituaries of his friends pinned to the top of his jewellery box. They meant so much to him.

Aside from feeling my parents energy around me, there was one occasion when i was shopping in a store that my mother and i went to quite often,there was a Van Morrison song playing, Into the Mystic, and i could definitely feel my mother holding my hand and dancing. She was very happy that i was buying food and going to take care of my Brother and myself and she was happy that i had just come from the hospital chapel where the pastor and i prayed for my parents. I also told the pastor how i had a personal relationship with Jesus when i was very young, although i had very little experience with religion. I miss the wonderful connection we had. It was a time of gentleness and innocence that i want to rediscover. I also want Jesus to come into my life to help fill the void that has been left. I want to have a permanent connection, one that will continue through my life and after. I don't care who you have the spiritual or love connection with. I think it's important that we connect with some spiritual guide or master.

My Native American friend taught me a few other things that i have found very helpful. He tells me that the spirits are always hungry. Aside from having a feast in their honour and setting aside food for them with every meal i asked that it be blessed. I ask that the earth be blessed and bless all those that made this food possible, especially the plants and animals. I ask that the food be multiplied and offered to my mother and father. I also offer it to the Grandmothers and Grandfathers and to the good spirits that they all may be fed. Many Horses says sometimes he will offer food for all the spirits even the not so good ones because they need to be fed too. I put food out a few times a week. I was told to put some tobacco out too. This will make sure they get it. He said there is a sign if they received it and don't worry about it if the animals or birds eat it. I think there is something to this and it also makes me feel good like i am still taking care of them. I have set-up a little alter and i try to keep a white tea light kept burning there as much as possible. I keep it in an ashtray for safety. When i light it, i ask that my parents be blessed and purified and taken and kept in the light. I also try to smudge their picture with sage and say prayers while i burn sweet grass. I feel that this all helps them.

I have some other issues regarding things that happened with my parents. It's very difficult to talk about because it seems so weird. I have some enemies who used negative energy against me, and i am very sure my family. Without saying too much about them, i often felt that the universe did not provide enough protection and help to my family. I will not seek revenge for i know that it's Jesus's place to deal with it not ours to respond to. This certainly is common knowledge to those that follow Christ and those that don't. I asked that my family be compensated now for any harm that was caused them and i ask that God please help me to understand and come to terms with the workings of the universe. I have to try to let go and let God. I feel though that my parents suffered a lot because of actions from others and that their lives were shortened and i don't think that that was fair. Do all things happen for a reason? Is the universe concerned about fairness? These were the types of questions that i will try to find answers for. I know that i need to find peace with God and to try to return to a place of harmony and love. I need to keep talking with God and expressing my feelings to the universe even if there is anger and resentment and i ask for help to deal with those issues and to understand. I do not want to carry those things with me for the rest of my life, but it's hard because of the great deal of love i have or had for my parents. Seeking revenge will not bring my parents back or change what has happened so i let it go and know that that is between God and them. I ask that God somehow make things right with my parents now, to bless them with divine love and light.

Last night i watched Deepak Chopra's movie the Seven Spiritual Laws for success and i came to a clearer understanding of where i failed. I did not follow my inner guidance and i became too attached to the outcome. I also believe that we are co-creator of our reality with God. So i guess i am just trying to bring myself back to being unattached and concentrate on doing the right thing in the moment. The Buddhists are right about attachment causing suffering. They say that when we attach ourselves to things that are external and we suffer because everything external is impermanent. We grasp onto things that we think will bring us happiness. We are attempting to fill a void within ourselves, which cannot be achieved by external things. We must find our happiness within ourselves and not let the external conditions affect this inner happiness or inner peace.

Dr.Wayne Dyer describes it well in his book Sacred Self when he talks about the difference between the ego and the spirit. Instead of letting the ego control things we have to connect to our inner selves and find peace. He refers to this 'silent witness' or soul as something that has always been there. When we operate from this deep part of ourselves we can remain peaceful, centred and balanced. We are able to let life flow. We can accept what comes into our lives and accept what goes out of our lives. This is nice and easy and we have to recognize when we are getting attached and possessive and gently bring ourselves back. Meditation is the best way to connect to this deeper part of ourselves. When i connect with this, i fill up with love and peace and i feel connected and powerful. When i operate from the ego i feel weak and i know i am giving my energy away. I also don't like myself very much when i am letting the ego control things. The best and easiest meditation is to relax the body a part at a time, observe the breath and to observe the thoughts. Realizing there is another part of you besides your thoughts, the one that is observing.

I am making a conscious choice to change the way i have been operating lately. I know the type of person i want to be and i am going to try hard to be that person because i like myself more when i am that way. To me this means being easy going, keeping things light and letting life flow. In attempting to transform myself i think of the qualities i would like to possess and i possess them. I know that it starts with changing my perspective as described before and trying to maintain it as much as possible knowing that i am human and can't expect perfection either. I also remind myself of what aspects i like about myself both presently and from the past and try to be my best self. I also reminding myself of what qualities i like in others and realize that i too can be that way in most cases. I do not feel that this is being ingenuine for if we see qualities in others we admire it must speak to us about an aspect of ourselves that wants to emerge. I think of my Mother's self-sacrifice for her family and her joy for life. I think of the respect my father's friends had for him. I also think of the character Atticus Finch in the book, To Kill a Mockingbird. It was said, "The highest tribute you can pay a man. We trust him to do right. It's that simple." "If your Father's anything, he's civilized in his heart." These people and characters have had a big influence on who i am and help to remind me to be my better self.

So the qualities that you like in other people can be used to help transform yourself. These qualities are one that we possess as well and they want to be expressed. This also helps you to look for and find positive things in others, helps you to be forever learning and growing and keeping positive attitude towards others and ourselves. I am constantly looking for self-improvement and trying to perfect my life is about self-discovery... The inward path is the only one worth taking. The qualities you don't like in other persons can be used to transform yourself as they too are reflections of your feelings towards yourself or aspects of yourself you don't like. These are projections or reflections of our own self-worth. If there are things you don't like about yourself then change them. By developing and nurturing our own self-love we will not be so needy or dependent upon others to fill the void. People who have this void i feel are constantly looking externally for ways to fill it and it's never enough because it needs to be filled internally. This self-reliant attitude does not mean you need to live in isolation but rather your self-love should radiate outward into the world like the sun. You are the source of love and peace, of light and strength. Many of our relationships too are reflections of our own inner state between our masculine and feminine sides. Our outward reality are manifestations of our inward state. It manifests these situations to come to terms with our inner selves. Use this knowledge to look deeper at ourselves and come to terms with all other aspects.

I read on the back of a bathroom door once a poem by Max Ehrmann entitled The Desiderata and i wish i could include the whole poem it's very inspiring but i better not do that, but it's something that's very easy to look up. Definitely a rare gem,very beautiful and peaceful. It begins…

"Go placidly amid the noise and haste…"

I realize i have lost my way in some ways and i wish i had followed this advice better, all i can do now is to bring myself back to a good path and try to do better. This poem is a good confirmation. Keeping light and following spirit has been very difficult for me. As another example of this i find spirit to be leading me in a direction very strongly with a lot of synchronicities, which i thought were strong indications of the path that is best to follow. On the other hand, it seems that every time i went to take action something was put in my way as a warning to stop me. This duality or mixed messages have been going on for a year now and i am still stuck on it.

I was in mediation that I needed to write in detail about this problem that i have been trying to solve for a long time. It started with me meeting a girl. She seemed to me to have a problem with an addiction I thought as she explained her life situation. Because of this, i was leery about getting involved and i put her off after she called. I ran into her again and she wasn't very friendly to me, which i didn't blame her for that. That night while in bed, i felt her energy come to me and i saw a vision on my right hand side of the two of us walking down a pathway holding hands and a hawk twice flew in front of us. I felt that that meant two children. But on my left side i felt an energy that was attached to me or more appropriately attached to her or this situation and this was clear to me that this energy was that of a demon. I sat there for a long time feeling this to make sure. I am familiar with this energy due to the high number of times i have been attacked by, i am presuming by the same demon. I was given guidance at the spiritualist church from my Father that i could walk around this situation if i wanted but i felt he wanted me to proceed because the girl was young enough to have children. I felt my parents kept telling me they would reincarnate as my children by giving me the message in various ways, 'field of dreams'. I prayed to Jesus to give me guidance and after church on Palm Sunday, i was watching t.v. and i came upon a show in which this girl was being offered anything she wanted. In this show, her parents appeared encouraging her to take it. The condition of this was that she had to join this woman and her accomplices by standing on the point of a star. In other words to join the dark side. I thought that this portrayal seemed to be uncanny based on what i had felt. As strange as it sounds, i had been having dreams and experiences, which i was approached by a certain group of undesirable type of individuals who wanted me to join them. This type of dream happened a number of times. Finally in one dream, i approached them and agreed to join as i did so, i saw an individual there who was watching over a group of people who seemed to be under the control of him and i saw him savagely and meanly beat someone up. Some others and i went to the aid of this person and helped them escape. I was then walking next to this person and i casually pulled out a knife and cut his throat. I felt energy leave me as i awoke.

There had been alot of guidance i believe from my parents and Hawk to proceed with this relationship. At one point, i felt my Mother was telling me she would be over the moon if i were to proceed. When i asked the spirit world what would happen if i got in touch with this girl and they showed me very clearly a horse's behind. A few times i was about to make contact and something signifying caution seemed to be put in my way. I eventually did reach out and when she called me, i knew my Mother was present as i was talking to my Mother when the phone rang. I talked my way out of it and immediately i felt my Mother respond by saying goodbye to me. I heard the song Forever Young by Bob Dylan. This was heartbreaking for me. I wanted very much to help my parent's dreams come true, for me to have children. I felt that i was put into an impossible situation. I do feel that Jesus guided me by telling me it was a deal with the dark side because the girl was under their control with her addiction. I felt i was shown this by seeing a movie on t.v. on Palm Sunday. I had asked Jesus for guidance. In this movie this girl was promised she could have anything she wanted she just had to come join the others by standing on the point of some kind of star. Her parents were encouraging her but at the last second she refused. This is when i decided to try to manifest another girl who was young enough to have children but was safe, clearly in the light, and hopefully on a similar spiritual path. I had one reading at a spiritualist church in which the medium seemed to pick up on this situation as he mentioned my desire for a family and guided me to keep moving forward. I decided to try an exercise from an Edgar Cayce book where you get guidance from your dreams and in the dream i met a girl who was on a spiritual path and it happened in the early fall. Again, i recently had a strong visual experience where a child was being handed to me. I had this happen twice and i clearly saw an angel's wing brush my face. A good teacher of mine felt that this meant a new start.

But this happened the same day that i bought a large angel, as well as a couple of religious cards, with the purpose of helping me to bring children to me. I asked how do i make this happen and i saw a highway with a billboard ahead that said, 'life'. This is what that one reading said as well. I'm trying to feel what is the right thing to do and i am not clear on what feels right but i do feel myself being moved from side to side as if to say no when thinking about pursuing that other girl.

I recently had another dream where a person i know who seems very knowledgeable about the dark side was dragging me trying to take me into a house across from where i used to live. He was saying "you don't know what you've done." This confirms to me that they are still after my soul or energy. These things just drive me closer to Jesus. You don't need to be religious to be close to him and the angels.

I've been having a very hard time lately. Beating myself up for not following guidance in the past and feeling that by doing this, i failed to save my Mother when she went into the hospital. There's not much else i can say about this.

I saw a movie called Powderblue, by Timothy Linh Bui that seemed to help a bit. The characters were all broken but in the end found redemption. I feel i can only be healed by Jesus. A little while ago, i was watching the movie, the Passion of Christ, produced by Mel Gibson. While watching this, i decided to send energy to Jesus during the time when he was crucified to help to take away his pain. Shortly afterwards, someone from a spiritual church gave me a message from Jesus who said, "that's when he was carrying that cross i was with him." The spiritual reader had no knowledge of what i had previously done. To me, this proves it is possible to go back in time and affect events as Reiki is an interdimensional healing technique and when you send energy distance does not matter. Apparently neither does time. As Einstein claims, about linear time being an illusion that can be transcended.

My spirit desires fun and freedom and an escape from worries and problems and at times control of the demon. The demon wants me to be unhappy, by me gambling and losing money and when I follow suit i am allowing that demon even more control. The demon that i am talking about is very real and i believe these spirits have the abilitry to attach to people and control them as they feed them and influence them. These spirits are very dark and want to hurt because of envy. They have no empathy for anyone else only hatred, bitterness and jealousy. They have contempt for others they see as having happiness, joy and walk in the light with wholesomeness. I awoke one night at my parent's house to see it standing there beside me and it grabbed me by the throat. Whether it is a thought projection from someone else i don't know. I do know that this spirit has done everything possible to make my life miserable including attacking my parents who were completely innocent, defenceless and very frail. This spirit should be very proud of itself. I reminded myself that Jesus teaches about not being veangful towards people but he does say to me "condemn the spirit not the person". Anyone under the spell of darkness has weakness and they don't feel well about themselves and there lives. This is what allows these spirits an opening into there souls. That's why the best solution is to keep positive about everything. When something you do makes you unhappy about yourself, examine it in detail understanding the intention behind my behaviour helps me a lot. I understand myself better. I know the reasons behind actions are more or less innocent. I forgive myself. I love myself even more and attempt to choose paths that will lead to me feeling even better about myself. I move from a place of self-loathing to a place towards self-love. My friend Many

Horses is right when he says "with self-love you can overcome anything." That's the problem if you don't have self-love you could be tempted to hurt helpless souls to feel your worth. This low self-worth is so great that one can actually take pleasure in harming people. It's hard to believe that anyone could be so sick but it's true.

I learned through experience that figurines bring in certain energies and you have to be careful what you possess. One of the experiences i have had was when negative energy was being sent to me and i saw dolphins swimming around me to try to block the attacks. I believe the dolphins came from a little globe with dolphins on it. Trying to decide whether to keep certain pictures or figurines has often been very difficult for me. I had a powerful guide and totem that i felt was no longer healthy for me to have for reasons that are complicated and unclear and i broke connections with it. I realized that part of the problem was that a few people i know attached themselves to it. They were some other things that made me feel it wasn't beneficial. While undergoing attacks i on a few occasions, tried to reconnect with this guide and it seemed when i did my Mother had a negative reaction. When my Mother was in the hospital, i felt one of my totems guided me to reconnect to this former totem. I did so and the energy felt very good but my Mother had some problems with her heart rate; so i removed it.

I was also told by a renowned psychic that my mother made it her last soul's purpose to go out the way she did along with other souls to help them bring to light the poor sanitary conditions of hospitals. I think in particular, the one she was at.

All i know is that the only way to heal is to be honest about things and i am finding that writing things out is helping me to heal as well. While in the hospital the girl next to my Mother gave her an angel with a trumpet after i sent her mother some energy. I felt afterwards the angel was calling my Mother home. When in her hospital room, i had two angel figurines in a bag on the windowsill. My friend and mentor, Many Horses, told me over the phone that i had two angels standing behind me. He was in British Columbia while i am in Hamilton, Ontario. I don't think that i can really heal from all this but i try to make it easier by understanding everything that took place and to ask Jesus and the angels to help carry the burden of this experience. I do know this much though, i wish i was more like my Mother. She is a gentle and innocent soul and i never met anyone like her. No one was more fun to be with and she loved doing anything. She was so easily pleased. I think she was this way because she loved herself, grew up modestly, and i am going to strive to live a simpler life so i do not have to keep going through these periods of self-loathing.

My Father was my good friend but his weakness was that he didn't love himself. He needed too much love from others to keep himself going. I felt that this had to do with the way his Mother was so tough on him. If you're not shown love by your parents it's very difficult to love yourself.

I had another fall. I was on vacation and went to the casinos too often. My luck seemed to have changed as i was having some good fortune and seemed to be getting help from spirit as i would win enough to get my money back. Things seemed to change after i began letting the energies of the others affect me too much and i became too lustful and flirtatious. I feel that this cuts me off from the light and help from the positive spirits. I had also bought a picture with an eagle fighting a snake and it showed a human figure overshadowing the snake. I thought this closely depicted my situation and might invoke the help of the eagle. I got mixed messages on whether or not it was beneficial. I thought it might also invite the negative energy unintentionally back into my life. I returned the picture but i felt the negative energy was back more strongly than of late. It knows when things go poorly for me as it seems to be attached to me as well. It also seems to negatively influence events. When i am upset, i can feel this demon grabbing my throat. I was also in a negative frame of mind lately berating myself for choices i have made that may have been important and i recently had a dream of a snake as well. In the dream i had an exotic pet snake i remember it was wrapped around my left leg and biting me. It seems that i was better off not buying that picture. This demon thrives on hurting me in any way and sometimes influences mine and other people's behaviours. He is able to attach himself to people. He's just a mean miserable loser, no pride. This demon is actually helping me. He is giving me lots of things to write about. At first, i didn't mention too much about him. Now i realize that it's best to explain these experiences in detail. I have been told by three mediums/psychics that i should write. At first it was my Grandfather's idea, which i received in message service which is part of the normal service at the spiritualist church. So this demon may one day result in helping me to get lots of money when i write a book. Again, i will not let these demons get the best of me. I will turn this latest fall into a positive and let it propel me on a path of light and a positive attitude. They say that living well is the best revenge, so this is what i am going to do. My happiness is my control and knowing that it will just piss him off and it helps to motivate me to enjoy life.

I was upset with myself the other night and i asked why i have this problem with gambling and lust. I had a dream that same night in which i met a girl. This seemed to be in present day even though i haven't seen her in 37 years. The girl and i had a crush on each other for 3 years from when i was ten to twelve. She moved away and i was crushed. What made it worse was that on the last day of school, her cousin invited me to a party for her and i said no. I was upset because she hadn't talked to me for a while and didn't seem to care much about me. She didn't ask me herself to go and maybe i was afraid to go to a dance. I don't really know why, but it was a terrible thing to do. A few years ago, i went for a reading at my teacher's place and she told me that something happened when i was twelve and it was almost like i stopped living. I didn't figure it out for a while but this is what happened. In the dream, i told an old friend of mine loud enough for the girl to overhear that she was the one that i never got over. She seemed happy to hear this and her and i were together holding hands and i think i kissed her. It was a wonderful experience i will cherish forever. I knew that we were really together on a different realm. I can still feel the love we had for each other and i can feel her energy when i think of her. Distance doesn't matter with these things. The love we have is so pure and innocent. Whether she is consciously aware of what happened, i don't know. Without this latest fall i would not have had this wonderful experience that will hopefully help me to change my way by allowing me to be more present and involved in life and to learn to love again. I know that she has forgiven me and still loves me too.

During the same time, i picked up a figurine one similar to those i had in the past. I got rid of it a few times because i felt there were some other people attached to it. It happened again, other people attached to it. It keeps happening and it's one of the reasons i didn't keep it when my Mother was in the hospital. No sooner do i pick it up that this particular person starts calling me all the time. This is the same one that i frequently have dreams where he is living in my house. There is one or more other acquaintances as well. I don't know how it happens but as soon as i return to this totem or guide they are attached to me; trying to live off my energy or karma. I have felt i had to avoid a few of these individuals who were sometimes in my life. I can often feel something attached to my left hand and left side of my head. It is especially through my dreams that i am made aware of the situations. Like i said, there are a few individuals who are frequently living in my house. I interpret this that they are trying to live in my energy or take the benefits of this relationship, as it is usually when i connect with this guide, for themselves. I believe our dreams let us know what is going on and that we don't need anyone else to interpret them for us. I'm trying to decide whether or not i should keep this figurine-guide. On one hand it must be beneficial if so many are trying to attach themselves to it but i find myself being very tired lately and just wanting to sleep. I don't know how much my contact with that girl when i was young, had to do with this guide because the guide can be very powerful and at times, when its presence is felt, there is a dreamlike quality to everything. Connecting with her has brought back feelings from that time period where everything seems magical. Like from the movie Hearts in Atlantis when Anthony Hopkins says "when you are young, it seems the world is a magical place, like it must have been in Atlantis. Then you grow old and your heart breaks in two." I also remember when i was a child my parents had a similar figurine in the basement. It was a happy Buddha. I'm sure it was no coincidence that the basement was the location of frequent fun filled parties. I realized that the energy of this was part of my life too at any early age. I should also mention that i had a close personal relationship with Jesus as a child, so one did not take away from the other. It's funny but i think one of my favourite books To Kill A Mockingbird by Harper Lee and this too brings back memories and feelings of my childhood as it is told through the eyes of a young girl.

A few other examples of experiences with figures are when I purchased a large bear. I had a vision and saw how i was connected to a constellation. One time i had a dream of a deer. In this dream, the deer talked to me. I had just finished reading a book by Tom Brown Jr. and on the cover was a deer with a star on its chest. This book was very significant for me as it encouraged me to try to positively influence the course of events by sending energy to the earth and to man's consciousness. As Grandfather (Tom Brown's mentor), "The present is like the palm of your hand,with each finger being possible futures." I choose to believe the future is going to be beautiful. I remember the song,

"This is the dawning of the Age of Aquarius", and it blew my mind when someone told me the name of the group was the Fifth Dimension. I don't know exactly what a dimensional shift ensues but i believe it's about operating from a Christ consciousness; and a whole world consciousness. A blessed new beginning that has been prophesized about including in the bible. I believe it will see a oneness of all humanity and we as humans will operate at a higher level both consciously, intellectually and spiritually, having and using our more powerful minds to manifest, heal, and communicate both with each other and the spirit world. It is also said that the veil between the spirit world and ours is becoming thinner and thinner and time is speeding up. It is definitely a very unique time in our history.

In any event, the deer in the dream said, "we would like you to come live with us in nature." It was walking through a desolate land that seemed to be the aftermath of something big. One thing i observed was the power in this gentle and innocent creature. I had just finished reading a book by Tom Brown Jr. that had a deer with a star on its chest. This was no doubt a magical being. I believed there is great power in gentleness. On another occassion, in a dream, a Rottweiller spoke to me to warn me about three people who were up to no good. I was trying to put a parcel behind a door and this rather large dog kept jumping up on me wanting me to pet it, he was very friendly. I noticed three small dobermans in a neighbour's yard and i commented that there not friendly. Much to my surprise the Rottweiler spoke and said, "No, there not friendly!" The only thing i think i might have done to connect to this dog was that during that day i had helped a small dog to get untangled as it got its leash wrapped around a tree. It shows that good deeds are recognized by God and the world of spirit and they help you in return. When animals speak to you in dreams i understand they are dreams of power. I have had numerous occassions when animals have shown themselves to me to offer guidance.

I have not always taken this advice and i am not sure if i did the right thing or not. My awareness of the possible relationship between the animals and us started when i read the well-known book Animal Speak, by Ted Andrews. While reading the book, a large number of crows showed up on my mail route where for the previous two years i hadn't seen any. There happens to be a crow on the cover of the book. The book tells you how to ask the universe to show your totem. I did so and 45 minutes later i heard the cawing of a crow. I looked up to see a hawk 30 feet over my head flanked by two crows.

I have had a lot of experiences with Hawks and other animals, which i know, were totems or helping spirits. There are many synchronicities where i feel they were trying to provide guidance for me. I know my totems have appeared to lead me when buying a house, trying to decide what to do with the house i bought, leading me to relationship possibilities and when my Mother was in the hospital. Like i said before, most times, i stubbornly did not listen and most times, have regretted it.

When my Mother's obituary appeared in the paper, there was a picture of a hawk on the classified section cover with the caption "time to migrate, i guess."

I have learned to pay close attention to my dreams as i feel that they tell me quite a lot about what is going on in my life. To help me to dream, i have a large dream catcher and i keep a notepad beside my bed to record briefly what i dream. They say that having an intention of recording your dream helps you to remember them. I feel that dreams can tell us a lot about what is going on. I have had a number of dreams with certain people living in my house and i feel i know what it means, and i take action to try to correct the situation. To me, this means these individuals are attached to my energy. In most cases, i feel that the dream is given to me in ways that are understandable to me and therefore, i don't want to go to someone else to translate it for me. Although some books can help with what things mean, like water for example can represent, i believe emotions or our spirituality. Often times, i have conversations with people in dreams and i trust the information that i receive as valid and truthful. We often enter into a different realm.

I have had many dreams where i am with my parents. One of the first dreams i had was where i as bicycling with my Mother. I remember that she was a little shaky on hers and as i reached out to try to steady her, she pushed my hand away and pushed ahead. That was definitely my Mother; very independent. She was also showing me that she was fine and that she can now do things that she hasn't been able to do for years. I had a dream where i confronted an individual and i said, "You're harming my parents", and that person admitted it in the dream. I had a dream where two of my Dad's friends were bumming cigarettes off me. There was another friend there who was an alcoholic and had recently passed. I realized that addictions are something that we can carry with us to the other side. Another significant dream is when my Mother's friend, stood in front of me and just turned around and walked into the light. The message for me was very clear; just try to lead a life like he did and it too will go into the light afterwards. He was a minister but even more significantly was how he and his wife adopted a number of children with disabilities. It's one of the most amazing things that i have ever heard. Besides being my Mother's friend and co-worker, he was the minister who baptized me before i got married.

Sometimes your spirit or higher self operates and performs some amazing things while you are asleep. One of those things was when to my own surprise i cut the throat of the demon after he had beat somebody up. Quite a few years ago myself and a friend of mine who had cancer chased a spirit and when i caught up with it in an alley, i took out a gun and shot it six times. I feel that her cancer had a spirit and i think maybe that we killed it. I had another dream in which a friend of mine threw a person out of a glass window. I feel that person that was thrown was causing some harm and the other came to help. I feel that through our dreams, we communicate with others on a sub-conscious level. That we operate in other realms and that our energy bodies carry on with various acts. I have dreams where i have been in schoolrooms and yes, there are romantic dreams that seem very real.

I have been told that sometimes the demon is attached to me and i know this from a few times when it punched me. Once a medium made a reference to my evil twin and i feel he was talking about the demon. Sometimes it influences me in negative ways, mostly lustful behaviour and gambling. But it doesn't mean i have to allow it any power over me. I feel this demon can attach itself and have influence over others in my life. Definitely my own Father near his end. I have recently discovered the healing power of the Bible. I feel that i was healed physically by holding the Bible against my chest and solar plexus.

I had another close encounter with a deer, talked to my mentor Many Horses and he confirmed that i needed to be more like the deer, like in Animal Speak (by Ted Andrews) being gently and innocent, but he also told me that the deer is intuitive and cautious. This may relate to how i need to be right now in regards to my involvement with a girl that i have recently met. There seems to be signs both ways and i am not sure what to do at this point so i need to take things slow.

I called my friend and mentor Many Horses and he talked to me for quite awhile and while talking, he is doing clearing work on me. That's the main thing Many Horses does. He clears negative energies or negative spirits that are attached to people and affect their behaviour. The guy is pretty awesome and i am proud to call him my friend. One time, i was going to get some healing from him and it started a few weeks before i saw him. I started getting very strong emotions for him like a Brother connection. I mentioned it to him that i think i was remembering one of our past lives together. He said "that's right", and talked a little about a time where we were children together playing in a kind of magical cave. One thing we talked about was letting people be as they are; accepting them and their behaviours. Not judging them just accepting things the way they are. He talked about some men he knew who were married to women who slept around and those men knew about it and accepted it and loved their spouse anyways. This has often been a thought of mine because of all these type of situations i have found myself in. I sometimes wish that I could be able to be strong and accepting enough to stay centred and loving no matter what. To walk in peace no matter what others do. I read a very important book once called, Care of the Soul, by Thomas Moore and one thing that i got from this book was not to judge a person or their actions because no matter what they do, it is their souls that need to act this way. Learning to accept the soul of a person and of a relationship. To me that speaks to real peace and freedom.

I went through some of my old mailman stuff and i think i felt my energy from the past and i miss it. Whether it's the job i had or the way life was back then or my energy was stronger. I feel like part of me is missing and i want to try to bring it back. Maybe i am having trouble accepting that some things may change and can't be the same again. Maybe it was a guide that helped me to be stronger back then. I'm going to use a rattle that i was given to try to bring back some of my soul or energy that i feel i may have lost. I may also try to do some dowsing on this as well. Isn't it funny how babies are given rattles to play with? Is this to bring their souls fully into themselves? Again i find myself with the prospect of a relationship or two and i am not sure what to do because the one is a long distance situation. I have recently had a number of readings by mediums and have been told three different things regarding this so i am confused. Again i think the only way to get guidance is to go inward and see how it feels or what visions i get. It's one thing to accept a person as they are, but it's also up to us to decide if we want certain experiences in our lives. I wish i were more easy going following the path that is laid out for me. I don't feel it's always that easy. I believe we are co-creators of our reality and i believe we always have choices to make. At least that's how most things have seemed to me. If we don't like what we are being offered, than we need to clarify with the universe what we want. Again, i have to see how something feels and i have lately found myself being moved from side to side as if my guide or angel or a higher self were telling me no. Or sometimes, i will ask to move one way if it's a no and the other way if it's a yes.

Aside from this, i have started doing some Reiki again and it feels great to be doing energy work. Part of me maybe didn't feel worthy or my ego was telling me i wasn't good enough to do it. But after being given a message at a spiritualist church, telling me I would be doing lots of healing work, i decided to start working on some friends and this has helped my confidence. I know that the healing energies are not my own and i am just a channel but i still need my confidence built up. Now i am finding that it has released a large block and i want to jump more fully into the whole thing. I'm looking to get somebody to help clear people, the room, and myself. I'm interested in reading related books and meditating. I feel that i am getting hooked onto the healing and spiritual path again. I feel that we all get hooked on something. I know i was hooked on drinking and smoking and before those drugs. More recently i was hooked on gambling. It feels good to be hooked on something healthy again. Along with this is getting hooked on going for nature walks and getting hooked on going to church.

I was very fortunate and had good parents. My Mother was very civilized in her heart. She was a tremendous caregiver who quit work to take care of her Brothers and Sisters when her Mother died. When my mother was only 17. She took care of three boys; one who had some serious health issues as well as her husband as well as a house while going back to school to finish her high school then going to college in social work. She had a good career at Big Brothers. My Dad was well respected by his numerous friends. People trusted him to do right. He ran everything from being a baseball coach to company fishing trips, poker games and golf tournaments. In many ways he was my hero growing up. My Mother and Father were very important role models to me and were my best friends as well.

I was reminded about the importance of service and caring for others as i witnessed a friend caught up in bragging about her material world. I realized that she needed to do this to feel better about herself and i remembered about how good i felt when i did something for my parents and now for my Brother and how i need to extend that out more to others. I did share that with her but i realized it was something that i needed to hear, to other people are always teaching us. Another friend and i were a bit at odds over the cause of cancer. My belief is that all disease begins in the mind or the emotions. I believe most if not it was Edgar Cayce who said "what man thinketh, so shall he be." I also believe a lot can be known about a person by where the disease is manifested in the body. It is no surprise with my problems with relationships and my own feminine side that i should have issues with my prostrate. My Father developed cancer in the lungs, which is where sadness is manifested. My Father was very depressed and had lost his will to live. This though wasn't totally his fault and he was bothered by a very negative and evil spirit or entity that was dark who was trying to hurt my parents to get at me and he was somehow able to work on my Father's mental and emotional level. It's hard to believe that that kind of evil exists can but unfortunately for this world we live in it's absolutely true. I'll get more into this later if it feels like something i need to include. More importantly, i know my Father is fine now and he is with me helping me quite often and certainly every event is well noted by our heavenly Creator.

Anyhow, it reminds me of the importance of staying positive. I find it helpful to say positive things to yourself. To remind yourself of the good things that you have done and remind yourself of that. There is always something positive to focus on. Sometimes it isn't easy but find a positive focus. Being where you are and enjoying what you are doing. If what you are doing is monotonous than think of something good that you enjoy doing or someone that you love. Or send energy to the earth or someone who is sick. The point is, you are choosing to be happy! I find it very helpful to have something in the near future to look forward to like going out for dinner. I find it very helpful to set goals, to write down what needs to be done. Prioritize and accomplishing them. I find writing them down takes them off my mind and helps me to feel more organized and in control of these things. I have been reminded of the Reiki principle (Reiki is an ancient healing technique where the practitioner channels divine universal energy into the client to promote healing and well being.) "Just for today do not worry", by Dr.Mikai Usui. I'm finding it very helpful to identify to myself when i am worrying. Another good thing to do is think about something you can say or do for someone else to make them happy or i often remember things that i have done for others in the past and it gives me great joy. So doing for others is really for you. The point is we have control over our happiness, attitude and peace of mind.

The most important thing that i do whenever i can is to send energy to the earth. I like to visualize holding the earth in my hands and surrounding it with healing energy or light of the sun. I feel that our minds are powerful and we can use them to help make a difference. I also feel that the earth needs our help right now. Much of my motivation came from some of the Tom Brown Jr.'s books where his mentor, Grandfather, talked about us being able to affect the future of the earth and mankind. He also talks about spiritual power being given to those who use their energy for a greater cause. I love the Native American teachings and the importance they place on being caretakers for the earth. But i feel that it is not just their responsibility it is all of ours. I remember a quote from the movie 2001, A Space Odyssey, when the message from the monolith was "Remember you are just the tenants, not the landlords."

It is a common opinion that the earth and everyone on it is experiencing a very unique and significant change. Often referred to as a dimensional shift. There have been many doomsday type prophecies but I prefer to think positive about this long ago predicted time in history. I remember a song from the 70's, "This is the dawning of the Age of Aquarius." What really gets me is the name of the group was the Fifth Dimension. I feel good about connecting to the sun and using its energy in helping the earth. In Wayne Dyer's book, Sacred Self, he in his dedication says about his wife. "I thank you as the earth thanks the sun." I have always felt very good about that. I remember what it is like to be outside in nature first thing in the morning when the sun is just coming up when there's wet dew on everything. Everything just feels so appreciative and welcoming of the warmth and light of the sun, and there is nothing more uplifting and positive than the promise of a new day. I suspect there is much more to the sun than i know. Sometimes i will focus on surrounding the earth with sun energy using my mind. Other times i try it with white light, or green healing light, sometimes a purple transmuting plane. There is also a crystal rainbow earth healing exercise in Sun Bear's Dancing with the Wheel that i really like and i think influenced me in developing the technique i choose to use.

I find myself thinking a lot about the power and importance of water. It really is a sacred thing that we badly abuse. I guess the farmers would know all about its importance. The life force energy that it contains. It rejuvenates us whether we drink it or shower or swim in it. You take a seed and add water and it blossoms. This doesn't work with any other liquid. It has life giving qualities in it. Something else about water is that it is easily programmed, or that it responds to our thoughts and intentions. My teacher and friend J. always tells us to bless your water. She also tells us that we can program it to heal anything. It sure doesn't hurt to try! Another friend and important influence, Raymon is involved in a worldwide action to purifyand raise the energy of the waters of the world.

Right now, i am finding myself depressed. It's mainly because i am stuck on a situation and i can't find my way out. I can't decide on what to do and it's taking a lot of my energy. Confusion is my biggest problem and i find myself continually getting caught in confusing situations. I had a number of readings with mediums and i have been told three different things regarding my path with a future partner. Again, my parents want me to go in a direction that just doesn't feel right and it's difficult because they say if i do go down it there will be a child. I feel that my parents are telling me this through the message "field of dreams". (like from the Kevin Costner movie). I keep seeing this and i feel my parents are telling me, if i create a situation where there is a child, they will come as a reincarnate. In trying to meditate as much as possible to get my own answers but i also have an opportunity to get more readings and i am desperate for them. The one they want me to take is a long distance relationship. I don't want to say too much about any of it but in meditation i may have seen another possibility in the near future as well as something developing with this girl maybe around Christmas. Like i said, it's confusing and i feel that when it comes down to it, i have to trust what I feel is right.

Although these readings have caused me quite a bit of confusion, there are other things about my future that the readings have been pretty clear about and there are things to feel very positive about and it helps me now to remember those and try to focus on them when i am in despair about the uncertainties.

When i am in a negative mood, i often become aware of the presence of negative energy. When i am aware of this, i try to clear my energy. First a technique shown me by Many Horses. Take a deep breath, push down like you are going to the bathroom. Grab the back of your neck and as you exhale pull up like you are pulling off a shirt. Do the same to your third eye, throat chakra, chest, solar plexus and when you do your naval area, pull down to get your lower chakra as well. Then, take both hands and wipe the top of your head. You may also want to brush each wrist and ankle, as well as your tail bone also your ears. Many Horses talked about demons that cling onto your back and you have to make sure you remove them. A nice lady teacher, Rev.Jean Toward who stood by my side for a long while, would have us clear ourselves by brushing our zone lines. Starting with the left arm, brush from your shoulder down to your thumb. Do this five times, moving over to get each finger. Do the right side as well. Then do the front of your body down your left leg five times. Again starting inward finishing at your big toe and working outward. Then do your right side the same way. Then do your head by turning your head to the right and with your right hand, start near your forehead and brush over the back of your head and back of shoulder. Do five times finishing at your ear. Then turn your head to the left and take your left hand and clear the right side of your head. Then she would have us clean our auric fields with our minds. Starting with the one closest to the body and working outwards. I do it with white light or sunlight. She says to do seven auric fields in this manner. Then she says we should look at our grid, which is outside of these fields and make sure there is no openings. If there are, then seal them with your mind using light.

It is a good practice, though i have to admit i don't do it enough, to surround ourselves with a ball or egg of white light. I was also taught a Native American technique by my old friend and at one time teacher, that by using a drum and facing the four directions starting with the east to bang the drum and call Kway. Then she did it three more times, once from downward to the earth, then upwards to the sky and then once in the centre. It is also a good idea to smudge yourself with sage or cedar or dried pine needles or whatever you feel works for you. Another important thing is to ground your energy by visualizing sending energy down through your feet deep into the earth. Instead of white light, i seem to prefer to surround myself with the sun, whatever seems to work for you. Certainly prayer and asking for help from our guides, angels and ascended masters is always a good idea. I feel that i tended to do this more than putting some effort into it on my own.

A few other techniques that i have learned along the way is after cleaning our energy out by flushing it with white light, sealing each chakra by placing a white or gold saucer with a white cross inside over our crown, forehead, throat, chest, solar plexus below naval and underneath (don't forget to do the back of them as well!) It is commonly known that the Lord's Prayer, when said, stimulates all of our chakras, and the 23rd Psalm seals them.

I remind myself of the importance especially when negative energy is around to stay positive.

Whether a negative attitude draws negative energy i believe this to be true but i also feel that the energy i am dealing with wants me to be unhappy. So i will say screw you! I'm going to be happy and i focus on things that feel good. A good meditation tape or prayer or going to church, finding a positive thing to focus on because there are things that it doesn't want me to be doing. Always turn to the light for the way out.

Lately, i have been upset with myself with some regrets i have over how i treated my parents. Then i remind myself that my relationships with my parents are not over. That i can still talk to them and if i try i can sense them and hopefully will learn to communicate better with them. I know that i have had some communication. It is an on-going thing and i know they are very aware of the circumstances of my life. Certainly spiritualist churches are good for getting a message from them but i have had some direct contact from them and just need to spend more time in the quiet talking to them. Just an example of this is when i went for one reading and the reader made a comment about my interaction with one girl saying how i put all my cards on the table and this kind of scared her away. I had another reading with a different medium at a church in another city. The medium said my Father was there. She identified him as looking like me except for having less hair. She asked if I liked playing cards and told me that my Father had said, "that i never was much of a poker player." My parents both had opinions about a relationship possibility. This i witnessed through four different readings with four different mediums. I did not agree with my parent's advice but i know that they are aware of my life and in fact are very much alive. This knowledge is a fact and it does help me dealing with my grief.

I certainly miss being with them in a more physical sense, but this knowledge is encouraging me in wanting to develop my own abilities and awareness more so i can have more direct communication with them. I have had too many readings probably and with all due respect to the mediums and those in the spirit world, i know i have to rely on my own guidance the most. I have to go by what feels right and by what i see and experience in meditation and dreams. I frequently berate myself for mistakes i made and missed opportunities. Most of the mistakes i made that bother me are regarding my parents. What i am getting from my Mother to help me deal with this is that everything can be forgiven as long as you have a good heart. This includes forgiving ourselves. Mistakes were made but the intention was good. It was based on love and wanting the best for those we care about. Nothing can destroy the love we have for them. I again remember the poem that i mentioned before.

"I am standing upon the seashore..." and i remember "she is gone from my sight that is all."
Henry Van Dyke

I had a dream last night that i feel was very significant for me. It may have tapped into a past life or maybe i was dealing with my own feminine side. But it exemplifies many of the relationships i have experienced in my life. In this dream, i was visiting France and i met a woman and we were living together and we were having what i thought was a good relationship. It was a very exciting life. Then she informed me that she had met someone else. They were in love and he was going to move in with her. She informed me that she did not love me. I also noticed that she was subtly rubbing it into me that their relationship was very sexual. Before i was leaving i was heart broken and feeling very heavy. Then i said to her "for me there is only the travelling on the paths that have a heart, on any path that may have a heart. There i travel and the only worthwhile challenge for me is to traverse it's full length.... looking, looking, breathlessly." I then said to her that she doesn't have a heart. I then left and i felt light and ready to leave. This is a quote from a Carlos Castenada book that, although probably intended to mean something different, it helps to remind myself what i am looking for and what my motivation should be. I have to raise myself up to focus on love. Like i said, i have had a few relationships with this type of scenario, usually though the other person does not tell me there is someone else involved. I have understood for a while that we draw onto ourselves in our relationships an aspect of ourselves that we are trying to come to terms with. At least one of these girls i was involved with was a soul mate. They say that our soul's mate is not necessarily the most harmonious relationships but ones that we can learn the most from. I realize that these women reflect an aspect of myself that is usually repressed. Whether it's my feminine side or my own shadow self that Carl Jung talks about i am not really sure. But obviously i have to keep working on coming to terms with it. I know that i have to try to purify myself to focus more on love than on the physical or sexual aspects. Something else i considered is that if i were involved with someone else who was sleeping around, maybe i should consider accepting them anyways and try to remain in a relationship with them. Maybe i should just accept that they need to do this and look at releasing my own attachments to their physicality and possessiveness of their sexuality. Obviously this is not easy to do but it would be the ultimate in remaining unattached, balanced and peaceful.

Ultimately it's about addressing my own shadow self and being aware of how i am operating. Am i operating from a place of lust or love. Being aware and honest with myself. Raise my own self to a place of unconditional love. I am currently in Atlantic City and i am putting this to the test. I probably shouldn't be here but i felt that need to see the Atlantic Ocean and i also wanted to have some fun. I've told myself that i am allowed to gamble only on vacations or special occasions. I realize that gambling and drinking can also bring lustful behaviour and i do not like operating like this. It makes me feel cheap and unbalanced. I am much happier when i can connect with the simpler things in life like getting up early and watching the sunrise, walking and meditating on the beach. Being outside and walking along the boardwalk. I am currently sitting on a bench on the boardwalk. This morning i did a sunrise ceremony standing in the ocean i said a prayer and put a portion of my parents' ashes into the water. I told them how lucky i was to have had them as parents and that i loved them very much. I asked God and Jesus to take them where they needed to be. I did an earth healing meditation and dedicated it to my parents and dedicated all healings to benefit of my parents in any way they needed or desired. I offered myself to God, Jesus and the light to be their service for this life and all time, as long as at some point i would be reunited with my parents either here or in the spirit world for eternity. Then the sun came out. I felt that was a promise from God. I was told that i needed to release my parents, that i was holding them back. I don't know if this is true or not but in a meditation i saw myself as my native female guide carrying a baby into the light. I handed it to an angel with large wings before entering into the light and the angel handed it back after i entered. I saw myself on a beach facing the ocean at sunrise. I carried the baby into the water and we both went under the water briefly, like a christening or baptism. Then i saw myself rising upward looking down on the scene as i continued travelling upwards. When i came back i was standing as a native male shaman facing the ocean holding some sort of medicine stick raised in my right hand. I know that a baby could represent new beginnings and this coincides with spring. May 4th and sunrise and i have to look up about seagulls as there were many around and i know i need to know more about the east.

Giving the baby back to the angel and the light and being told i was holding my parents back made me feel quite upset as i felt that i blew the opportunity to have a child and give them a chance to reincarnate with me as i felt they were telling me they wished.

As i was travelling to the Toronto airport, i was again going over these latest events and i saw a big sign by the highway that said Life. This is what i saw from spirit a year ago after the angel handed me the baby. I did some healing work at a benefit to raise money for Haiti. One person i worked on had on a shirt that she had made that had the left eye of a woman. This reminded me of a vision i had when i did my second level Reiki attunement back in 1996. According to Don Juan (as told by Carlos Castenada in his writings), it is a sign one sees when "a warrior is about to lose his human form."

Coming to Atlantic City reminds me of my parents as they liked it here but it reminds me of all of our trips to Virginia Beach. This i feel is another step in recapturing the energy of my past. It is called recapitulation and something Carlos Castenada talks about to regain lost energy so one can retain their awareness after death by darting past what they describe as something like an eagle which takes back your awareness after dying. A friend at the spiritualist church also told me that i needed to do this and in my own meditation i saw a rattle, which to me meant to use this method to pull back lost energy.

Recapitulation not only pulled back energy lost in the part but also gets rid of toxic energy associated with past events. Castenada talks about a different method of doing this using the breath and moving your head back in forth as you recall past events, to expel the toxicity and regain lost energy. There are a number of other events that seem to be doing the same thing. Recently i saw and purchased a Centennial silver dollar with a goose on it, which is a coin i used to have as a child of seven years. One birthday i gave it to my father. Goose can also represent travelling to legendary places from Animal Speak (Andrews). Atlantic City i wonder about my past connection to Atlantis and funny how my meditation on the beach included crystals which were prevalent in Atlantis. It could also represent my parents returning home, another meaning for Goose.

I was offered free tickets to a hockey game and this reminded me a lot of the times spent with my father. I saw his friend there and i felt this was a sign of my Dad at work. I also bought a $2.00 hockey card of my favourite hockey player when i was a child, Dave Keon.

It seems, too, that i am being guided to reconnect with spiritual teachings and powers i had in the past. I was given the Mahatma book. This was a powerful weekend workshop that i did a number of times to anchor the higher rays into the earth to help with the dimensional shift, it was written by Brian Gratton. Also i had a dream where i met the Dalai Lama. Carlos Castenada has come up a few times lately of course my native guides are there in my meditations as well. I have also recently been calling upon the direction keepers and had a powerful dream, which i believe involved Mudjuwinkas (large black bear) and Wabonoose (Buffalo). I was riding on the back of Wabonoose hanging on for dear life.

I knew the springtime was going to be significant and in a few meditations i saw new flowers just beginning to come up. Apparently on April 3rd a powerful spiritual shift had taken place around 7 pm. At the time this happened i was at a church watching a performance of the resurrection. Again representing new birth. Just prior to the resurrection of Jesus in the play, the pastor came on stage and asked if anyone wanted to accept Jesus as their saviour, to repeat what he said. I have accepted him twice in the past few years, but the first time i did i was a child at a camp. As a child i felt i had a close personal connection with Jesus after i asked him. As i repeated what the pastor was saying, i felt the presence of Jesus standing beside me. I actually did this twice on the 3rd and again on the 4th which was on Easter Sunday. It was on Easter where i felt his presence. Again this is reconnecting with my childhood and the energy of that time. The peacefulness and love i felt by having Jesus as my close companion was wonderful and i welcome the return of that. This is also the best way for me to deal with my missing of my parents. I am also excited about bringing back joy and love and innocence into my life again. Like i said the simple things in life are the greatest. It keeps you centred and peaceful as well. Even when in a place like Atlantic City. I was walking along the boardwalk and people were talking about Christ. The sign said, "Sin is death.

Christ is life." Maybe that's what the vision i saw was referring to.

I did some dowsing work while here on removing negative energies and raising the spirit of love in this town. I also did some work on the ocean by raising its energy. I'm going to take a sample of the water home with me. I believe that all water is connected and that you can affect it all by blessing just a portion. Through dowsing you can also raise the energy level of it. I also want to have ocean energy in my home and life. This type of dowsing is a method taught to me by Raymon Grace. I had a dream and i was preaching to people at my church and i was talking that no one was 100% pure. That we all have dark sides or shadow selves and it was okay. That we have to get in touch with that side of ourselves and allow it an expression. A Native American elder i met said, "If you have a black dog and a white dog, which one are you going to feed, if you don't feed the black dog as well it will bite you in the ass." I believe that has been a lot of my experience in some relationships. No one is perfect. From Care of the Soul, Thomas Moore talks about loving yourself in your entirety. I will love and accept my own imperfections. I will not feel shame but i will accept myself. Of course i will not permit myself to ever cause harm to another. That is not within my nature and it is not acceptable. If you love yourself, you cannot harm anyone anyway. I am allowing joy into my life.

At my house there have been three blockages in drains that needed clearing. Some corroded pipes and leaks and the main drain was blocked. I also had to replace the water pump in my care. It is surprising i was having all kinds of trouble with my prostate prior to fixing these. I gladly had them fixed as i feel that my physical health will improve. Especially in regards to my own plumbing being renewed. I also feel the cleared blockages also signifies a clearing of blockages in my life.I feel there is a correlation or metaphor between ourselves and our homes and even our vehicles. I am also aware that water represents the emotions and spirituality and these two have been calmed and rejuvenated. I also brought home some ocean water and sand. I wanted to bring the peacefulness of the ocean into my home and life. I met a psychic in Atlantic City and the main thing she told me was i was blocked or was being blocked.

I was looking up goose in animal speak and it talks about legendary places reflecting a stimulation of the childhood thrill and belief in legendary places. In the movie Hearts in Atlantis, Anthony Hopkins says "when you are young, you think the world is a magical place, like it must have been in Atlantis." I can really relate to this. It follows by referring that our hearts often get broken as we get older. Atlantis appeals to me for some reason. That coin with the goose on it takes me back to the magic of childhood. The goose talks about "communication through stories" and i have started writing again after a long layoff. It is also "a harbinger of spring representing fulfilled promises that great quests bring." It also represents "new paths, greater vision and time to come into my own," Animal speak Andrews. This all seems relevant to my life and is very exciting to me. The blocked drains could also represent the blockages i had in writing may need to be at the ocean has to do with "the connection to the shoreline." It is a place of a great mystery and magic. The presence of gulls may present this and may be "opening up my ability to work in other dimensions." Animal Speak Ted Andrews. Certainly the poem about the shoreline and the sailboat weighs on my mind quite a bit as well.

Lately i feel like i have been focussing too much on personal belongings like clothing. I have been having a lot of fun shopping for and getting the things i need. Included is looking in thrift shops. I know this is self-indulged but i need it right now and i am enjoying it. I've also decided to get what i need no matter what. This includes doing whatever i have to to enjoy life. I am making me and my happiness a priority. I certainly, at the same time, do whatever i can for others, especially my Brother and i send energy to the earth and do other energy workings, i.e. raising the energy of water bringing in the spirit of love, etc. (as taught by Raymon Grace) whenever i can. I feel this is related to the blockages being cleared and also is a type of rebellion against an energy that has done everything possible to block my happiness.

I know that you have to be careful when buying used items as to what type of energy from previous owners might be attached. If i get a good feeling when i hold it i know it's probably okay but i like to smudge it with sage as well. I know spirit has led me to some items i have found.

When my brother and i put flowers on my parents' grave site on Mother's Day, the sun came out the same instant and i feel it was a sign from my Mother saying she got them. I went for a coffee and a walk down by the waterfront at one of my Mother's favourite places and i was thinking how much she enjoyed this and how much joy she had for the simple pleasures. What a wonderful happy soul. I could still feel her happiness and i felt she was with me. Even after returning home i had a strong sense of her pleasure and could almost see her with her hair ruffled and cheeks red from being outside and the fulfilment she had from the sun and fresh air, and don't forget the coffee. I have been putting food outside regularly and wondering if i had become far too eccentric. When i returned from being away, i had a dream of my mother sleeping in the other room and she was extremely hungry.

I don't want to turn this into a diary but I feel these events are significant. I felt these events are significant. I felt a drawing to return downtown. Partly from getting the hockey tickets and i enjoyed myself when i was wandering around down there even though the downtown has become dilapidated. It reminded me of a period of time that i used to go down there. Partly it may be another recapitulation thing and it's also an attempt to live life more fully and allow some excitement and new activities in. I bought a spiritual item down there and it became apparent to me that for whatever reason, it wasn't appropriate. This happened as i was attacked and felt somewhat vulnerable or exposed when I had this hanging in my room. I checked and it seemed that i needed to get rid of it. At the store where i purchased it i saw a figurine in the window. It was of a Native American chief together with a Native American female. It was made by the same company as another figurine of a Native American chief, which i bought at a hotel in Mississauga where i took my parents. It quickly became obvious to me that i should try to exchange what i had purchased before for this, as i felt this was a significant thing for me. I don't know if owning it represented meeting a partner or maybe a coming together of my male and female sides or a joining of two of my guides that i recently know have been active.

For a short while, i felt some guilt over my self-indulgence. I feel that this could just be another trick of the dark side. It's okay to enjoy things and to treat yourself well. It's a fine line between getting enjoyment from things but not becoming too attached to the material world. For attachment causes suffering. I'm looking at it more as gifts from the spirit world and allowing joy to be in my life and every opportunity, i also feel that i am battling an energy that wants me to be unhappy. I feel the psychic picked up on how someone was trying to block me and part of what's going on now is the releasing and overcoming of blocks whether self-imposed or influenced by others. It's not just material things that the spirit world is giving me, it's finding joy in the moment. It's trying to get a sense of where it feels right to go and what feels right to do in that moment. For example went for a hike on a perfect May day through a meadow and reconnected with nature, finding my new place to go close to my old place and while there sending energy to earth and nature. I'm also doing this now, sitting in a coffee shop by the waterfront in the sun writing. I'm trying more and more to create sacredness in my everyday life by living and finding joy in the moment. I am trying to follow spirits guidance and my own intuition to determine my activities and I am trying to live a balanced life and making sure i include service to God and the light. I remember a poem about "planting your own seeds and growing your own garden rather than waiting for someone to bring you flowers." It's called, Comes the Dawn, by Veronica Shoffstall. You have to be a provider for yourself as well. Earlier this week i seemed to be getting attacked on all sides. I realized again that this negative energy is able to attach itself to others and or influence their thinking and behaviour. This energy also tries to control you by trying to make you unhappy. Sometimes it's almost comical because it's so bizarre. There are a few certain individuals that their energy especially works through. And i know neither they nor this energy wants me to be happy. Aside from the desire to control, it's also because they are so miserable and they don't want anyone it seems, especially, me to be happy. They are so miserable they want to spread misery. What sad people they are they waste their energy trying to destroy others or positive things rather than to help themselves. Their only joy seems to be in hurting others. Again, a person cannot hurt others if they truly love themselves. These people are sad because they must be filled with self-loathing. They are jealous of others by their possessions and happiness and they have to be better than you. They get angry that you are full of joy and happiness, so the best way to combat these individuals is to not let them get you angry or intimidated but to show them they have no effect on you. Show your joy and happiness, it just makes them mad, they can't take it. And usually walk away.

We have to be aware of our own negative thinking as this also may be the work of the dark side. Replace negative thinking with positive. One thing i found that helps when troubled with negative energy is to send light and healing to the earth or to someone who needs healing. Another thing i have been trying to do on a regular basis is in my mind take a person's hands and joining them with Jesus and holding them there until i see white light making their connection. I also find it helpful to sing a hymn and certainly prayer will help to push the dark side away. A couple of times at work while talking to people about Jesus i felt Jesus standing beside me. I kid you not, Jesus is real! In talking with other people i love harmony, i want to make the other person feel good to try to find a positive focus. I also find it important to find things you like about people rather than dislike. But i think this happens naturally when you are filled with love and feel good about yourself. You just want to share it. I think that spirituality is also about freedom. You are above the controls and powers of other people, who are like Castenada talks about, petty tyrants. Freedom is an attitude and others can't control it and they don't like that.

A lot of it is about remembering who you are and not letting the world or others make you deviate from being yourself. To me that is victory if you can still be yourself no matter what. The recapitulation process is about remembering who you are. I feel that the powers that run the world want to control you and that society is geared to do just that, right from school on upwards. Like the group Pink Floyd sings, "We're just another brick in the wall." It's all about controlling us so we can be the workers who scrape by and never question anything so the elite can have the good life. John Lennon's working class here says, "when you're born they make you feel small by giving you nothing instead of it all." And certainly his song, Imagine reflects the power and control of government and many religions. It will be interesting to see how that changes with the changing energy in the world.

Anyways if you are depressed, your energy is trapped somewhere and you must take action to unblock it. My desire is to become as much spirit as possible to connect with that higher energy, the unconditional love. In doing this, i can fill myself with a love that no one can take away. I can find the peace and healing my soul needs. I have suffered too much and now only desire to be one with love. I have found that connecting to Jesus to be important thing for me and to offer myself in service to him and the light. In return i often find myself filled with love and peace and am often floating along feeling connected with spirit.

I'm still dealing with issues of worthiness. I have to remind myself that i deserve to be happy and to have a good life. To have things and to have a good partner. I'm trying to learn to go with the flow again and give up trying to control or worry about things or the future. I'm trying to live more fully in the moment. Someone referred to me as happy, go lucky and that's exactly what i am trying to be. I used to be that way and i am trying to return there again. That's how i liked myself best. The Buddhist teachings are so simple but profound when they talk about how the grasping mind causes suffering. To control things in the larger sense or the word is to try not to control anything. Suffering is caused by attachment to people and things. You must think detachment letting life flow. Attachment implies needing, possessing, ownership, control. By letting life flow is allowing the universe to unfold naturally. When you are filled with self-love you are already full and are not needing anything.

My philosophy is that life is a journey. It's a journey of self-discovery. You begin it alone and you end it alone. No one travels the whole way with you. Life is a constant separation. I guess if we want something permanent than work on our connection with God and our spirits because what else is permanent, other than this. When i talk about always separating, obviously even with a lifelong partner you must separate at death. But often our loved ones are still with us. I'm frequently having dreams where i am with my parents. I feel that in another dimension we can still interact with each other. I also feel that my parents have been communicating with me in different ways either through synchronistic events or through readings i have had with mediums. Sometimes i can hear them as well. The night my Mother passed away when i went home i felt she talked to me. She at first was angry with me saying that i lied because the last thing i said to her was that i told her that her Sister who is in spirit was with her and that i promised that she would be okay. I think she mistook what i meant was my healer teacher, Jean. I explained this to her with my thoughts, i then heard her say immediately "no regrets." She was very close to her Sister and it's a comfort for me to know that she stood by her. The first dream i remember with her was us riding bicycles together. It was very realistic and i know it wasn't just a dream. She was a little wobbly on her bike and i reached out to steady her and she pushed my hand away. This is just like my Mother, fiercely independent. I also know she was showing me that she could do things now that she loved but wasn't able to do them in the physical. Since their passing my parents have been communicating to me the message "field of dreams." Which i know is from them. It took about two years and numerous readings before i found a medium to confirm this. I know that they are aware of the goings on of my life through the comments that are sometimes made in the readings. In another reading my Father was identified. The medium asked about cards and then said my Father stated that i "was never much of a poker player." That is my Father's sense of humour exactly and it was a carryover from a previous reading commenting on my habit of saying what's on my mind rather than sometimes the wiser choice of keeping things to myself. I have known about the continuous existence of the spirit since 1980, 30 years ago. I went to a psychic and she had said there was someone there who passed away 2 years previously. She said he drowned. He was a Brother of a friend or friend of a Brother. He was both. I knew exactly who she was talking about and he had drowned 2 years previously. I had the proof i needed and i had never questioned it since. My Grandfather and Cousin also appeared at the first of my readings. During a house cleaning the individual that I was referred to also described my Grandfather Williamson, a short guy with a kilt. During this house clearing my teacher said a previous owner now deceased was still in the house and she helped him to leave. This actually happened in both of my houses. In my second house i once felt this energy rush by me when i went to get the door and the house inspector who was at the door suddenly became angry, i could tell he was later taken aback by this sudden feeling of anger that came over him. Some other personal experiences i have had was one time when i was half asleep i felt my aunt whom i was close with and is in spirit, visit me and she grabbed my leg and shook it. I had a dream of 3 of my Dad's friends and 2 of them were bumming cigarettes off me. The other had recently passed over and was a drinker. This showed me how addictions can be carried with us in the afterlife. In another dream, my Mother's friend, who was a minister and co-worker of my Mother's just stood in front of me and he turned and walked into the light. I knew that he was guiding me as to how to live my life and the reward that lay in the afterlife. I know that he and his wife had adopted a number of children who were physically and mentally handicapped. He was an amazingly giving person and a gentle easy going spirit, bless him. Shortly after i first began a spiritual path, i booked a past-life regression with a person i will just refer to as J., who later became a great teacher of mine, and many others. The song on the radio right now: "I find it hard to believe we're in heaven ..." by Eric Clapton.

During the first life i visited during the regression i was laying on a funeral pyre. She instructed me to observe what i was wearing. I had on a long dress and old fashioned laced up boots. I was a female missionary i feel in Africa. I took my mother to see her once and the only past life she managed to experience before she got frightened was that of a missionary. I feel that we were best friends during that time. The second life i felt this incredible joy like i have never felt. Jean asked, "What's happening?" I could feel myself being thrown up in the air. It was just like i was there. I could see other children standing around in a circle under me holding a blanket and throwing me up in the air. I could see the view at the height of my travel. I knew i was brown skinned and i could see the top of a cross on a mission or church. Unfortunately i missed the blanket and i ended upside down where i broke my neck. I feel that the neck problem i had in this life originated back in that life. The third life i was their big huge guy that barely fit on her healing table which was oversized. I saw a lot during this time of the life i had in this regression where i was a viking. I also saw my two children. I recognized immediately that my son in that life was my Father. The girl i didn't recognize right away and she informed me to look into her eyes.

After doing so something like a silver rod shot out her eye and hit me in mine sending my head back. This happened in real life a few months later with a girl. We went out for a short while and i feel she was a soul mate of mine. It was a difficult relationship but i feel we almost made it work. I read in a few places that our soul mates are not necessarily the easiest of relationships but more the ones that we learn the most from. In any event, i feel that life is about learning and that's best done by learning about yourself. Past life regressions i feel are an invaluable tool to help with self-realization. To me, i went back as a female, a child and a male. I feel this was significant as it showed the ideal of each part of myself and i should strive to bring those positive aspects together in my present life. Obviously it also shows how we are connected with others in our lives so deeply we frequently reincarnate with them. Jean also took me back to what she referred to as the Holy Grail. Although i didn't see anything she told me to keep working with it. After doing so, i felt i experienced my birth before coming down here. I saw myself inside of a large dome like building and i was coming out of a pool of silver liquid and taking physical form. I remember the intensity and sense of purpose i had at this time and i need to reconnect with that energy. I have done other quick regressions in classes which contained a group of people and on my most recent life i felt myself floating down through a squadron of British bombers and i was on the ground as a child pulling bricks from a pile. Between this and my other recalled life when i died very young helps to explain the severe separation anxiety i had as a child. Sometimes in meditation or dreams i have slipped into past lives and i have awareness of myself living in the desert, of being a solitary monk maybe with leprosy writing calligraphy of the scriptures, as a female Native American woman. I saw myself out in a valley at nighttime by myself holding an infant and looking at the stars, very serene. Another i witnessed myself living in New York City or some other large metropolitan city as a single wealthy man enjoying the theatre and listening to music. After going out with one girl who said she was having memories of us as a native couple together i had two dreams of the same thing. In one of them, i was tying two feathers to an adorned tree and i knew it was my marriage ceremony. Realization of past lives has helped me to understand different aspects of my personality as well as to why i have such passion for certain things or ways of life. I want to mention how when my Father was nearing the end of his life he often talked about being with his Mother and he also talked about a good friend of his. In the presence of myself, my Brother and sister-in-law, my Dad said matter-of-factly that his friend was sitting right there in a chair next to his bed. Interesting how none of us had choose to sit there, but left it vacant.

Like i used to say to my Mom its right there in the verse of Amazing Grace, "When we've been there ten thousand years bright shining as the sun, we've no less days to sing God's praise than when we first begun." Written by John Newton. I was just going to comment on this and other references to the sun, like Neil Young's, After the Gold Rush…"flying mother nature's silver seed to a new home in the sun."When on the radio comes Peter Gabriel's Salisbury Hill "grab your things i've come to take you home." Neil Young also sings in Harvest…"as the days fly past will we lose our grasp or fuse it in the sun." I have wondered about myself sometimes and the answer is to connect to the sun. I feel the sun is the source of all things. The sun is the source of energy and life, love and maybe God. I am reminded of a sunflower that will turn to follow the sun. I want to keep my face directed into the sun, filling up on its energy and love and radiate this outward. Again, what else do you need when you can get it from the source, anything else is just a bonus. Keeping connected to the sun will keep you strong and grounded and healthy. The simple pleasures we have to return to. I think of Chief Dan Evehama from the Hopi's Survival Kit, Thomas E. Mails, who spends hours in his cornfield touching and talking to the corn. I think of grandfather from Tom Brown Jr.'s book and how he appreciates the sacredness of the water. I want to have this attitude of love and appreciation when sending energy to the earth. I can see how different musicians and writers have influenced me and i guess what they said somehow resounded with my soul.

Two or three times i have seen a circular rainbow around the sun and each time it was after doing energy work or prayers. I feel it represented source of God's energy becoming manifested. I find rainbows interesting or isn't it strange how if you hold a prism to the sunlight it gets refracted into a rainbow. A rainbows colours are in the same order as the colours of our chakras or energy centres. I feel that it shows in this way how we are all expressions of the light. I brought home a container of ocean water because i wanted the peacefulness of the ocean to be brought into my love and life. I feel that it will help me also to give over to God and to go with the flow letting spirit take control and for me learning to go for a ride. It has occurred to me i am blessing all the water in the world as i drink a cup of water that i feel all water is connected. This occurred to me when i brought the ocean water home and also when drinking from a water cooler at work that seemed to have a different taste some days. I believe we can, therefore, heal or bless the water by blessing a small portion of it. I also thought too of the parallels between us and the ocean. We are like a small sample taken from the greater ocean and how we are still all connected to that ocean and how one day we will return there. In that way, we are all the same. I have heard that said many times and maybe it is true. Not only are we connected to the great ocean of God but to each other as well. This reminds me of what Carlos Castenada talks about how we are all connected to what he refers to as the 'sea of intent.' If this is true, then we can affect mass consciousness by raising our own consciousness. Can we affect or raise everyone's consciousness by sending energy, prayers, etc., to raise mass consciousness? A friend and kind of a teacher of mine, Raymon Grace has for a number of years been doing this type of thing there by getting as many people around the world as possible to send healing and prayers ever solstice. One reason why i connected with him was because i was sending energy for this purpose as well. I was influenced by a story by Deepak Chopra about I believe it's known as 'the 100 monkees experiment', where they were trying to teach monkeys a new skill. What i think happened was that when the monkey finally learned the skill all monkeys around the world were born having that skill already. So it reflects that there is a consciousness that connected them all. I've thought this or read about how a flock of birds flying together like a cloud changes shape and direction all together that the flock has to have one mind.

I have been told years ago by my teacher to bless water. Many others have talked about how water is easily programmable, that it responds to our thoughts. I know that Raymon Grace works a lot with raising the energy of water, the movie, What the bleep do we know by Betsy Chase, Mark Vincent and William Arntz, talks about this as well. I believe it was my teacher J. that told me as well that we can program our water to heal anything. I've been trying this and i believe it works. I'm finding that being near water, whether the ocean or Lake Ontario, to be very soothing, calming and healing on an emotional level.

Just remembered another Neil Young song that had a big influence. I believe he sings in Cortez the Killer about the Aztecs "... and i know she's living there and she loves me to this day, and i still don't remember when or how i lost my way." Sometimes Neil was very connected. I think we get a lot of guidance from spirit through music, certainly through writing and movies as well. I'm trying to work on this and find that a lot of times i will get an impression and i am learning to trust it more. I know that i need to spend more time meditating. This will help to connect me to spirit and i can get many things. In this manner, by going to spirit i can get guidance and answers to problems. You can receive healing, gifts and knowledge. You can raise your energy and consciousness and connect with peace and divine love. You can also talk to your loved ones. It helps you to develop your own spiritual abilities.

Recently i found myself in a very negative mood. I recognized this and started to find positive things to think about. I changed my attitude, then i treated myself a little by having a milkshake and i went to a peaceful place with good energy, which was near water. I had to recognize what the underlying issues were. I was again blaming myself for past mistakes and i found it very effective to remind myself of all the good things i did for my parents and more importantly for the love and time i spent with them. I also realized that at times lately i have not been focussed on love and i had to realign myself with love. I also did some prayers and energy work to send out my intentions of what i would like to manifest in my life. I brought back my focus on love and felt filled up with this energy. I feel that when you walk through life filled with love and connected with God you will draw good things to you. When you try too hard to draw things to you, you become desperate and off balance and seem to repel people and things from you. Again it's about not being needy.

Just like past life regressions can help with self-awareness i feel that many relationships are an attempt to do that as well. I believe we draw to us in relationships an aspect of ourselves for the purpose of working out our own inner conflict. So once again the focus is within to come to terms with all parts of the self. For me, realizing it and knowing what to do with it are two different things. Infidelity, real or imagined, has at times been an issue on the part of some of my partners. I understand that underlying is a desire for love and acceptance and there also exists sometimes a fear of intimacy and fear of rejection and of getting hurt. We have to love and accept ourselves in our entirety (Care Of The Soul). Through love and acceptance we can grow rather than blame and chastise ourselves. In part, there is an aspect of me that wishes to be unattached because i desire freedom. I don't like being controlled. I don't like being told what to do. In a sense i am a free spirit who likes to come and go as i please. At the same time i yearn for love and i have a lot of passion that i would like to share. Maybe part of my problem is i am a Gemini.

My desire for freedom has been integral to leading me on a spiritual path. I have learned from many sources but have made my own mind up on what i believe based on what feels right and what i experience. I also believe that much of society is oppressive and about control but i believe that a spiritual path is the way to freedom. Freedom of the spirit. There is a certain part of me that cannot and will not be controlled ever.

I see other people who seem to have such a great life, wealth and material possessions and i have to admit sometimes it's a little hard to take. Much of society bases people's worth and importance on this. In the event i have to observe myself and see that my energy is low and i was falling into self-pity and jealousy. I needed to re-examine my life's goal and get back on track with what i think is really important. What is my soul's purpose, what makes me unique? I need to embrace that walk fully: sometimes i am not putting enough heart and energy into it and therefore i feel like i am a phony because i am not walking my talk. There always seems to be a lesson from life.

Again i see people with addictions and both this and materialism are ways to get fulfilment from external things. I think they are a replacement for self-love. For me, i feel connected and on purpose when i spend time praying for the earth, sending energy to the earth, listening to a meditative c.d. that connects me with my angels (from John White of Lillydale, New York) and doing my own meditations to connect me with my guides. The spirit world and the light. I'm also finding that this carries on with the regular time of my life. I'm feeling good about myself as i am sharing with the people in my life. I'm being more present. I'm saying prayers for others as well and i am making sure i express my gratitude to God for prayers answered even before they materialize. I'm treating each job or chore as sacred instead of feeling negative i am inviting in love and joy. When i feel i don't have the energy i will push myself even to do a little and this seems to bring more energy and incentive to do more. I often find that if i do things in bits, splitting my time between chores and personal time to do something i like going for a walk or a coffee to work best. I need to have that balance as i often find with working night shifts time and energy are more limited. If feeling overwhelmed i am prioritizing and focussing on one job at a time putting my energy and focus only on that otherwise i tend to feel overwhelmed if i am thinking about everything that needs to be done at once. Often i will make a list and this helps to take things from being on my mind. Being in the moment and present in life, full of joy comes from feeling good about myself and being involved in life and taking action also lends to feeling good about myself. I'm taking a lot of joy from the little things in life. I'm remembering my mother and how little it took to make her happy. I'm seeing the little gifts coming from spirit as rewards for my efforts to help and it feels good to be appreciated and have spirit helping you out. Besides praying for the earth, nature and the animal i am also saying prayers for my parents and my Brothers and myself. I am asking God for what i want to manifest in my life and i feel that i am deserving, because i am also giving of myself both through energy work and in my daily actions. I also dedicate the benefit of my healing work to go towards what i want, which is usually to help my parents on the other side, to benefit them karmically, to honour their dreams and wishes,etc. Aside from prayers and dedicating my healing or energy work for a specific purpose, i am also focussing my thoughts on manifesting a loving relationship. I know that thoughts are real and manifest in the outside world. I was shown this proof by a psychic years ago. She put a paperclip on a string, draped it over the back of my hand and told me to push it back and forth with my mind. After doing so, she got me to move it side to side, then in circles. First one way and then the other, then stopping it. I have shown this to a number of people and everyone has the same amazed reaction. They know like i did, that it moves with your mind. The mind is indeed a powerful thing and should be used carefully to manifest the life we want to create for ourselves and i think for the world as well. This is supposed to be used for the good.

Someone can use this type of knowledge or persuasion to do evil, like voodoo or curses, etc. it's the insane that would attempt to use it in this manner. I can't say too much about that but does someone who has love for themselves take pleasure in hurting others? Of course not! A person who deep down hates themselves would want to spread this self-hatred, self-contempt and meanness towards others they see as having things they doesn't have. Like i said, you can't harm others if you love yourself? This self-love you get mostly from your parents, from their love. A person is a fool because they think they win by hurting the ones you love. One day, they will have to face God and answer for there actions. They cannot escape this inevitability. Then, they will find out what karma really means. In spiritualism we believe whatever one sows, then that's what one will reap.

I know my parents are fine now, they're happy. I am now closer to Jesus who i sought for healing and my spiritual path has been made firmer for the dealings with this creepy stuff and people that use it. I have often thought hard about how Jesus' wishes for us to leave it to him to deal with the evildoers. A lot of people will think that i am crazy but i know what i experienced and almost everything i believe in and write about it from that. I also had confirmation from others, especially my mentor Many Horses. He said the first time i talked with him on the phone "Ya i see him." The demon, I mean. The first time i became aware of this energy, a girl told me she woke up and saw an ugly face superimposed over mine. One night, i was sleeping on my parents couch and i awoke to see this thing with horns standing beside me. It grabbed me by the throat. My Father was attacked and wound up in the hospital. He was there for six weeks. At one point, the doctor told me my Father was extremely ill and i decided it was time to call this individual i met at the Toronto Health Show. Raymon Grace, he uses dowsing in a unique manner and he worked on my Dad from a distance, his place down in the States. My Dad didn't know about it but the following day my Dad was completely better. Prior to then when the physiotherapist took my Dad for a walk, the oxygen level in his blood immediately dropped. After Raymon worked on him it remained very high. The doctor, a well-known head of his department, told me he didn't know what was wrong with my Father and he didn't know why he got better. As Raymon later explained, it was my Father's will to live. I have knowledge that i cannot share about certain partners to this crime who work with the devil. Not long after that, my Mother was also in the hospital and yes there is much that went on that i am very aware of that i cannot say too much about!

One time i was doing Reiki on my Mother and the demon must have been attached to me and jumped onto her because she started having trouble breathing and we had to go to the hospital. They decided to operate on her heart. I have reason to believe that there were intentional acts that went on behind the scenes. My Mother survived the operation and was walking around the halls when i visited. The demon must have been attached to me again because immediately after i arrived, the artery in her leg where they opened started bleeding. It took her almost another two or three weeks before she got back out of bed and this almost killed her. The attacks against them and myself went on until their deaths. I know the demon was involved. My Mother knew something was wrong with me as well. My Father was having nightmares where he was being chased by it. My Father had dementia and i feel the demon was affecting his mind. I could see that he was depressed and jealous of the relationship with my Mother and i. My Father wanted to die and i had a dream where he told me he would miss talking to me. One time when my Father was laying half in bed and half out covered in feces looked at me and smiled and i could feel the demon; i could feel it in the left side of my head. This destructive energy was attached to my Father and found an easy target. He took away all the things my Father cared about until his quality of life was gone. He couldn't do the things he loved anymore and he already was a person with a low sense of self-worth and therefore lost his will to live. The demon, i believe, somehow caused the problems with infections that my Mother was having. I know it sounds crazy but i was there. I saw that when my Father was taken into the hospital laying on a bed, my mother reached forward and it was like the demon jumped from him on to her and she grabbed her shoulder. The infections killed my Mother. If i had took that guide when my Mother went into the hospital i think it would have saved her. At one point, my Mother seemed to be doing well and then they moved her. She was in a tremendous amount of pain and the nurse would not give her any pain medication. The doctor in the other ward had okeyed this and i told her so. My Mother had a horrific night and she told me she didn't think she could handle another one like it. My Mother was asleep and talking to someone. I believe she was talking to an angel. She said "in a wheelchair." Then i heard her say that "Lonny will have to do everything." I had to leave to go to the doctors and she told me she had something she had to decide. When i was in the doctor's office a song came on the radio and i knew it was from her saying goodbye. Through dowsing i increased her will to live and she tried to fight right to the end but it was too late. I was with my Father the entire next day doing Reiki on him. I left him for a little while and i shouldn't have. When i came back to the room he was gone. At his death, i was in the chapel crying/praying to Jesus. About a week before this on our last trip outside, my Father shook my hand. My Father knew my Mother had died and he followed the next day. The battles i had with this demon are well known to my teachers and friends Jean and Many Horses. They helped me all they could.

I had only one medium who seemed to see the situation for what it was. It was at a different Spiritualist church and the person giving the message made a reference to my 'evil twin.' This gave me confirmation that negative energy was attaching to me somehow. Another Reverend i know said in a reading asked "who was sending me negative energy all the time."

Many Horses taught me how to pull an energy from your back, and how to wipe the top of your head and pull it from your chakras and tail bone. Many Horses spends most of his time pulling spirits out of people. And i too believe that people who have addictions are possessed. I feel this contributed to a large part to my gambling, although it started off as a reward from spirits. I feel this spirit started to cause problems for me. There have been a few occasions where i have felt an energy punching me in the kidneys. I knew who was doing it. It happened one time right when i finished praying to get rid of someone. Another time it happened when i realized how much money i had actually lost because of my gambling. I saw this demon one time and it was green and had horns, hooves and a tail. I believe the green represents envy. There is the time that i was doing some experimental work i had learned about a method of dowsing on someone I believed possessed. As I was doing this she got in a car accident at the same moment. So that just showed to me it's ill intent. It had no courtesy to someone who was ill or elderly. It was so filled with anger and spitefulness. My harmless Mother, what stupidity! I will tell you something positive in all this, right away i called my teacher Jean and she at that moment was watching t.v. and on the news someone was showing a grilled cheese sandwich that they had that they believed was a depiction of Mother Mary on it. At the time i didn't realize the connection or the significance as i was not really Christian. But now I swear by it. I can't explain how these things happened just tell you what i experienced and what i know happened. I have seen only a few things but enough to make me realize that the world of energies and spirits are quite bizarre. I was having trouble for a while with energies referred to by Raymon and Many Horses, as 'noogies'. Once i saw them, they were small energies flying around the air above me then i saw them all enter my solar plexus. I have since learned how to remove them with dowsing. One time i saw an energy come through my bedroom mirror, this may have been a 'noogie' as well. It looked like a tentacle of an octopus and hit me in the solar plexus. The energy was too powerful for me to block. I then began having a lot of trouble with my intestinal area, i contracted diverticulitis. My teacher Jean and i did a lot of healing on it. I had a dream of her putting on gloves and i feel she did some psychic surgery on me. I did a lot of visualization of replacing what i 'saw' with my third eye and tried getting rid of the old 'plumbing' with putting in new. I also saw tentacles going through my parent's bedroom mirrors and attaching themselves to my parents' chest and back respectively. I discovered that this particular energy seemed to be attached to a good friend of mine but i don't understand why it came after me and my family. I later found that it was connected to someone i knew and had this confirmed by my teacher Jean who also knew the individual and set up a meeting afterwards to speak to the individual about this spirit.

The main thing i can say is that it's very important to stay in the light. That negative energies are all around and are often responsible for a lot of things. They can even sometimes control our behaviour or thoughts. I find it's important to smudge myself with sage or cedar; sometimes sweet grass. I thought sweet grass was more for prayers but a few people say after using sage to remove negative energies smudging with sweet grass helps to bring in positive ones. I was told by a friend that making sweet grass into a circle and putting it above your doorway will help clear your energy as you come into the house. I can't say for sure how effective it is, but it sure doesn't hurt. I also put sea salt around the outside of my house at the corners of my property and sometimes in the corners of rooms. I like to keep garlic handy and i find even smelling garlic salt or powder helps to clear me. Some people use small mirrors facing outwards to deflect negative energy. I like to use mirror balls. I pray frequently. I find hymns to be helpful and i like to connect to sun energy. This is easily done by visualizing holding the sun in my hands or sending this energy to the earth or visualize putting it around my head or see myself walking into it. I keep Jesus close to my heart as well as the Holy Mother and i also call upon Michael the Archangel. I learned that lighting a blue candle is helpful to invoke him.

According to Edgar Cayce's readings The Lord's Prayer is supposed to stimulate your chakras while the 23rd Psalm is supposed to be a protection to your chakras. See sometimes it's the simplest things that are our best friend. Like i said before, i have found a very helpful c.d. from Rev. John

White from Lillydale on connecting to my angels and i play this often. There are many books to help you connect with the angels. I have one by Silver Raven Wolf that is helpful as well. The most common advice you hear regarding protecting yourself is to ground yourself and surround yourself with white light. You can ground yourself a number of ways by connecting your energy to the earth by sending your energy down like the roots of a tree, for example, with your mind. Put white light around yourself like you are inside a big sphere. The more you practice, the better your protection. You can also visualize white light in front of you and walk into it. I have also been taught to surround myself with mirrors facing outward to not take on any negative energies or conditions. This could be done as protection for psychic attacks although some are uncomfortable doing this. You could also instead send it into the light or negative energies could be returned with love. As well as doing those things mentally, ask your guides and angels to help you do this as well.

When i say the 23rd Psalm i stop after the part which refers to the 'annointing' and i ask that God, Jesus, the Holy Mother, the Holy Spirit, angels, friends, ascended masters, guides anoint mine and my families' heads with oil. Thus removing all negative energies and entities, negative spirits, negative disincarnate beings, negative connected souls, demons, psychic cords, negative thought forms or anything else harmful. I ask that they ground us deep into the earth. I ask that they join our hands with Jesus and that we be taken into the light. I ask that we be filled with the pure golden/white light of protection. I ask that our chakras be sealed with a white cross on a gold and or white disc, especially the crown (top of head), third eye (front and back) and the solar plexus. I ask that our entire energy fields be filled with this pure gold/white light for protection and that all holes rips or tears be repaired. I ask that our energy fields be sealed with light and mirrors be placed around facing outwards in all directions. I ask the same for my premises and my vehicles. This is put together from various learnings. I was also told by a Spiritualist minister that visualizing a cross inside of a circle over the solar plexus is a useful protection.

When under attack i will often hold a crucifix or a cross, sometimes garlic or a sage wand. Holding a Bible is helpful especially i find over the solar plexus. I command negative energy to leave immediately in the name of the heavenly Father and to repeat it three times. So, i have been guided by spirit to use a technique taught by my friend was using a drum to call the direction keepers. Facing each of the four directions drumming once and calling the word 'Kway,' Then three more times, once for below one, for above and one for the immediate space. When calling spirit either this or Michael or other ascended masters i do not do it lightly. Hematite jewellery can be helpful as it helps to ground your energy. I don't know if the magnetic type is any good or not. My mentor told me to get some parafree. It's supposed to be used to get rid of parasites. I feel this is helpful for psychic parasites as well. Sage tea is something i have also found helpful. As is having certain brewed coffees when dealing with mental attacks. Too many aren't good. Omega 3 is helpful mentally. I have not taken dream catchers seriously but i am starting to be sure to smudge them. I feel they may be very helpful especially when kept near the bed. I am no expert in these things, i have had frequent attacks and i use whatever i can until something works. I often have to use a variety of things that seem to work in degrees. I still think one of the most effective techniques for me is with dowsing as taught by someone i learned from, Raymon. I also find myself mentally trying to cut energies as it attaches to me with an imaged knife or pulling it down to the ground and mentally putting a cross over it as i ground it. This is similar to a technique my teacher taught us to clean an object by pulling the energy down with both hands to the ground and making a cross on the ground, being sure to do all sides three times.

As mentioned earlier Many Horses taught me how to pull energies off myself by grabbing at the back of my collar and pulling upwards as i take a deep breath and exhale and push down like you're going to the bathroom (sorry but it's the only way to describe it). Then you do the same to the third eye, throat, chest, solar plexus and you do the navel and pulling downward to get the root at the same time. Wipe the top of your head, wrists, tail bone, ears, back of the knees and ankles. Many Horses also said if you feel negative energy is around ask if it "comes from the light" and say "if not, then leave immediately." You can do this mentally on another person so they don't hear you and i have seen it work. Many Horses says he often sends love to stop negative energy. He will eat a garlic clove and feels this is effective. I've found smelling garlic powder or ground sage effective if negative energy is attached to me. Also, cinnamon is supposed to be effective for mental entities. When having trouble with an individual i have heard of surrounding them with pink or white light. It was also suggested by a psychic, whom i sought help from that mentally putting them in a golden birdcage would be helpful in containing their energy or preventing them from causing harm and would not be harmful to them because you're using golden light or sunlight.

I just remembered a good example of how an energy can affect you without you realizing what's going on. I just met this girl and after talking to her i had an incredible desire to give her a lot of money. After talking to Many Horses, he said "sometimes an energy can attach itself to you and make you want to do illogical things." I also realize that playing poor me is a way of getting people's energy, many people are 'energy suckers', needy.

Self-pity is one of the ways to draw from others rather than being responsible for your own life. I'm sure we all do it sometimes, especially when our energy is low. But some do it routinely. I have noticed on occasion that sometimes other people will hear my thoughts and i know there have been a few occasions when i know i have heard others. I feel badly because i thought something negative about somebody and i could feel that it hurt her.

I don't know a lot about astral travel but i have had experiences where i felt that energy of a particular girl being with me and sometimes we have had conversations mentally. It seems this girl can attach herself to me and i know she can see and feel what i feel. We have a unique relationship. I wonder sometimes if she is a guide of mine because i know there have been times where she has provided protection to me when i was being psychically attacked. One time, years ago, in meditation i saw myself in nature sitting against a tree. I was at my lowest for some reason. I was surrounded by animals and nature spirits when a woman surrounded by bright white light appeared. I can't help but wonder if it was her because i was at my lowest when we almost connected. I also am quite sure she's connected to the fairy realm. I feel that many of us have spiritual powers or abilities. I think we are much more powerful than we realize. I think a lot of our being resides in the spirit world and we have access to that. One time i was at my teacher's place and she talked about there being fairies in one area of her property. She is a big time seer by the way. I walked over there and soon everyone else who was there helping with chores joined me. She said the fairies were up in the trees wondering why we were there. She said one was taking a reed of grass and rolling it and blowing in it so we could hear. At first we couldn't hear anything. Then all of us heard it clear as day.

Another time, after a meeting i had with a girl i could sense her energy or spirit with me as i travelled home and i know once i got home she spoke to me mentally. My teacher Jean does astral travelling routinely. One time i was very upset over something that had occurred at my new house. I was lying in bed and i clearly heard the voice of my teacher saying, "Lonny what's wrong," i kind of ignored her then i felt her take my chin and turn my head to face her as she asked again, 'what's wrong." I swear to God.

Again, some confusion over what spirit is telling me. It seemed like signs and synchronicities were trying to tell me something but when i asked the spirit i felt myself being moved side to side as if being told no. I had a reading with a reverend at my church and she told me that my desire to manifest my parents' wishes was so strong that i was misinterpreting signs. I still feel the best way is to go within and see how something feels or, in my case, i feel my angel or guide or higher self physically moving my body to indicate yes or no. In a sense, i think my body is being used like a pendulum. I can't use a pendulum for yes or no answers because i know it is affected by my thoughts. Just asking a question and feeling, especially in the solar plexus. If i get a positive (open) feeling or a negative (clenching or tightening feeling), trying to understand signs drives me crazy.

Summer vacation brings about a frequent dilemma of should i stay home and do chores or should i take off and have some fun? It reminds me of the name of the Moody Blues album a Question of Balance. Balance is the key in life. I think of the Buddha's teaching of the middle path is the way. I feel it applies to day-to-day living, when to have the discipline and when to take time for fun as well as spiritual activities. I feel it also applies to spiritual teachings. It seems most places will say there's the correct or best path and not think that other teachings also have value. Man seems to need his way to be the best way. I feel there are many truths or different versions of the same truth. I like to look for commonalities between teachings. John Lennon's song Imagine he says "There's no religion, nothing to kill or die for." I feel this is certainly true when you look at all the wars that have been fought because people have different understandings of God. How can there be a thousand different religions in the world and only one of them being right? The middle path brings harmony. I like to explore different teachings and take what feels right to me and leave the rest. You have to trust what feels right to you to find your own truths rather than rely on others to tell you what the truth is.

I saw the movie Lovely Bones by Peter Jackson and it struck me especially because someone recently told me i had to let my parents go. The little girl in the movie comments "I was there for an instant and then i was gone." Recently i had been spending my time shopping looking for things at thrift shops and enjoying hunting for treasures. It really hit me again about the frivolous nature of a lot of activities, how pointless it is to be so attached to material things when what that girl said is so true. It's time to remind myself to fill my actions with things that are meaningful. Love and spirit is all that matters because that is all that is permanent. But by letting our loved ones go maybe even our love, i have to still believe it isn't permanent. In the movie Little Buddha by Bernardo Bertolucci, a comment is made, "in a hundred years from now everyone who is currently alive on this planet will all be dead, that is impermanence." In the Carlos Castenada books his mentor Don Juan Mateus, teaches to "live every moment like it was your last moment on earth." Can you feel the power in that? Although i was told to let my parents go in a reading i had last week the medium identified my father as being there and someone i can still ask for advice. It's come to my belief recently that much of ourselves resides in spirit whether that's the soul or higher self or whatever. In my reading a Reverend confirmed this; that i could communicate with my parents in spirit and, at the same time, they could be reincarnated and living another life. There is more to what she said but i will let you read about it in her book. In that movie Lovely Bones, the girl says, "when i decide to go as you won't even know it except for maybe a whisper." As i write this last line i am still in my Mom's car at my Mom's favourite place as the sun is going down over the water and faint music from the ice cream truck playing a whimsical song, lullaby and good night, by Brahm's. A very peaceful feeling surrounds me and i make a promise that i will search heaven and earth until i am with them again. In the days that follow while sitting in the front room after dinner and the sun is diffused by the tree in the front of the house filters light and i swear i can feel my Mother's energy is with it. It just feels like love. Afterwards i felt fearful of being alone. I guess i took a lot of comfort in that my parents were still with me and in some ways being actually closer to them than in the physical because they could travel with me and see all aspects of my life. It's time to face this fear as well as any other that i have. I have to get closer the divine spirit, Jesus, my guardian angels and guides to help with that feeling of loneliness.

As part of completing the first year development class at a Spiritualist Church, normally, we volunteered to help out with the last Sunday service of the year, but this is especially significant as the church is moving after 62 years and this is the last Sunday service there. I volunteered to read scripture and was guided clearly to read The Lost sheep and the Prodigal Son from the bible. I found a small booklet at work and my friend and i were looking at the various scripture, when i read this one, i felt it was the right message as it referrred to "the lost sheep", and "the prodigal son." I'm being careful not to quote from the Bible, but i find it so profound how the Lord continually 'searches' for the missing one, not the 'found' one. He doesn't give up on you! I hope that you will take some time to read it yourself, just let it sink in. It's easy to forget that it's not about condemning, it's about love!

Afterwards someone at the church gave me a message from spirit saying she got, "Michael rode the boat ashore." I don't know exactly what this means but i feel that this parable in some ways applies to me as well, that i have found my way back. This is a very old hymn, first published by Allen, Ware and Lucy McKim Garrison. I remember that it's okay not to be perfect. Jesus forgives us so why can't we forgive ourselves. But i know that the spiritual path is what i need to now and i need to walk it fully ottherwise i feel like a phony. It's time to walk the talk, i heard a Native American saying "that you can't go down a river with a foot in two canoes." It seems to me that so many activities that don't involve service on some level are useless and are a waste of time. I see how people, myself included, do things to just amuse ourselves and it feels so empty and meaningless. In any moment i can make choices that will involve me spending my time in powerful and meaningful activities, i feel i have been given gifts. I had to do an energy test at the spiritualist church in order to receive my healing certificate. A Reverend there felt that i was a "natural healer." She also told me about the guides she saw working with me. The bottom line is i feel that healing work is what i should be doing and maybe i was born to do it and it would be a waste of a life if i didn't put more effort into practising this. Remember that the dark side loves it when you go off the path and the light rejoices when you are on it. What type of connection to spirit do i want? One that is pleasing to God and the light and makes the dark side cringe. Of course, i have been told a lot of things about through readings so let's try and see what happens. A couple of days later, i had a message at the church and the medium confirmed that i was at a fork in the road and the path that i had chosen to take she saw was lined with oak trees which to her meant strength. Taking positive actions that make you feel good about yourself is very satisfying on a deep level. I was told in the message that for me spending even a few moments by water is re-invigorating. Which is why i have been drawn there. When by water i always pray that it be blessed. Water i am finding is also very calming of the emotions to me. I'm also reminding myself to use my breath to a re-energize myself. Deep breathing pulls energy deep into stimulating all of your chakras and is also very calming.

My Native-American shaman friend taught me to put food out for my parents to do a special meal. I have taken it too far i am sure, by frequently putting food out. I will continue just in a case to get aside some food to feed their spirits. I was told by him that the spirits are always hungry. I don't think you have to put a lot aside. I usually do, but i think a small amount is all they need to get the essence of the food. This i believe is a Buddhist belief as well. I especially put out their favourite meals for special occasions like birthdays, Mother and Father's day anniversary. I make sure i get flowers for these occasions and for birthdays i even get cake and balloons. I just want them to know that i haven't forgotten them. I was told putting a little tobacco by the food is like putting a postage stamp on it. It makes sure they get it. On a daily basis, i light a candle on a memorial i have in the home and i say a prayer for them to be taken and kept into the light. In the fall i put some winter coats and hats and stuff in the backyard. I also hang out a wool blanket on the line. I keep it out for a little while and then i bring it back in. I hang up the blanket on a wall and i pin their picture to it. I get a really good feeling about this. Maybe this is all for my benefit but i want to make sure they are provided for. The other day at a festival i heard the song "Somewhere Over the Rainbow...." and i wondered if it was a message from my mother? "That's where you will find me..." Written by Yip Harburg and of course performed in Wizard Of Oz.

I was at another festival recently. It was a hocky little country fair. I took a female friend with me and as we sat listening to the bands playing with only a smattering of an audience, there was a feeling that we were in the flow of things. It occurred to me that i had at times wished to have a partner who also would be satisfied spending her time going to things like this. As my friend and i went to sit in the grandstand to watch the fireworks, i couldn't help notice this very attractive women sitting behind me noticing me. I felt too awkward to talk with her but as i left I looked at her and i could feel that she felt me looking. I just wondered if that was the girl i was looking for and once again i failed to act. Some people say if it was meant to be you'll meet her again but in my experience opportunities seem to only come once and they're gone. I don't know why i keep missing these chances. I will do some ceremony that includes prayers and burning sweet grass to carry my prayers to the Creator. I will write down what qualities i am looking for a partner. I will visualize putting it in a pink box, with it wrapped in pink ribbon and see pink balloons or pink wings carrying it upwards to God as i light the paper with a white candle. I will put some tobacco on the ground beside it as well. This except for the tobacco and sweet grass was told to me by a compassionate psychic.

Remembering other ways besides the breath to raise my energy, one is joining my thumb and my forefinger or middle finger, making a circle like you see in the Buddhist figures. Using a rattle, like i mentioned before, to pull back lost energy. I was taught a technique by my friend who learned it from her friend who is also a Native American Shaman. They call it the 'tower of power.' Standing with arms down and palms facing outward bring arms slowly upwards imaging you are collecting energy from the earth trees, and sky and putting the energy high above your hand then bringing hands down in front of body imaging the body being filled with this energy. This can also be used for protection from mental attacks by manually putting energy around your head. Also i want to mention again about grounding yourself for protection and strength by sending imagined roots or rods coming out of your feet and sending them deep into the earth. Then see yourself going upwards until you connect with and are filled and surrounded by the white and or golden light. This last one is the most common teaching that i have heard but it's important.

I am dealing with a few injuries and i remind myself that i can use my mind to help to heal. I'm not saying this is a replacement for any traditional treatment or medications. I just believe we can help ourselves by using our minds intentions and visualization. For example, focus on pulling out negative energy from a problem area. Focus on the area as well as around the body in the auric fields outside of the injured area. A lot of times the problem lies in the emotional or mental or spiritual areas or fields around the body. Use whatever works for you manually reaching in or around the area and pulling it out or doing it with the mind. You could imagine a white spot light, and/or white or purple flame. A fire hose blasting light. In your mind use a vacuum to suck out any darkness. Maybe see a shower of white/gold light going through and around you washing any negativity away into the earth. A good chi-gung technique either using left handed or even visualizing the left hand going into an injured area kept the right hand lower pointed towards the ground into a visualized green flame on a copper pan. See the negative or darkness leaving via gravity and going into the flame. When finished always fill an area you worked on with the light visualized white/gold. This was another technique i learned from friends and i have had some success. It's definitely worth a try. Sometimes i have visualized the strings of an instrument like a harp running through the problem area and see myself playing the strings with the sound and vibration loosening the negative energy of the problem area and the motion of my hands strumming the harp helping to pull the energy out towards the surface. I had a Buddhist teacher who taught us to see the problem area as dark smoke and with your breath see it lifting and dissipating. When i was having problems with my intestinal area i thought through meditation i saw old, rusted and leaking pipes. I visualized removing them and replacing them with new golden 'plumbing.' I believe it helped, it certainly can't hurt.

The other day, i saw an opossum that i was concerned that may have been trapped on this bridge. When i said a prayer asking my angel to help it, the animal, judging by his reaction i felt heard it or at least sensed i was not a threat. It reminds me of a few other incidents where i felt i had a communication with an animal. One time i saw an injured seagull and every time i thought about calling the humane society he shook his head like he was telling me no. I killed a centipede once that was in my house and i distinctly heard a voice saying "why?" I've talked about dreams of talking animals and i would strongly recommend the book Animal Speak by Ted Andrews to learn to connect to your animal helpers and totems. I know that i have gotten a lot of help and guidance from my totems but unfortunately a lot of times i don't listen. Hawk guided me to buy a certain house but i let the logical mind talk me out of it. They were guiding me to rent out my house instead of selling it. With the illness of my parents, animal helpers were trying to help and guide me.

When in the midst of my grief i was walking by the water and there was a white swan close to the shore. I could feel the tremendous peace that emanated from this animal. Around the same time i was at a Thrift store and i had thought to look for some of those green animal figures (Blue Mountain Pottery). I turned around and saw two swans that were the exact kind i had in mind. I knew i was guided to buy them. I feel it has helped me in bringing that peaceful feeing, going with the flow energy into my home to help both me and my Brother, who is not well. This is just one of many examples where animal helpers have come into my life. I need to meditate and build a stronger connection with my spirit helpers so i can clearly understand what they are telling me. I don't have any more room for regrets.

The importance of staying positive is not just in regards to ourselves but towards others as well. I need to see people's positive sides. Put my focus on that rather than on being critical and judgmental. If I focus on the negative aspects i won't like anyone because everyone has them. It's a reflection of my internal state, why do i need to see the negative in others? Obviously i am not feeling very good about myself or my life. What do i need to address about myself to change how i am perceiving the world around me? I heard it said and it's probably true that when we see things in others we don't like it's because it reminds us about the things we don't like about ourselves. I'm sure i have brought this up before but it pops up once in a while and i need to pay attention to what my state of being is like on a regular basis. I need to stay in tune with myself and making corrections is an ongoing project.

I'm appreciating the help from spirit these days in my life. The other night while i slept someone in spirit gave me a chiropractic adjustment to fix my sore back. I'm once again finding that spirit takes care of you when you put effort into serving and working with them. I had made a commitment and now i am putting myself out there to do spiritual healing after taking the course at a spiritual church. In this you allow your guides, healers, angels to work through you to do hands on healing. I am also sending energy to people in my life that i know need healing via Reiki and am offering a friend or two to do healings in my home. Some people make a big distinction between Reiki and spiritual healing but i, at this point, can't say which is better. I think there both good and it's although ones more from spirit and ones more from energy. Reiki channels divine life force energy. I have been told guides sometimes work with me when i do Reiki so i don't know if there's a lot of difference, i feel that there both compatible and overlap.

I was told in a recent reading to remember an upcoming anniversary. Today is my parent's 60th anniversary and i was reminded in a reading to remember, so i made sure i celebrated it in what i hope is an appropriate way. I had a vision of my Mother receiving the flowers. My Brother and i went out for dinner and brought home a meal for each of them and put it out with the tobacco. I don't know if it's still necessary to put it outside. I bought a cake and balloons and did the same. Of course i had to leave a coffee as well. It feels good to show them you haven't forgotten them and it's healing for you as well to provide for them and share in special occasions.

I know i talked about how others seemed to have been able to take away some good karma or gifts from spirit and it occurred to me that anything they gained in this manner was probably quickly lost, i think.

In making decisions of how to spend my free time, i feel so much better when i make choices for activities that are innocent and wholesome in nature. Some will say it's boring but it just feels good that i want to stay with that good feeling. I feel that a lot of this good feeling comes from spirit as well. In making decisions i am trying more and more to focus on what feels right and also in what i perceive as guidance from my higher self or guide in the way my body is being moved (i.e., forward or backward or side to side). I'm working with this a lot to test it so i become more proficient at making decisions. It seems to be working pretty well. There were times when i needed an answer very badly and it proved to be correct.

I have had a number of strange experiences in the past and i haven't found a good place to bring them up. So i am going to now to show some of the other types of energies i have had encounters with. One time i was lying in a bed and i heard loud buzzing sound outside my left ear. Something entered my ear and then it hooked around my eye and into my cheek bone area and started to actually tug me. I don't know if it was a psychic attack or came as the result of doing some energy exercise by Carlos Castenada, but i have had trouble in this area since. I got a tattoo and on one occasion i had a dream where another person and myself were in an attic and up through the opening came some strange creatures. We were fighting them. The fact that this person was in my attic was also a cause for concern. I had one of these creatures and i was choking it. As i was doing this, a long sharp protrusion came from one part of its fingers and it pierced my shoulder right where i had the tattoo. Again i am guessing but i wonder if by having a tattoo your auric field is compromised and maybe an entity that was in that place somehow attached itself to me. Another time i was sealing up a hole in the back of my house when something invisible flew out and hit me in the mouth. One time, i was getting a healing at my teacher from the past place and i saw the hand of a man take my hand and joining it with a girls. I later screwed up my meeting with this girl. My teacher had said to me after i had already 'saw' this that there was someone there. She identified him as Raphael, one of the archangels. I was doing a meditation with a friend once and in it i went down into the earth. I saw a lot of bright gold light and my energy had the embarrassing reaction of getting a large erection (believe me it was not of normal size). Not long after someone in the class had returned from Arizona and bought stores for us. I reached in and grabbed one without seeing and pulled out this odd figure of a hunched back flute player. I thought i may have seen this figure before on my Sacred Path card book by Jamie Sams. And when i read that his name was Kokopellli, "he lived in the underworld and is often depicted with a large erection." I couldn't believe it. He is not a mythological creature but actually exists, as do angels. I strongly recommend these Sacred path cards.

I saw a play tonight that paralleled some things in my life. This individual was paid a visit by some imaginary creatures that were encouraging him to return to his dream of writing. They came also to help him rediscover his childhood dreams. This individual had a wonderful happy life with his family and after losing his child, he lost his will to live. These creatures came to help him to heal his soul and to move onward in life. They forced him to face his demons and to reach the Phoenix. The play was called In Between Places written by Aaron Joel, Craig and Ryan M. Sero.

When i talk about psychic attacks, some won't know what i am talking about or will think i am imaging things. I know what i feel and that's what i trust. I don't need anyone to tell me what i am experiencing. Just as a note to this, most times when i feel i am attacked or the presence of negative energy the next day or two a pimple will appear in the exact spot of attack.

In life situations, i find that you can't let failure get you down, you have to keep your head up. I believe that you have to take a negative situation and find a way to turn it into a positive one. Otherwise, you can get too down on yourself and go into a downward spiral. Mistakes and slip-ups are going to happen along the path but take a positive perspective. Use mistakes to adjust behaviour and get back on the good path as quickly as possible. Once again i wonder sometimes if mistakes aren't somehow necessary to push you in a certain direction.

I asked to be shown a hawk or a crow on my way home from work if there was a girl out there for me. I was driving along and saw a large bird on the ground on the grass medium as i drove by i saw it was a large red-tailed hawk and it became airborne just in front of me.

I know that my energy is down a bit and feeling too needy by wanting a relationship. Get back to mediating and filling myself up on getting centred and balanced to try to stay on the good path and trust that i will be led to where i need to go. I have been experiencing some negative energy around and i came across a Tibetan ornament known as a 'Dorje.' It is supposed to dispel evil and attract good fortune. It seems to me that it does some good. Buddhist things were something that i had felt a need to release in the past because of a negative influence upon them by another very negative individual, who i believe is into witchcraft. I was surrounded the other night with this wonderful loving warmth and it was the first time i carried with me this little figurine of the Mother Mary. Experiencing this loving energy felt so good. I wanted nothing else but to remain in its presence. I wasn't raised Catholic. It doesn't matter what religion you are. You can call upon Jesus and the Holy Mother and they will come. I know that you can call upon Ganesh as well, who is a Hindu deity and is kind of like Michael (the Archangel). Doreen Virtue's book, Archangels and Ascended Master, tells you to connect with some of these beings. I am reminded of my past connection with Melchizedek (See Mahatma 1 and 11 by Brian Gratton) who also can help with protection. In doing so, i am careful to remember for me Jesus is the most dear to me and whom i make my strongest allegiance with. Some people, including me, sometimes feel that it is not cool to talk about Jesus and the Holy Mother. Sometimes it's cooler or more exotic to follow other teachings or beings. Like i said i was not brought up in a Catholic environment and i am not talking about religion. I'm talking about making a personal one to one connection with them and personally feeling their loving presence. You don't need any intermediaries to do this and, to me, nothing i have ever experienced feels 'cooler.' I was doing some rather intense healing work, sending energy to the earth using a crystal. I felt i was guided to do this. I was reminded that the use of crystals was popular during Atlantean times. As i was trying to decide whether i should keep this crystal, on t.v. a movie was just starting and it was made by the Atlantis Alliance and part of their trademark is quartz crystals. Then, at the beginning of the movie, it showed an angel holding a ball of light. While adding energy i called upon Jesus, the Holy Mother, angels, Archangels, friends from the light, other ascended masters and guide. Afterwards i was lying down and i saw that i was lying at the feet of someone. All i could see were his sandals. I felt it was Jesus. I also felt wings attached to my back. I picked up a couple of books and in it they mention many beings of light. Names that i had heard first when doing something called the Mahatma initiations. The point is that it is fascinating to discover that all these beings of light exist and i believe they are all focussed on raising the energy of the earth and i just want to be a part of it no matter how small that part may be. We are not alone. There are many who are among us and we are working to heal the earth and us and i believe they need our help. When working with crystals it's important to clean them. Placing them in salt, rinsing them under water, putting them in a freezer for 24 hours, smudging them with sage and placing them in the sun are ways i have heard of doing so. Also you should visualize white light filling them.

I read something that i feel verifies what i have said about understanding and accepting our own dark side. In the book Archangels and Earth Angels by Petra Schneider and Gerhard Pieroth (pg. 132).... "It is protection for people who can accept the evil in themselves and in the outside world. It is for people who no longer must protect themselves against evil because they recognize that the dark side is also within themselves and wants to be accepted and loved."

It goes on to say that "only then our vibration is high enough to connect with the power of Metatran as protection." Other than that it suggests connecting with Michael. I feel this is similar to what i was saying about understanding and accepting our own shadow selves and not condemning ourselves, for not being perfect but trying to understand what the motivation is behind it and coming to the realization that it just seeks love; but somehow is not able to get it in more appropriate ways. The most important things are honesty and self-understanding as keys to transformation. I am reminded that a lot of people do not understand the things i talk about and i can't be worried about what they think. It's important to follow on your own path and your own guidance. There are still a lot of times when it hurts because i miss my parents and i believe if something hurts you have to let it bleed. Instead of trying to deny it or avoid it, allow it. The more times i allow myself to grieve the more i heal and the less it hurts. There is a person close to me who was far from the spiritual path. It was suggested that i be a beacon for him and i believe that the praying and visualizing i have been doing is starting to work.

After i got home from work i was shocked to see a praying mantis on the inside of my car door ledge. I looked it up in Animal Speak. My first thought was i need to pray more, but the main thing i got from the book was that i need to go into the 'silence' more. It talked about 'prophecy.' I also have not had much success in trying to heal a condition of mine with my mind. I probably haven't been putting enough effort into it and need to try harder. I have a book on meridians and i will look at some of the pressure points to activate by pressing where i am having trouble. I also tried putting accupeds on my foot that corresponds with the troubled area and i believe it helped as some toxins were pulled out of the area. I also put a pad (all natural detoxifier) directly on the troubled area and this too seemed to help somewhat as something definitely was removed. I have something she tells which i need to use more to help break up and negative energy outside of the problem area.

This reminds me that maybe i would be more successful in healing myself if i focussed on the area outside of my body, removing negative energy and filling it with light. Anyhow, my motivation to heal myself is high and i have begun exercising and stretching and have seen some good results which has, again, increased my energy level and desire to do more. I have been tempted to seek more treatment but i first want to try my best to heal myself first. I find that it is empowering when you take action in this manner. I picked up a few books on yoga positions at a book sale and feel that maybe a few of the positions may help heal the problem area i am having. I even started to do some jogging. I'm not recommending yoga as i understand that there can be problems caused by it. I'm not sure but i do believe it has to do with what is known as kundalini energy, that realeasing ones can cause imbalances. I'm just curious to do some stretching to help my posture, loosen some tightness and to strengthen.

I was sitting in church in a quiet meditation and again i thought about my future path in regards to relationships and i opened my eyes to see a little spider on the ledge of the pew in front of me. I watched as it wove its web onto the hymn book and then climbed up an unseen thread to the ceiling. The Animal Speak book and Medicine cards (Sams/Carson) explain the native belief that spiders are weavers of our destinies and i am certainly very pleased to see this happening as there seem to be lots of these types of messages from spirit lately. In meditation i was shown what i believe was my left hand and it had a wedding ring on it. In the next meditation i noticed a lot of dancing going on and it seemed to me that Kokopelli was present. He is a being closely associated with the Hopis in the south-west and is said to help bring fertility. On my way home the other night driving along a quiet dark road i saw a large bird in front of me that was standing on the road and flew up into the air as the car ahead of me scared it off. I have only seen an owl once before and if this sighting was meant for me it could mean "silent wisdom or an ability to see in the dark" (Animal Speak) it could also mean the "presence of magic or an omen." In any event, i always find these types of occurrences very exciting and i am hoping that this time they materialize into something concrete. I know in the past i have gotten my hopes and expectations up and nothing seemed to happen. The only thing i can do is to spend more time meditating to try to understand what these things are telling me when i feel that the spirit is paying attention to me. I feel that the least i can do is to put more effort into my spiritual path by focussing more on healing as well as going into the silence.

I had a bad cold and i decided to put these accupeds on my toes because in reflexology this corresponds to your head area. During the early morning i awoke very dehydrated but my head cold was mostly cleared up. I'm having a health problem and i have started to work out to make my body stronger and i can really see the results. Just curls with a dumbbell, push-ups, various squats and i picked up a few books on yoga to learn some stretches. Once again a negative is turned into a positive as my overall health is much better. I also find taking hemp hearts which are very high in protein and omega 3 to be helping as well. While doing some healing with my mind on the problem area i imagined that my left hand is going into the area acting like a vacuum while my right hand is pointing at the ground. I found this effective. Afterwards i filled the area with sunlight. I then worked around the body about an inch outside and then put the light over my ears where, apparently, you catch the flu from. I heard this from a person who is a friend or guide i saw a black demon inside of me. With my mind i burned it with a fire hose that shot flames. I watched it burn. I stated that this body is sacred. I have been getting attacked at the back of my legs. In prayer when i ask that my chakras be sealed with a white cross and a white or gold disc i ask the same for the back of my legs. I find that dowsing is effective in removing these 'psychic cords.' I also visualize taking a sword and cutting these as i encircle my body with it. I also feel that skunks showed up to guide me to use smells for protection. I feel i can't go into detail over what i use for this. I was reminded of a few techniques to use while being attacked. One was crossing my arms, legs, fingers, and even toes. I also find it helpful to put on a light at the head of the bed, especially a warm yellow light that reminds me of the sun. I also know that wearing a hat is a simple and easy protection but i don't think a black one is best. I also surround myself with light. Sometimes i find this a little hard to imagine so i will see a ball of light and put it over my head like an astronaut's helmet. Then i will imagine a shirt made from light and put it on. Then i will do the same with pants, i sometimes forget to tell negative energy to leave. I will have to do this on a regular basis. I know i have mentioned a few ways others have told me how to do it. In dreams i have seen myself doing this with a crucifix commanding negative energy to leave in the name of Jesus Christ. Whatever works for you is the right way. I feel that between the Kokopellis i have and some angel figurines in prayer as well as a few pictures of angels (one is cupid and the other angel is carrying a woman) i brought out of storage, are helping me to manifest my desires. When i start to worry over details i remember what a very good psychic told me when i was 20. She told me then i would be married twice. I let go of worry and fear and maintain a positive attitude. I remember the power of intention and state my desires and try to let go. I know that the attacks make you appreciate the simple things like feeling healthy and i am content in doing simple wholesome activities. It helps to keep you on a good clean path. Suffering also teaches you to have more compassion for the suffering of others. I find myself getting very angry at some things that have been happening in government. First they bring a new tax that they say is going to save us money because it combines the two previous taxes but now they have things that are subject to this tax. They think we are stupid. Then the Members of Parliament give themselves a 15% raise. I'm shocked at the greed. I do not believe our government or society in general cares about anyone or about the earth! There is no compassion. I remember a song by Rush - Closer to the Heart.... "and the ones who hold high places must be the ones to start, to mould a new reality, closer to the heart." And remember a line from their songs …"and the meek shall inherit the earth...." Remember that this is what is said in the Bible as well. In my regular prayers i have been asking that two big angels be sent to myself and my family members as well to remove any negative energy, to keep negative energy out and to keep us in the light, to protect and guide. When asking this i definitely feel a loving presence.

I have further proof of how this demon attaches itself to people and attacks me through them. I had a dream of this particular person walking in my house and i apologized to him for what i consider minor incidences, but the attacks continue, i remember at my previous house and i saw this person standing at my back door and he was green, which i interpret as green with envy. I also find that when this energy is around insects such as centipedes and flies will be quite noticeable. Now i will say the Lord's Prayer and the 23rd Psalm.(Again i also call upon help to clear away negative energies and entities, spirits, negative disincarnate beings, negative connected souls, demons, negative thought forms and psychic cords). I also ask that mine and my family's chakras be sealed with a white cross and white disc and gold disc. I ask that we be grounded to the core of the earth and join hands with Jesus and ask to be taken into the light and completely filled with this white and golden light. I also ask that we be surrounded by mirrors facing out. I feel i need to focus on doing this more with my own mind. I have been reciting a prayer called the Mantra of Protection from the Fellowship of Universal Guidance of Glendale, California. To try to clear others i command negative energy to leave. I mentally hold a cross in front of this person as i do so i try to mentally pull it out as told to me by Many Horses (grabbing it by the upper back/shirt collar area and pulling). I will use Reiki symbols or Raphael's (archangel) banishing star (see the book Angels, Companions in Magic by Silver Ravenwolfe). I mentally put a white cross and discover their solar plexus as well as mine if being attacked. I will mentally surround them with white light. I will mentally shine white light into their eyes. I will light a blue candle and call upon Michael. Sometimes i will just mentally see a blue candle. I also mentally take the person's hands and join them with those of Jesus seeing white light as their hands join. I will then take the person or push them with my mind into the white light. I believe lighting white candles are also beneficial (of course you should never leave a candle unattended and I always sit it in an ashtray). I like to use those little tea lights. Sometimes i draw a figure of the person and put sage and/or garlic or sea salt on their picture. Cinnamon is supposed to be good for mental abilities. I will also draw a cross and circle over them or over certain areas that need protecting. Sometimes i will draw the five pointed banishing star of Raphael around them. I'll try anything I can think of that might work and watch the results. Again dowsing as taught by Raymon Grace is effective in removing negative energies. Sometimes i will put their picture inside of a Bible. Especially with the 23rd Psalm. I also find it effective to mentally put the sun or white light around the person. I also sometimes, when i feel i need to, call in the direction keepers by using a drum and asking for their help. I return the favour for help received by sending energy and prayers for the earth. I find it helpful for me if i am having trouble with negative energy to connect with the angels. One way to do this is by listening to an Angel CD, the one i have is by Rev. John White from Lillydale. I think it's also beneficial to call upon the Angels of the person that negative energy is connected to and ask for their assistance in clearing the person. A clearing and protection taught by Jean is done by using the forefingers of both hands. You start above the person's head with fingers together, draw a half oblong saying "all evil shall depart, never to return." Then complete the bottom half of the oblong bringing the fingers back together saying "no evil shall enter." Draw a cross at the bottom of the oblong with your fingers saying "in the name of Jesus Christ." Do three oblongs to cover the entire person. Start at the top and overlap the oblongs going under their feet. Then do one more large oblong to cover the entire person. To be sure i do all four sides of a person. This can be done on a house as well. You can also do it with windows and doors, inside and out, to be reinforced you should do it from the inside as well.

Sometimes i will mentally draw white light around the property as well as visualize the house surrounded by white light or sunlight. In sending energy to the earth, like i said before, i like to see the earth between my hands surrounded by light. Often i use the sun. Sometimes i have to use my solar plexus or throat chakra to push the energy into this visualization. When doing this, i ask in return for something like protection for my family and myself. I again remember what Grandfather swayed from one of Tom Brown Jr.'s books, "the present is like the palm of our hands with each finger being possible futures." It's up to us to help determine that future with light and love.

I saw a movie last night with Robin Williams. His children were killed, then he was also in another car accident. It shows him in the spirit world where he eventually reconnects and rescues his wife who is trapped because she committed suicide. At the end of the movie, they both go back down and reconnect again in another life. I don't know the name of the movie but it was very powerful and i felt i was guided to see it. It made me think that my parents are together and that they may be moving forward so they can reconnect again in another life. It also helped me to keep trying in my personal battles by reminding me of the determination i had before i came down here in this life. This vision i had was made after having a past life regression done and by working with it quite a bit. I had a recollection of myself before being born. A skunk has moved under my porch. At first i thought about getting it out then i began to think what are skunks know for? Their ability to protect themselves i thought. Maybe it is protecting my property against seen or unseen energies. Maybe it is showing me the best way to protect myself is through the use of smells. Once again i referred to my trusty book Animal Speak and the keynote is "sensuality, respect and self-esteem." Maybe the skunk is helping to draw to me a partner. In any event, i am greatly honoured by the presence and help of all animals.

The other day i went for a drive to St. Jacobs i was kind of lost and i had a thought for hawks or crows to give me direction. A short while after about 100 crows flew in front of me. It turned out that the exit i needed was the next one.

I had a dream i was at a casino and i hit something i thought was good on the machine and it paid hardly anything. I was very upset feeling that i was ripped off. That i was being treated unfairly by the universe. I thought about this after i awoke and i have seen how the universe has offered me guidance and opportunity on a number of occasions and i usually failed to follow it or take advantage when the opportunity presented itself. Where i felt hard done by was when i tried to force the universe to reward me. It seems that the universe presents an opportunity and if you don't take advantage, it's gone. I don't think it's fair but it doesn't matter what i think. I can't blame the universe for my failings can I? Another example of this was after i sold my house, i kept getting the impression to invest in gold. At that time, gold was selling for about $800 Cdn. an ounce. It is now roughly $1,400. I cringe every time i hear the price. The one thing i know though is that the universe has helped me in the past and is continuing to help me. I'm finding that the spirit is working with me a lot these days providing me with an abundance of the things i need. Especially things that i find useful for protection. These include hats (i use them only occasionally) hematite rings and bracelets, a certain type of oil, a few new angel figurines and animal figurines, a picture of Padmasambava (from the book The Tibetan Book of Living and Dying by Sogyal Rinpoche). A Tibetan figurine, some more mirror balls for certain areas in the house and also some long sleeve red shirts. According to Many Horses the colour red is very protective. He even recommends wearing a red ribbon around your neck. He feels at nighttime it is especially good as it stops negative energy from entering him. I like to wear a haematite bracelet when i sleep (non-magnetic). I find it very soothing and protective. It also stops my leg from twitching when i have too much energy and need it grounded. In my prayers lately i have included that two big angels be sent to each one of us to remove negative energies that may be attached. To stop the other ones from entering. To keep us in the light and to protect and guide us. I want to mention that i feel sage tea is good to drink when having psychic problems with negative energy.

The way i am noticing or taking advantage of spirit guidance is that i am paying attention and following impressions or feelings that i get. I had a strong impression to go into a certain store where they sell mirror balls. I often ask to myself where should i go now and see what feels right. Sometimes i may hear something. I used to think that what i heard was my thoughts but i realize now that that is not always the case. Just this morning i hears the "okay ace." That's what my Dad used to call me. I rarely feel alone. I have also noticed that when i make an offering of food to my parents i get a good feeling that i believe comes from them. When sending energy to the earth with my mind i see myself holding the earth with my hands and then i see sunlight filling it until i am holding a ball of sun. I wanted to mention this again because i think it is very important that we do what we can to help the earth, nature and the animals. Sometimes i feel the need to push the energy out of me into this vision. A lot of the time it seems that i am using my solar plexus. Sometimes my heart and throat chakras or energy centers. I remember my former teacher Jean, saying to "use everything you've got."

I went to the Royal Winter Fair in Toronto last weekend and there was an exhibit from the Ministry of Environment or Ministry of Natural Resources and they had some animals on display that are endangered and i find this incredibly painful for me. This shouldn't be the case. The reason so many animals throughout the world are endangered of becoming extinct is because of the loss of habitat. Because of the encroachment of humans. The Haudenosaunee, meaning people of the long house, Grandfather's people (Tom Brown Jr's mentor) as well as the Hopi Indians and probably all aboriginal people believe that they are caretakers of the earth. With no disrespect to them but i believe the reality is that we are all responsible for this. I remember the movie 2001 A Space Odyssey and the message of the monolith was "remember you are just the tenants not the landlords!" Our money and possessions are left behind when we depart this world but to too many of us that is all that matters. There are times when i have let money become too important as well. I am starting to get my old motivation back to get busy to try to fulfill my life purpose and try to help the earth. Spirit helps those who help.

In a recent meditation i saw myself carrying a heaping bundle of gifts in my arms and i know that it represented the gifts that spirit was giving me for my service to helping the earth.

I know that my Mother's spirit is still with me. The other night i was extremely upset about something and i felt her take me by my left hand. This had become a trademark that i have come to recognize as hers. I found my other hand stroking my hair and the side of my face. I know that i would not be doing that on my own, it was her doing it. Shortly after, i had a dream where i came back to a house that was full of water and my Mother was standing there trying to get rid of it but there was too much. I knew the house represented me and water emotions. I saw that the house had cracks all around the foundation. After thinking about the dream i went back in my mind and patched up the cracks and put in a pump to get rid of the water.

I ran into a girl that i used to know. Funny because i was thinking the other day of an embarrassing situation that happened with her. I notice more and more i am getting these types of things happen when i seem to get a glimpse of the future. I don't know why i ran into her but i feel that many people that i used to know think i went kind of crazy. I have to laugh because in some ways i can't blame them. This girl seems to be doing well financially or materially but i don't think there is any spiritual awareness with her or most people i used to know. I don't care about what they think. I'm not going to let their opinions have any importance to me. They don't have power over me. I know my path is different than most but it is based on the truth and the heart. It is the only path that i could have followed. How can you have some awareness of spirit and energy and not want to incorporate it into your life? I remember clearly as a child looking up at the stars and wondering what is out there? I remember thinking is there an end to the universe? Does it have a sign saying dead end, turn around? Does it go on forever and, if so, how can anything go on forever? I had the intention even then of knowing the truth and experiencing it first-hand. My life has been extremely difficult at times but it has at times been wonderful as well. I have so much more to learn and experience. Like Don Juan Mateus (from Carlos Castenada) says "...for me it's the only path worth travelling..."

Cassino's To Cardinals Part 1

I went for a massage today and, after i talked her into doing an extra half hour session and listening to a Native American flute c. d., i am sure i had an out of body experience. I felt like i was viewing the whole scene from above.

There is a skunk living under my front porch. I wondered at first if i should try to get rid of it, but i thought what are skunks known for? To me it's their ability to protect themselves. I felt that maybe the skunk was protecting the front of my house from seen or unseen unwelcome energies. I also thought that maybe it was telling me that the best way to protect myself was by the use of smells, i.e. oils. I looked in Animal Speak (Andrews) and the keynote is "sensuality, respect, and self-esteem." Like the cartoon Pepe la Pew, maybe it is helping to draw to me a partner. In any event, i feel that the animals are great helpers to us.

One thing that seems to be kept getting thrown in my face, and it makes me very angry, is when i see the selfishness of people. When things keep happening, it must be there to show me a lesson. It probably means i need to take a look at my own selfishness; i don't really think i am selfish, but i must be on some level, otherwise i wouldn't keep having to see it. I need to develop my own compassion more and try to do more for others.

There are many things that are uncertain in my life, and when i am feeling needy, i just think of my connection to Jesus and that fulfills me. If there's more to come into my life, that's great! But if not, i have something very special and permanent that will remain of supreme importance. Like i said before, it's a very real connection and all i need to sustain me.

I am aware that i have a habit of kind of collecting things and living a safe life in seclusion. Certainly my focus has been on protection for me and my brother, and this obviously contributes to a more reclusive life. Much of my life i think how this has kind of been a pattern and it's time to make an attempt at living a fuller life. To take risks and see what happens. I know that life will go by and that i will return to spirit soon enough.

Speaking of this, i am really becoming aware of how fast time is speeding up. It just goes by so fast. I like to sit back and think about things and plan them and i know that i have to change that strategy because things come at you so fast there's just time to take action. I feel that this speeding up is all part of the changes that are taking place with the shifting energies and the 'dimensional shift' that is under way. It's going to be an interesting ride: live from the heart, try to emulate Jesus, and live with the Christ consciousness.

I was talking to my old friend and mentor, Many Horses. I wanted to get his permission to pass on his teachings if my writing turns into anything. He says "no problem." He is happy that other people might try it for themselves, to remove negative energies. He mentioned how he had to return home because all his helpers were being attacked by 'noogies', which i talked about before. Many Horses also told me that it would be good for me to get my brother a cross and chain. With Christmas coming it gave me the opportunity, and much to my surprise, he liked it! Many Horses also told me that i needed to go see on of those old time Chinese doctors to get my kidneys looked at. I didn't realize it at the time, but i had been getting attacked by a 'noogie' as well. I had been getting a pain in my solar plexus which is where i had been attached before by this thing that had tentacles like an octopus. I am cognizant that it was significant that a friend asked me to sit in his car after he got out of the hospital; he was in there with diverticulitis, which is what i developed after my encounter with these things. In any event, a few days after talking to Many Horses, i had a vision of one of these things and i reacted in my mind by taking a sword and putting it through its head. I remember now that, last year in meditation class, spirit handed me a sword. I feel that my higher self is now ready to operate like previously it was doing so in dreams. I'm not sure but i have been listening to a different Rev. John White c.d., this one on the higher self, and maybe this cd is exactly what i needed to bring my higher self into action. I have also been sorting mail left handed more frequently to help prevent injury, and i noticed how different i feel when i do this. I'm using a different part of my brain and at times i feel almost like a different person. Whether it's right brain, masculine side, higher self, spirit guide, it's an interesting, and i feel significant development for me.

The following is kind of hard to explain or connect the dots of seemingly unrelated events, but i know they are connected and, although very personal, it is also very powerful in showing how much my parents are helping me and i think have saved my life. I give a ride to work to a friend of mine and i noticed a mouldy or musty smell from her. I wonder if she has black mould in her house. I know that she has a lot of health problems and i can't help wonder about the connection. I had been told that black mold can kill you and that it has a spirit that goes with it. At Christmas she gave me a present that had an angel taped to it. The angel was blowing a horn. When in the hospital, my mother was given one and she did not react well. My former teacher said the angel was 'calling her home.' I had wondered that as well. I guess it was God's wish but my Mom knew it and she had such a desire for life she didn't want to go…i didn't want that either. I felt this mouldy smell was definitely negatively affecting me and the angel kind of made me wonder. On Christmas Eve, i felt good about taking a drive out to a certain mall just outside of town. On the way there, i took the scenic route, which was my Mother's favourite ride. I made it to the lift bridge and was stopped there as a large freighter was coming into the harbour. I was the first one at the edge of the canal. To me this had a lot of significance, although i didn't quite know what it meant. See, there was this one time my Mother and i were sitting at the back of Henderson Hospital on top of the mountain. We were looking at the city and harbour below. There was a ship heading towards the lift bridge and my Mother didn't want to leave until she saw it go through. I knew it was a sign to her that she was going to live. She never told me this, i just knew it. See, her Brother had a big part in building this lift bridge years ago, and i think she was asking him for a sign. I knew my Mother's energy was with me while i sat watching the boat go through, but this is only part of it. I did some dowsing on this situation with the mould and the spirit. I don't know if this made a difference. I feel my parents did something. When i got home from my other Brother's place on Christmas night, i flipped through the channels and stopped at this movie i never saw before. I believe it is called Meet Joe Black. For those who haven't seen the movie, Joe Black is apparently death and he has come to take away Anthony Hopkins. In the meantime, Joe Black falls in love with Anthony Hopkins' Daughter and is going to take her with him as well. She is willing to go. Anthony Hopkins tells him it's wrong and that he should tell her who he is. The Father convinces death to take him but leave his Daughter behind and Joe Black does so grudgingly. After Joe Black takes Anothony Hopkins away, Brad Pitt appears, apparently the one whose body that death had used. He and the daughter of Anthony Hopkins were obviously connecting and making a new beginning to have a life together...i believe my parents are behind the scenes directing things between this girl and me. The same one that they tried to bring me together with over a year ago...i also feel that maybe my parents may have sacrificed themselves so i could go on preventing me from leaving so i could have a life. Just to confirm this, the song at the end of the movie was Somewhere Over the Rainbow, this is written by Harold Arlen and E.Harburg. I knew this was a message from my parents as this was a song that i heard last summer at a festival and felt it was from my Mother. I felt this so strongly that i wanted to name the book (if it happens) On the Other Side of the Rainbow. A couple mornings later as i was taking this all in, and getting very emotional, i heard 'dreams really do come true'.

I can't believe how much i love my parents. I can't believe how much they are still helping me. As i went to the shopping mall, after being stopped at the lift bridge, i felt that my Mother's energy was with me. I was on the alert for something to buy for my Brother. I walked by one store and a sign dropped in the show window as the girl cut the string as she must have been changing signs. As i glanced into the store, i saw a set of Rolling Stone collector's glasses. When i gave them to my Brother he said "that was a good present." He usually doesn't say anything.

In meditation prior to Christmas, someone was putting a coat on me. I feel it was the leather coat that i found at a thrift shop for $15.00. I know that this was a Christmas gift from my parents. There was another jacket and a rug as well that i got incredibly cheap, the rug i bought at a Pow Wow.

On Christmas morning, after lying in bed for a little while, i heard the song Hark the Harold angel's sing, glory to the new born King. It is written by Charles Wesley.

I went for a drive out of town to a place where my parents and i used to go a lot. There is a small outlet mall there. As i was walking, i got a very warm feeling like someone put a coat of love around me. So i went into the store and i found a pair of shoes that i have been looking for for a long time. Just wanted to share how they are working with me.

I have found the need to seek out some new energies to help me with negative energy. I am convinced the buying figurines, often animal ones, help to bring in different energies that can be helpful. I won't talk about which ones I have bought, but i have been buying a lot of different ones, testing them out and getting rid of some that no longer seem to work so well. It's an ongoing process that i do by trial and error or the scientific method of experimentation and observation. Like i said, it's an ongoing process.

On a lighter note, i have been ready a few times to try to move forward in regards to going out with a girl. It seems that turtle keeps showing up, both on t.v., then seeing one in Value Village, it seems to be telling me to be patient. I pulled a Medicine card and it said 'Be patient.' When talking to Many Horses before Christmas, he talked about a possible relationship and told me to be patient. Just to make matters more interesting, one of the turtles i saw on t.v. was a story about a Gallopogos tortoise named George who was 100 years old. He apparently is the last of his species and they are trying to hook him up with one or two female tortoises to see if they can get him to successfully reproduce. It seems weirdly like my situation. Maybe i feel like George, it is hard to find a compatable mate who can understand my life and dreams.

When i found negative energy attached to me, i found it helpful to hold a crucifix towards myself and command negative energy to leave. I have also experienced some problems with crucifixes. I was told before by my teacher that sometimes when you have a crucifix, you can end up getting crucified. The other day, i saw this with my own inner vision. I had a crucifix on my bedstand and i saw a vision of me being hung up in a similar manner. I find crosses to be better for having around, although a crucifix may be useful for some purposes. I know that for me, i will keep most of them put away unless i need to use them for clearing.

I also find crystals to be sometimes a hazard. In experiencing a psychic attack, it seemed to be helpful to me to put the crystals in salt and cover them up. Whether it's because crystals magnify things or that they can be used as openings by negative energy, i am not sure. I'm not going to get rid of the ones i have, but just be aware of the potential problem and know what is helpful when experience psychic attack.

I met someone who told me that Michael the Archangel sucks negative energy out of people like a vacuum. I have found this knowledge useful in helping someone who is not completely capable mentally. I call upon Michael, was told that lighting a blue candle helps, but i also use my own mind to suck out negative energy, and i found it effective. Something else i have been trying and found effective was with my mind i bless water and i dip a kind of septre in it and i make the sign of the cross with it towards the person that negative energy is attached to. With my mind i see that this 'holy water' is landing on the person, and as i do this at least 3 times i also bless this person in the name of Jesus Christ. I also do the room, all sides, ceiling, and floor, and the bed as well. I keep doing it until i feel they are cleared. I then join the person's hands with Jesus. I ask also that Jesus take him into the light and clear all negative, unclean energies from his with his light.

In dealing with negative energy, i have found it most important to have a strong, clear connection with Jesus. In a meditation, i walked down to the edge of a river and met my guide who is standing by a boat to take me across the river. I saw it was a native guide and the boat was quite small and i felt the water was going to contain some large waves (which to me meant some type of spiritual trouble coming). Something told me to continue walking along the bank. I saw a statue of liberty (to me representing freedom). Jesus was standing there by a huge boat. It became very clear to me the route i needed to go. I have also been hearing in my head the song i believe by Triumph: "Hold onto your dreams and i will take you there." To me this was clearly the words spoken to me from Jesus. In the same meditation, i was walking with Jesus ad he pointed to the side and i saw Ganesh as well as the Buddha. I feel he was telling me that they were helping me as well, that it was fine with Jesus if i sought and received their help at times, it was a 'good connection'. Clearly i need to focus on my partnership with Jesus first. In any event, i certainly appreciate help from any masters, they are welcome friends and do help, but i know that i need Jesus to be first and his connection is the most significant part of my spiritual path and connection to the light as well as my confidant.

I've been getting attacked from various people. Part of me wants to send negative energy back, but i have to remember that it's not them doing it, at least in most cases. On some level, i think that there is some negative feelings towards me and this certainly doesn't help. I have been working on reducing this through dowsing. I feel that when people are not happy with themselves or their lives, it leaves an opening for negative energy to take hold. Jealousy seems to be the underlying emotion. I feel it is the same negative energy working through many people and i have been looking at mentally cutting the connection between these individuals and negative energy, i am not saying i recommend this, i am getting attacked and i am trying anything that works starting with the least intrusive measure. I have been dowsing to remove negative energies, spirits and demons. I have been sending white, gold, and sometimes pink light to them. I have been calling upon Michael to help to clear them. Again, i myself will sometimes try to suck it out of them like a vacuum. I call upon the Angels in a way described by the Angel book by Silver Raven-Wolf. Again, i found that mentally dowsing them with holy water in the pattern of a cross helpful. There is a clearing method talked about in the Sacred Path Card book by Sams where you use a whirling rainbow. I have found this to be quick and effective. I will occasionally place them in a golden cage to contain the negative energy. After clearing, it's important to fill them with light.

I will sometimes ask for help from Jesus as mentioned before. Sometimes i will surround them with white light and then mentally place a glass jar over him to hold this good energy to keep the positive. It's not to harm but to assist being more positive and 'in the light.'

Again, i have found a huge difference made by what figurines i have. I have found that some of them i had to get rid of immediately as they seemed to make me susceptible to psychic attack. I realized that i had to remove any that were too feminine or small and vulnerable. I had to make sure that the energies of these figurines were strong, yang, or male to help with protection. Like i said before, i was shown and believe it to be true that i have to make sure that Jesus's energy is clearly demonstrated as being the dominant one in my living space. I have also done this in my a loved ones living space as well, although other energies are helpful and supportive. I also have to be careful as to where i put and how i use crucifixes. For example, i don't put them too close to someones bed; i like to use a cross instead. I just feel i have to be careful when assisting others. I like to hold a crucifix if i am commanding negative energy to leave in the name of Jesus Christ but as mentioned before sometimes we can take on the symptoms. We have to be very aware and vigilant in this manner as to not be attacked. I often hang things up and frequently move them.

In meditation, where i am looking at whether there are future problems coming, i realize that sometimes this is influenced by my own thoughts and i have to be confident that the future problems are minimal as this influences sometimes what i see and therefore allow to happen. Jesus showed me that he will take me across the water in a large boat and that is where i have put my trust, and i am confident that he will do this.

I did a past- life regression and i saw a few things: first was a knight in armour with a crest on my front. I later saw myself on a white horse fighting a black knight with lances. It sounds kind of corny but that's what i saw. I also saw myself as a child, i believe during the Depression, or it could have been during the industrial time, in England. I think it was the first because i believe i saw my spirit entering into my mother in this life.

I decided to do a past-life regression on my own the next day and saw myself as a Native American chief being chased by cavalry. I chose not to hide but to stand up to them. Afterwards, as i was coming back, i felt some of the energy of that life connected to me. I saw myself in my temple (part of my meditation) and i saw Jesus there. I prayed to Jesus and made a strong pledge to him. I saw his right arm go up to block any negative energy from that life coming forward. When i woke up, i had an impression of being out in the bright sun and going to a certain thrift store. I went there and there was a figurine of Jesus giving communion to a female. I knew that this is what i was guided to buy and i later prayed in front of it, strengthening my connection and commitment to Jesus. Just buying a figurine or picture isn't enough. Afterwards, i saw on t.v. a freighter travelling towards the open ocean with the sun behind it. I pulled a few angel cards and they both talked about release. One said to call upon Raphael to help me release. I knew it was talking about my sometimes thoughts of lust. I thought why is it there, what is it replacing? I realized that my shyness and sometimes introvertedness was behind this. I saw how this kept me from walking through doors of opportunity in the past. I saw also how fear, bad relationships, and low self-esteem contributed to this as well. I went deeper and remember my parents fighting and the feeling that there may have been an issue of faithfulness. I remember the separation anxiety that i had as a young child and feel that a lot of this was because of some early deaths I had in past lives. Also, a major issue for me was when i was young and a particular girl moved away. I know it sounds crazy, but the feelings i had for her were so deep that part of me stopped living after that. I didn't even realize this until Jean pointed it out in a reading. Even then it took me a long time to figure it out.

I found that a Buddha figurine, as well as a Ganesh figure, each holding their left plam up with the right palm facing outward, was helpful in blocking negative energy directed toward me or my home. I found it useful to mentally put a white cross in front of the person sending negative energy, and, if needed, to mentally throw blessed water on them in the shape of the cross.

I decided to buy a Jesus figurine and put it in my Brother's room. After i bought one, i stopped at a thrift store and found a mug from East Side Mario's that had a statue of liberty on it. (It reminded me of the meditation in which one was there beside Jesus). My Mother and i used to go to East Side Mario's a lot for their appetizer specials. It was one of our favourite places. I know that it is my Mother guiding me.

In my prayers, instead of asking for 2 big angels to be sent to each of us, i have been following what Rev. John White does in his Angel Guides c.d. and asking that we be surrounded by 3 angels with Jesus standing behind and above to complete a circle of protection. I ask that they remove all negative energies and spirits and to surround us in the light for protection. I would definitely recommend getting this cd if you get a chance.

Sometimes prayers don't seem to be enough and i need to focus on surrounding myself with light, or sealing chakras, or grounding. I find it helpful to do this with others i am protecting. I will ground them and take them into the light. I have been using a purple flame lately to help remove negative energies and it seems to be effective.

The Buddhists talk about life being an illusion. I kind of think it may be like the movie The Matrix. Think about it. Even as a child, we're told this: "Row, row, row your boat, gently down the stream. Merrily, merrily, merrily, merrily, life is but a dream." Written by Eliphaet Oram Lyte. This is kind of similar to Carlos Castenada when he talks about the nature of reality or maybe it's not quite what he's saying, but reality is not as fixed and secure as we believe it is. This just got me thinking that if what they say is true, then we should easily be able to affect or adjust the dream we're having. Maybe this is not exactly what the Buddhists would recommend; they would say 'be detached.' Something to think more about.

I have been under a great deal of attacks. I was getting attacked by animals in my dreams and on 2 occasions i saw that they were killed. On the one occasion, my teacher was in the dream with me, i think giving me instruction. One time i saw a bear skin rug just before i woke up. The other time i saw a lion that i had strung up, upside down with what looked like fishing line. This was wrapped around its neck and it was dying. I became aware of this and had compassion for the lion, so i cut it down. This was not a good idea as all hell broke loose until i finally had to string it up again and kill it using my mind. I heard the expression 'lucky charms.' I am aware of that some Native American people use 'charms' to cause trouble for people; i feel it's a type of black magic or voodoo. I found myself also getting attacked by every animal figure, emblem, and picture i had and even ones i encountered outside the home. I did a lot of smudging as well and clearing on them, going around them on all sides, pulling down negative energy and making crosses on the ground, as i was taught by a teacher who frequently clears negative energy. I also cleared and sealed them using another technique taught by a longtime teacher and friend Jean where i make 3 circles commanding all negative energy to leave and commanding that no negative energy shall enter, and i made a cross at the bottom of each circle in the name of Jesus Christ. I talked about this technique in more detail earlier. This whole situation also made me realize i had far too many figurines and it was time to let go of some. I realized i had to pay attention to the energy coming from various human-like figures and even some angels as well: letting go of some, clearing others, and sometimes temporarily putting some away in the shed or trunk of my extra car.

I was also instructed by my former teacher's husband's guide during a healing session in which he channeled to cut down on the number of figurines that i had, as i was giving them too much of my power and it made me more vulnerable. He also instructed me to regularly smudge them and to ground them, mentally connecting them deep to the core of the earth.

One positive result of this ordeal is that i have become closer and closer to Jesus. I kept finding spiritual items at the thrift store that i felt guided to. Across the street is a church with a large white cross. i really felt this cross has been shinning a light to guide me. I eventually decided it was time to visit this church, and my first time there was on Palm Sunday, and i took communion. I found it a very emotional experience. Although i have taken communion before, this was different. I remembered the meditation i had in which Jesus said "I will take you there." I have felt the need to let go of alot of my Native American things. The energy with a lot of them just didn't feel right any more. I gave away a couple of Native American figurines and it was an emotional experience as i felt i was saying goodbye to a guide that i was very connected to. I have a lot of respect for the Native American teachings and ways, but i felt i needed to do this to connect with Jesus in a more profound way. I had to make more room for him and also show him my loyalty to trust him as my guide. I have heard someone saying to me; "I will set you free" and, "I can move mountains."

On one occasion i was taking a drive to go to Toronto. I drove by someone standing dressed up as the statue of liberty. Then i noticed the car ahead of me had a Jesus fish on it. I ended up buying a Bible and a few books other books one on prayers and the other about Jesus.

One time i was having a really difficult time and i saw Jehovah Witnesses coming around. I met them outside and as i accepted the booklet to be nice, i felt Jesus's energy with them and the booklet. I'm not saying i am going to join, i am just telling you what i noticed.

That same day, i bought a figurine that i thought might be helpful and i clearly heard in my head "Go tell it on the mountain, over the hills and everywhere…go tell it on the mountain, that Jesus Christ was born", it was written by John Wesley Work Jr. Another time when i felt i made a good decision to get out of a difficult situation, i clearly heard the song Morning has Broken in my head. Written by Eleanor Farjeon.

I don't know if anyone else has the same experience regarding this as i do: many times when i feel negative energy attached to me and i can't seem to clear it, i have to look at clearing family members. The energy somehow becomes attached to me by attaching to others who are close. The people who this comes from are sick and I often wonder if it's intentional done for sport or if it's done by something that has a hold of them, by their 'spirit' that is not in good health. They are many possessed individuals and i have to remember this as well. I don't know how conscious they are of their actions! I do believe that some are stupid enough to use the ungodly spirits to give themselves some superior feelings of control or power because they lack a conscience, sad! It's silliness to use forces of darkness because as you control others you lose support in your life from the light of God and you will fail and you will fall. Life has to be supported by God's light to stay otherwise it with wither away. Like a fig tree supported by the light it will bear fruit. They don't even realize that God knows everything and there is a very heavy price to pay by the hands of God and Jesus Christ, not mine but theres for when you harm another being and take satisfaction in it... I'm just going to place my focus on sending peace and asking the angels to help contain the negative energy and to heal them.

I am definitely sure that you have to be careful about hanging up crucifixes. A few times after enduring an attack, i found relief by taking them down. It seems that you can take on the energy of the objects around you. I find crucifixes at other times to be helpful. It's just something that i need to be cognizant about i have also found that the Michael figurine with the demon under him to be troublesome.

i find that this allows or invites this demon energy into my home. Believe me i have worked with this one alot. Fortunately, i have found some Michael figurines without a demon attached. Not easy to do, but i feel, once again, that i received divine help on this. I had a vision of Jesus walking with his arm around a figure that looked exactly like the figurine i bought, and Jesus was very happy.

I just had a birthday and i am very happy because i saw some good things in meditation and got some good messages from my angel cards. But, i also know my parents are around. I was tired on Saturday and i usually buy a coffee and a pop to set aside for my parents. I didn't feel like going out, but as soon as i did, i felt like i was wrapped in a blanket of love. At the baseball game, i made sure that i 'shared' my food with them, and i had a vision of them both sitting there in easy boy chairs enjoying the game and the festivities.

I have been using these angel cards, some by Doreen Virtue, and these other ones called Karmic Angels, by Helen Saltarini. I love them all and should have been using them years ago. The Angel Oracle cards by Doreen Virtue actually give you actions steps to do. They really do seem to be aware of what is going on with you at that moment and what you need. Before picking one card, i felt this overwhelming amount of love and compassion. Then, i picked the card and it said the

Ascended Masters are with you and they're assuring you that there is nothing to be afraid of. These cards are cheap and are worth a million dollars, buy at least two of them!

In a reading, it was told me that i should use a bell to do clearing work. I have also found that using a white candle and commanding negative energy to leave, to go into the light, seems to be helpful. I have been told by a few people that what i need to focus on is to be more forceful when i feel negative energy around, commanding it to leave. Telling it i don't accept it and sending it back; sometimes telling it to leave in the name of the Heavenly Father or Jesus Christ, repeating at least 3 times. Sometimes like Many Horses says to say: "If you don't come from the light, then leave!" Also, telling things to "leave immediately."

I have to release any fears and knowing that i have the help of angels has helped. I am also aware of the importance of not feeling like a victim because this only encourages more of the same treatment. What i have also been getting from spirit, the angel cards, my one time teacher Jean as well as a psychic that i have found useful, is that it is very important to maintain positive thinking and visualizing a positive outcome. Both the cards and he encouraged me to spend time in meditation each day, to visualize success, create a positive perspective, and to take more control of my life rather than allowing outside events to influence me. A couple of ways that my psychic friend and ally suggested i do this is to get into a positive frame of mind, surround myself with gold energy, put mirrors around it and choose a colour and see it coming out of my solar plexus like a fountain, and observe how my day goes. He also told me to meditate with this attitude and stating to myself, "i am sitting in the middle of my world, and i affect it, not the other way around." He also told me to see a book, to turn the page, and mentally write at the top of it "Lonny's Chapter", and to write what i wanted to create in my life and, yes, make sure i smile and know the result will be beautiful. I have also found a visualization that personally works for me, but i don't want to share too much about it except you need to create one for yourself even if you draw a picture and go to this beautiful place often. I found that it's effective not to just visualize but to actually put yourself there; feel what it feels like, the sun, the wind, etc.

I have started going to a Baptist church near me as i felt guided to go there. I felt that this has helped me develop a real connection to Jesus. At times i have been almost overtaken by emotion, especially after i took communion. I have also gone a few times to a Catholic church and attended mass and i like it as well. I even prayed the rosary one night and i had a vision of Mother Mary turning to look at me and then i saw her energy above my home. I plan on continuing going to both of them as well as going back to my old Spiritualist church to hopefully start serving again by doing healing work.

I have come to realize that there are a lot of people possessed by negative spirits. I believe you leave an opening when you don't feel good about yourself. Just as a side note, that i know i had a demon attached to me, but i didn't realize it. So i am sure that most people don't realize it. I felt good about myself except for a certain behaviour, so i guess this is how i let the demon have some control. But, i also know it was there before i started doing anything stupid because others saw it. Anyways, i know that the demon can encourage bad behaviours and certainly addictions and the best thing to do is just stay in the light and you must keep yourself and your behaviours clean. I find that sneezing even is a way to dispel negative energy and i believe this is why people bless you when you do this.

If i find negative energy coming from a person, i will mentally put a white cross between us, or sometimes mentally hold up a mirror. I know that i need to focus daily on surrounding myself with white or gold light and putting myself and another i protect inside a mirror ball.

Like I mentioned before, if i have to i will mentally put them in a gold bird cage. If this isn't enough i will encase it is glass and put white crosses (or crucifixes) around it. The next step i don't like to take, but if you have to, put them in a box. I think sometimes the wood is needed, depending on the energy. This is not meant to harm but to contain the negative energy. I feel that i need to put more focus on my own protection.

I have been reminded recently of how we can become so attached to the physical world, whether it be possessions, money, or sex. I have been talking a lot to someone about this. I was telling her it's like an elevator that's operating on a lower lever, the sacral chakra or energy center just below the naval. We have to bring it up into the heart. We have to operate through the heart, to have a Christ consciousness. Love is all that matters. I want to use Jesus as my guide and just be love. To be a beacon for his love to shine through me into the world to help ease the suffering and pain that is all around us. I frequently visualize taking someone's hands, especially the elderly or handicapped, and mentally join them with Jesus and ask that Jesus take them into the light. I also find myself mentally saying prayers or asking for angels to go to someone or to simply bless them. Our attachments to the physical world are foolish really because all these things that we desire and cling to so hard are all temporary and impermanent. Only spiritual love is permanent. Just be love.

We all feel a void inside of us sometimes, and we try to fill it by looking outward for things. I think what we are all really looking for is love. When we realize that we are love, we won't need anything.

How can we need what we already are? We just forget what we are or do things that damage our self love. This is what we need to repair. We must love ourselves. We must stop doing behaviours that cause us to damage our self-worth. Many times we seek self-gratifying behaviour that temporarily makes us feel whole and content, but it goes away, so we go and get more of it. Connect to Jesus, and feel the love. He's there waiting for us. A lot of our behaviours make us embarrassed or feeling unworthy to go to Jesus. He sees everything already, and loves us anyways. He knows that what we really seek is love. We have just lost our ways. We have to understand that within ourselves so we can forgive our foolish behaviours. We just want love. We just want to be reunited with that love that we came from and will return to one day. We are part of that love, like drops from the ocean returning back to the source one day. I think we suffer from separation anxiety from this separation and don't realize it. We are connected to that love. I love to watch the sun rise and I fill myself up with the loving warm energy of the sun. To me, this is God's energy and it and Jesus are all i need. You can also just visualise watching a sunrise and feel it warm your chest and solar plexus, let it penetrate your very being, open up your palms, feel it fill your soul. Feel the love.

I had been feeling sorry for myself and one day at a baseball game, i saw a poor soul lying on a stretcher bed. His body was hardly recognizable as being human. I felt such compassion for her that i almost began to cry. I will never feel sorry for myself again. I want to go through life having compassion for the suffering of others and also gratitude for how God and Spirit provide for us on a daily basis. I'm learning to walk in the light and follow the guidance of Spirit. It's pretty amazing stuff how they lead us to things that we need. I've actually been doing it for a while. I'm just trying to tune in more. I think the Angel cards, books and tapes have helped. I was reminded at church, though, not to worship angels, but i have to remember to thank them more. Sorry! It's not just the Angels doing this, but also our guides and loved ones in spirit. Even though i am single, i never feel like i am alone.

I have recently joined a new meditation group and was told that i need to meditate on a regular basis, all the answers are there. I'm finding this to be true. Through meditation, i connected with my guardian angel, who is physically alive on this plane. Since that meditation and subsequent ones, her energy has been with me constantly and we have discussed whether a relationship is a possibility, this was discussed mentally but i know it registered with her. Although i care for her, i have to step back from the emotion- filled connection that i deem as important or significant and look at what type of relationship i feel i need to make me happy. What qualities are important in the person and what type of things i need to be there for me to be happy. I know that trust are important for me. Although i can still care for someone, i have to know it would be a healthy situation for me in the physical.

I went for a hike the other day and a deer stood in my pathway looking at me for the longest time. I know that deer represents gentleness and innocence. I know that i have to return to those qualities within myself as well, and that that is what i seek in partnership. I had a dream years ago of a talking deer and what struck me was the power of this animal, the power that is contained within these qualities. I was told in a recent reading that the 'keeper of the woods' would reveal itself to me, and i feel that is what happened.

When you have an inability to control yourself, something has power over you. I think you have to approach it like the Alcoholic's Anonymous 12 step program (i am not sure exactly what it says). You admit that there is a higher power and you admit that you are powerless over your addiction or behaviour. You turn to God and let God's power give you the inner strength to change, to take control of your life, to stop being a victim and to become empowered. I also pointed out that the dark side wants to prevent people from doing this, that it likes to have control over people's behaviour, to keep them doing things that are lustful and to prevent them from being in the light.

In another meditation with my temporary group, we went into the white light and the deer was there leading me down a path. I found myself with the Fairy Princess and at that point i made my decision to not pursue a relationship with her but to put my efforts in another direction. I should also mention that the 'fairy girl' is currently married. I have recently felt spirit guiding me to help her to connect with Jesus and God's light. This person is a guardian angel to me, she has come to my aid numerous times, so i feel the least i can do is to attempt to help her in this way by sharing what i have recently rediscoved. I hope that we can have a spiritual friendship/partnership of sorts since we have this ability to communicate telepathically as well as her ability to 'be with me' in a spiritual sense, but i am not too sure if she's cognizant of this.

During this i did a lot of meditation and i used Angel cards a lot. And, to be honest, i am not sure how helpful they are as i seemed to get contradictory guidance. I'm not sure if we may influence the cards ourselves. In any event, i feel the best guidance comes from your own meditation and for me asking myself a question and seeing how my body answers. I feel that i get yes and no answers by my body moving sideways for 'no' and forwards for 'yes.' This is not 100%, but i have worked with it a lot and this seems to work the best for me. I'm also finding for me if i hold up the pointing finger of my left hand while i do it i seem to bring down divine guidance. It seems to connect me to above like an antenna.

It certainly is beneficial having your guardian angel with you a lot, as i have noticed I have hardly had any attacks.

I had a dream a while back of a beehive and i saw a ship coming from the right side. The beehive to me represents fertility and the ship coming from my right is my future, meaning my ship has come in. I believe it was the next day i went for a drive and I thought about asking my Mother for advice, but i didn't. A few minutes later, i got stopped at the lift bridge because there was a large ship coming into the harbour, and yes, it was approaching from the right hand side. I feel that this was my Mother at work again because of her connection to this bridge and her Brother. I'm learning more and more that my mother intuitively knew a lot. She loved to wear white clothes and the house had mostly white/off white colours with white linoleum through the kitchen, hall, and bathroom. She also had numerous mirrors in the house, she used bleach a lot. All of these things seemed to me to be ways that worked for her for clearing negative energy. Obviously bleach cannot be recommended because it's a chemical and is so strong that some may have negative reactions.

In my meditation group, one person said there was a Native American chief standing behind me. (i was glad to know that he was still around!) She said his face kept changing and told her i can be nothing or i can be everything. This reminded me of what a Reverend had said in a reading i recently had regarding my situation and she said i had to choose between a physical life or a spiritual one. I saw it more as a choice between the soul and the spirit. After this girl told me this, we did another meditation in which we visited the Akashic records, where your past life records are stored. I saw myself standing there as a Knight in armour. When i said i want to be everything, i saw a fire become lit in the solar plexus. This reminds me of a vision i had years ago after doing a series of 3 past life regressions with my former teacher J. After the regressions, she took me to a place she called the Holy Grail. I didn't see anything at the time there, but she told me to keep practicing. I eventually had a vision where i was emerging out of a pool of silver liquid and was taking physical form. I noticed i was inside some large dome. I feel that i was having a memory that was just prior to my most recent incarnation. I remember the determination i had at the time before coming down here and i just want to regain that and keep it!

I realize that the issues that a soul mate of mine has i know them well because i too have them, at least on some level. I know i have to also ask myself what part of my own feminine side do i want to honour.

In taking a closer look at myself, i realize how i too have been focusing too much on external things, like food, coffee, and shopping. It seems like i am always buying something or ingesting something. Even though most things i buy may be spiritual, there seems to be an attempt to get fulfillment in this way on my part. We always have to watch ourselves.

Again, with getting guidance from ourselves, i sometimes make a statement and see how it feels in my solar plexus area. A good feeling would obviously be a positive affirmation, while a tightening or clenching would mean 'no'. You can also stand there and see if you move forward 'yes',or are you being pulled backwards, the opposite. I have found this to be quite reliable in the past, i also hold up my pointing finger to connect to above. Again, another way of getting guidance is i choose a direction and see what i see in meditation. Am I happy? What signs is Spirit giving me?

I did some healing work at the church the other day for the second week in a row after a long absence because of dealing the constant psychic attacks. As i am doing the healing work, we are just channels for the healing energies and healing guides to work through. I said to myself and Jesus that this was the only thing that mattered to me. Nothing else feels as good as this and i just want to keep doing it, to make it my first priority. In the book Follow Me by John MacArthur, he states "The best joys of this world are shallow and empty compared to service to the King of Kings."

A few months ago, i was listening to Doreen Virtue's c.d. set, Connecting to Your Angels. There is one part where you invoke Michael to help clear your house and i did so. I noticed that Michael was hovering above me, then i saw this energy standing in front of me and he was wearing sunglasses. I pulled the sunglasses off and broke them and i noticed that his eyes were just black. I held a cross in front of him and had no response. Then, i shone sunlight into his eyes and again, nothing. When i held a crucifix up to him, he bolted and i noticed him going up some stairs and as he opened up some door, light shone in and i realized that i had been held in some kind of dungeon. At least my spirit or soul was being imprisoned and i didn't even realize it. I made sure that his energy was contained in a gold cage. I ripped the door off of this dungeon, i filled it with light and i made sure no one else was there. I can't remember if there was, but prior to this, i kept having visions of my parents being restrained with handcuffs and things like that. On numerous occasions, i cleared these from them with my mind and would then take them to Jesus and see Him take them by the hands into the light. I have had it a number of times when i was unsuccessful in clearing myself and never got results until i did clearing work on close others. So this is something to be aware of how were connected to our loved ones and how are energies affect each other. I need to be more cognizant of this in order that i am helpful with them as well as towards myself. For these reasons, i have to be very careful who is in my energy and in my home as it protects others who are close to me when i am protected and clear!

The other night i had a dream where i was being held captive by 3 or 4 people. I recognized a few of them. They were building a cage in the basement. I don't know if this happened because of someone close to me had the negative energy attached to them or because my own behaviour lately had not been as clean as it should. I also went to a few casinos because i was on vacation. In any event, after waking and being bothered by this dream, i mentally went to the one i recognized, the same one the demon was attached to, and i told him he doesn't have power over me. I then saw him turn into a little old man and walk away. I feel that this showed that he had lost power and his power over me is only there if I allow it. I almost forgot that when i awoke and was lying there, i heard a voice say "fear not." This was the voice of Jesus, and i knew he was standing right beside my bed. Lesson: stay in the light and serve Jesus and there is nothing to fear, 'He' is always keeping an eye on me.

I find that my Brother needs to be cleared often, through no fault of his own he's like an open window. I'm not an expert and can't advise anyone what to do and don't recommend it to others because you never know what may happen! One thing Jean taught us to use on ourselves is clearing by using our minds. I pay attention to what i see, removing all negative energies and spirits, any obstructions or anything that seems to interfere or to be harmful. If i need to, i will call upon Jesus and Michael to help me get rid of them. I like to do various things using Holy water, smudging with my mind, smudge it with sage.

Sometimes i will imagine using one of those smudge pots you see priests using. I'll take a crucifix and command the negative energy to leave (3 times). Sometimes, i will physically remove them. Then, i will mentally paint everything white or gold, put white crosses on the wall and fill the room with white light or sunlight. I'll also ask Jesus to make His presence permanent here and i will ask that an angel or gatekeeper be assigned to prevent any more negative spirits from entering. When i remove a negative spirit, i will see myself putting him into a gold cage covered with glass, with crosses or crucifixes around it facing inward and ask Michael to take him away.

In a dream last night, i saw a friend of mine who i seem to be at odds with. Then, i saw many individuals shooting arrows at me. In my dream i went into a shed or barn and got a rifle out and started shooting back. Next, a Native American chief showed up and was handing me something to write. I felt he was telling me to explain the situation in writing. I can't remember the exact events that happened afterwards, but i awoke with a great desire to find and return to the cause that was greatest to my heart and that is sending healing energy to the earth. Without having a cause, then life just seems empty and aimless to me. It becomes centred around myself and finding pleasure rather than trying to do something bigger than worrying about myself.

What an awesome day! I felt guided to go to Niagara-on-the-Lake today and have a picnic (sub) and do some writing in the park at the mouth of the river. As i walked towards town i kept hearing the word 'fort', i walked around the town anyways. At one point i asked my guides and angels to take away the fears and worries i had been having that seemed to be preoccupying me. A few minutes later, i walked into a shop and one thing i found was an angel worry stone. The card said just what i needed to hear: "Give your worries to the angels…release your doubt and fear." Being there reminded me a lot of times with my parents. I was getting very emotional. I needed a coffee and and couldn't find one. After looking for a while, i screamed out in my head, i need a coffee now! Just then i looked to my right and noticed the café had take out coffee (which is what i wanted). I found a few things (spiritual) that i had been looking for and some i felt good about. I wondered about the time as my parking ticket was good until 3:14 pm. Five seconds later the guy in front of me told his girlfriend it was 1:30pm. I noticed a sign that said ghost walk. I thought about some friends of mine that went on one there and remembered about the fort. I personally didn't want to go on any such walks. I thought we should be helping spirits into the light, not profiting from them. Anyways, i had seen enough of the town and thought i had just enough time for a quick tour of the fort. As i walked in, i was drawn to the guard house. While there, i felt that i met a spirit. I believe his name is Henry and he is a British sergeant or guard, he has mutton chops sideburns. He was very friendly, and happy, and extremely courteous. We had a lengthy conversation. It was quite an experience! And, yes, i enjoyed the rest of the tour and just happened to be there as the main demonstration was on and it was the first time they had done it this year. After, i walked back to the car and saw that the meter girl had just passed. The time was 3:14pm, the exact time i had on my ticket!

I've been hearing the song "Can't Find My Way Home", by Blind Faith, a lot in my head. I don't know if it's coming from a spirit. In any event, i invited any spirits who so desired to go "home" to come with me to church. While there, i asked for help from Jesus and also Rafael. I visualized an opening of white light and Jesus standing there with hands open and I imagined that i was joining hands that were with me to Jesus. Like i said, i asked that the Archangel Rafael help as well.

Once again, about those angel cards, i am not saying they aren't good or helpful. I do think they help bring in the angels. I just think it's good to not become too reliant on them, especially if making big decision. I think it's best to get your own guidance through meditation and feeling.

Thinking about life and about how we live over and over and i guess the only thing you can really do about it is to share love and kindness to all you meet.

I bought a book on fairies as I promised my guardian angel (fairy princess) I would read to her so she could understand more about her spiritual nature. In the book, it talks about the character of a Fairy Queen in A Midsummer Night's Dream, by Shakespeare. I have always had this strong yearning to see this play, almost a haunting feeling about it. I guess this explains why.

Some years ago i bought a picture of a young woman standing in the middle of a ring of fairies. I didn't know why it appealed to me. I eventually got rid of it because i thought it was not good for me because i felt it made me too feminine and i needed to get more masculine to fend off attackers.

I was told in two readings that this individual doesn't have her feet on the ground. I was also told in one of them that very spiritual people often have this problem. This got me to thinking about some of my past relationships and that this was likely the case with some of them. I went to a resort for a few days on the guidance of Spirit. In a meditation in the sauna i saw my Native American Chief hand me a peace pipe. I need to relax and refocus my goals.

I've been hearing in my head "the life of Riley" and yes, i have been living it up pretty good because I'm on vacation. I'm single with no kids and no mortgage (thanks to my parents). But i would much prefer to go back 5 years when i had a mortgage with a house with all kinds of problems because my parents were still here in the physical. I think they are still around. It is probably them guiding me. I need to focus on connecting with them more. Part of me feels guilty or undeserving to be able to do things and spend money. I feel that my parents deserved to have had a better life. I remember my goal to try to have a child. I've been holding a pen and paper and i feel that the pictures that are being drawn are not from me. I asked my parents to be with me and i think it's good to ask Jesus and the angels to oversee any type of communication to make sure its coming from who you want it to.

Part of the feeling unworthy is i haven't been doing enough in the way of service. I know that i wll feel better when i go back to putting in regular effort into hands on healing and sending energy to the earth. Then, i can gratefully accept any abundance the universe has to offer and share it with others the best i can.

I signed up for a spiritual retreat in Lillydale, New York as i had a really good feeling when the program calendar came in the mail. I was standing in my driveway wondering if my car would make it down there. As i returned to the b.b.q., a crow feather was lying on the ground. I felt it was a confirmation that i was on the right path and i would make it there okay.

I've been listening to Doreen Virtue's Angel c.d.s and i have been finding them very helpful. I'm not sure if i am imagining it, but sometimes i hear her voice in my head.

I once heard Jesus say that he could move mountains. Jesus is freedom. It's very important to keep your soul clean. It's about control vs. freedom. I know that a lot of churches attempt to control as well and each tells you that their way is the only way. But, i go to a number of different churches and i do it to strengthen my connection with Jesus and other spiritual beings. I'm there to get what i need, it's very real and extremely beneficial. I go to a Catholic mass because i feel the communion is very important to do on a regular basis, taking Jesus's energy into my body and spirit. When at mass once, i felt an energy attached to me and when they were preparing communion, i felt something leave. I heard "i have them". I feel i was helping some spirits cross over. I also heard a thank you. There is a stained glass window at the church with Michael the Archangel standing there with a white horse with him. While at church one mass, i saw Michael standing behind me and he had a white horse with him. I've been hearing lately "lying in the arms of Mary". I had two readings at the spiritualist church and both mentioned the name Mary. One described her energy. That night i had a meditation group at a friend's store. I was kind of trapped up against a wall and i looked down and there was a card with Mother Mary right in front of me. I only get these benefits by attending mass. When i go to the Baptist church, i feel a strong connection with Jesus there and i think he referred to it as his 'temple'. The point is it's important to attend church, but take from it what you need, work on your own personal connection to Jesus and Mary while you are there. See it as a meeting place where you are demonstrating your intent to come to Him. I feel it's important to develop and build our own connection to God and the Lord, with no offence to the pastors and priests. We shouldn't give our power to them. I believe it's about our personal one-to-one connection with no intermediaries. When i was a child, i was lying in bed at the age of 10 or 11, and i used to talk to Him. I felt His presence and i felt like he was my best friend. I could feel His loving comfort. It was very real. You can't tell a 10 year old that it wasn't.

I want to also mention Doreen Virtues angel cards again. Sometimes, particularly with Michael's cards, i will hear him say something to me as i am picking a card. "I will set you free."

I keep thinking of that movie, Matrix, and the part where their plugged in at the back of their heads and they're living in some type of false world. Like that, i feel that our greater self resides in spirit, and i feel that we too are trying to become free from energies that are trying to control us. Freedom is all that matters. I believe that Jesus is the key to freedom. No offence to other ascended masters, who i do respect and appreciate.

Lately, i have been finding myself filled with love. The pain and suffering that i have endured has led me to the point, not always but usually, where i don't want to see others hurt, but just want to send out love. Just like Jesus. I'm not trying to pretend i am Him, but we're supposed to use Him as a guide and try to be like Him. I guess suffering can make you bitter or it can lead you to have compassion. I think it's Jesus that has helped to open up my heart. So maybe the difficult times were somehow necessary. Now all i really want to do is to be of service whether it's by doing healing or by passing on love everywhere i go.

I saw the movie, Our Idiot Brother, writters David Schisgall and Jesse Peretz, last night and i have to admit that Ned reminded me of myself and it made me feel good. He's this easy going, gentle soul, who's only real fault is that he's too open and trusting. I had a reading from these people who are Christian-based and believe they get messages from the source and i was told that God loves my openness. I love it too! I know it's resulted in problems, but i think it's the only way to be. Life's too short for bullshit!

I decided it was time to stop leaving food out for my parents. I wanted to make sure that i wasn't keeping them anchored to this world. I wanted to make sure that they were free. I heard the line "I can fly higher than an eagle"...from song You Are The Wind Beneath My Wings, by Jeff Silbar and Larry Henleyand I also heard "make us proud." In a reading i had the day before my Dad's birthday with a reverand. My father was saying, "That's my son, he's doing God's work!" Nothing could have made me feel better, and knowing that my parents are proud of what I am doing will give me more and more motivation to stick with it and to try harder. I reminded them that they deserve a lot of the credit for being the examples to me that made me strong and humble. Like I said, i chose well when I picked them, but i know it's not the first time.

An example of my parents' influence: I'm in Niagara Falls and i am choosing to stay in a lower-end hotel. I'm here to relax, write, meditate, etc. I went out for breakfast and i then stopped at a thrift store. Then, i just wanted to take a morning walk down to the falls and enjoy the weather. The simplicity of this and being in a tourist town when it's not busy reminds me of when my parents used to take me to Virginia Beach. The simplicity has a wholesomeness to it i like and maybe i got it from them.

In another reading, i felt that i have needed a few of them lately, one thing that i became aware of was the presence of a guy on my mail route!, a crusty older guy. I used to stop and talk to him frequently. Now, he's a guide or helper to me. "Some wild shit", i heard him say, in reference to what i am dealing with. He has a good sense of humour in a gruff way. I was going to go to the beach one day and i wanted to take this book on fairies with me that i just bought. I heard a voice say, "Don't forget your purse." Quite a character.

I think that it's probably a lot to do with being shit on by so many people and by being attacked so often by negative energy, that acts of kindness by people and by those in the spirit world fill me almost with an overwhelming sense of gratitude and love.

I've been hearing a lot from Spirit lately and sometimes it's confusing and contradictory. I believe part of it is interference and certainly there are different aspects to the spirit world with different levels of awareness. I don't want to shut down communication with my parents, but i also want to attempt to connect with the Master to get my guidance from because i know He will take me to where i need to go. I want to know and follow God's will. I'm not saying that others in spirit can't be helpful, but there have been a few occasions where my parents were wrong, but i wish i listened when they told me to invest in gold! Oh well.

I just want to mention one example that happened recently. I heard "Value Village" and i kept hearing the word "Mikasa", which I know is a brand of crystal. I was getting rid of a few things, so i dropped them off and went to look at the crystal, not really knowing what i would do with it anyways. I couldn't find anything and had a quick look at the figurine section, and there was a crystal angel with the label Mikasa on the side. Not only that, but it was the exact same angel my Mother bought for me once. I knew it was my Mother directing me there to buy it for my

Brother. The angel is playing a guitar. On the way home, i heard "celestial song." Thanks again, Mom and Dad.

Here's another example of how spirit leads when you let them. I had a feeling i was guided to go to Value Village again, (a thrift store where l have found an incredible amount of things i needed both spiritually and otherwise and i know are gifts from God.) I was having a coffee first at the mall and i heard the name "Raphael." I went to the thrift store and eventually decided to look at the jewellery case and i spotted a silver St.Christopher's medal. I saw also there was a depiction of someone on the other side, and it was St.Raphael the Archangel, the one who is in charge of healing.

I've been drawn again to gemstones. One crystal my friends talked me into getting, i heard spirit say "peace maker." So i felt i needed to buy it. I need to trust spirit in telling me what i need and i figure it's worth a try to see if it works. I have a collection of items that i buy to keep and use when appropriate, i consider them like one would a medicine, you have at your disposal to deal with all types of situation, you never know what you need and what works is what counts.

Again, i just want to mention that it seems that everywhere i go every church or course i go to, they all seem to say that their way is the only way. I go to many different places, all for different reasons, and God goes with me. I believe he guides me as to were i go, in most cases. You have to be discriminating and accept what feels right for you and leave the rest. Do not buy into what anyone tells you. You have to be responsible for your own spiritual path. For example, i love going to Catholic mass. I find it very important for prayer, for taking communion, which is extremely beneficial to bring in the spitit of Jesus into my body. I have brought the Holy Mother into my life in a real way and i have seen Michael standing behind me while there, he had with him a white horse, same as in the stained glass window and he put his hand on my shoulder. I find it very helpful in clearing away negative energy and crossing myself and i find it very helpful working with Holy water. The Baptist church is another great place. It helps me to connect to Jesus's energy. The one i go to has a great musical band and i find they're very inspirational and emotional. I saw my mother clapping her hands and dancing to the music in her own very unique way. I also saw her during a hymn at the Catholic church. Of course, none of these places would agree with Spiritualism. They should read Edgar Cayce who explains how the Bible was changed and reincarnation was taken out. Spiritualism, the continuation of the soul, is a fact. Going to Spiritualist churches gives me a chance to do healing work. For me, serving Jesus is important and this is one of the main ways for me to do it. Of course, you may hear people, even at Spiritualist churches, put down Christian Spiritualists, and to me they don't know what they're talking about, because it's the perfect combination. Also, you have people who do spiritual healing put down Reiki. It's all ego, peoples self- importance of needing to be right or better than their fellow man. All that matters is the truth, which you must find for yourself. It's what's in your heart that matters. A course became available that is like mediumship/healing, but more from a Christian perspective. I like the idea of getting my guidance from Jesus and to try to connect to the highest and the best. But, the person doing this course puts down the Catholic church as well as Spiritualist churches. It's very frustrating to me to see this attitude everywhere. I know that the Catholic and Baptist churches help me to connect with Jesus and the Holy Mother, and i am just filled with this rapture, it's almost overwhelming the love i feel. I find that i am getting tired because i am out a lot these days attending either meditation nights or doing healing work and i am signing up for other courses, but i am so pumped up because i feel that i am finally on my path! I'm feeling so fulfilled that i just want to do more and more. I feel that i am working with the Divine and i am following my life's purpose. I'm finding you can feel the angelic energy as well as that of ascended masters when you take a card. Often, i can hear them talk to me when i am doing this, and once i had a clear vision of Michael hovering above me when listening to one of the c.d.s. I feel like i am living life more fully. Even though i am single, i don't let it stop me from enjoying life and going places. I've been hearing from Spirit "back to basics." One way i have been spending my free time is by going to fall fairs.

I like the purity and innocence, the wholesomeness. Living a full life doesn't mean you have to be taking off on expensive trips. I went to an apple festival and walked around this nice little town. I bought some apples and cinnamon donuts and enjoyed a Scottish pipe and drum band. I think it's helpful to participate and take a little bit home with you. It's like going to the Grimsby Peach Festival. You need to buy a peach sundae. One other thing i have finally come to realize is that sometimes it seems that things seem to work out best when you stop trying too hard. When you listen to Spirit or trust impressions you get and go with it and things just seem to fall into place, it's amazing really how you seem to go to the places you need to or find the things that you need, even if you didn't realize that you needed them. I'm trying more and more to trust the subtle impressions i get, realizing more and more that they are guidance from Spirit and not my own thoughts which i often tend to dismiss because of this. Often it's a direction to say something to somebody and, when i do, it seems to open up an avenue of discussion that is usually very helpful to the other person and to me as well. As a side note, sometimes i will hear a humorous comment in my head to say to someone, and i know it's usually my Father.

The other night, i got talking to someone about favourite movies and it started a process for me of fond memories of my parents watching certain movies and i remember their laughter, i.e. Flirting with Disaster with Ben Stiller and Tea Leone, Richard Jenkins, Lilly Tomlin, etc.; John Cleese in Fawlty Towers. Then i remember sharing some of my favourite books with my Mother and Father, i.e., The Boat Who Wouldn't Float, Grey Seas Under isn't funny but there's something in the book that appealed to both my father and i and Farley Mowatt is such a great writer and when his humour does come out, it's hilarious, his wording, his wit, and his dry sense of humour. With my Mom it was To Kill a Mockingbird. It's so special to have shared the things that mean so much to me with them. I felt like i shared a deep intimate part of myself in that way. I also remember all the laughter they had with their friends, there was so much fun and laughter in their lives and it feels so good to think of their good times and know they had a good life.

When driving along and i see a dead animal i always ask for it to be blessed and taken into the light. I don't know how much it helps, but it doesn't hurt to try. The other day there was a dog or coyote and after doing this with my mind or prayers, i had a vision of the animal licking my face and running through a field, happy and free.

I feel that the connection with Jesus is very important to be successful spiritually. Since connecting more profoundly to Him, and also the Holy Mother, my healing work has taken on a new level. Also, with this was a greater commitment on my part to put myself out there to do His work and help people to feel this connection, love and energy that i have found. Like i said, i feel both the Catholic Church and the Baptist Church have given me invaluable connections. I don't totally believe everything about any religion. I take what feels right for me, and if i am not sure, i will meditate or ask God and Jesus or my higher self for clarification. I feel praying to the Holy Mother has brought her loving spirit to me. I feel taking communion on a weekly basis to be crucial as i am physically and spiritually taking the body and blood and spirit of Jesus into me. I know that the next step for me is to spend time reading scripture. I will open the Book or ask what i need to read. Having these connections gives me, through His power, not only ability to do healings, but to deal with the enemy as well by removing him from myself and others. I wish to make mention that this ability is mentioned in the Bible to.

Through worship i have the confidence and knowing that i have His power, protection and support with me to do these things that i feel i am guided to do, in His name. I have come to realize that when faced with negative energy, my first responsibility, besides protecting myself, is to try to remove that energy from a person before focusing on containing that energy. It would be wise for me to confer with Jesus what i need to do. Different ways to try this is to command it to leave; often helpful to visualize holding a crucifix or cross towards person, do this 3 times in the name of the Heavenly Father, command it in the name of Jesus Christ, and the Holy Spirit. Mentally or physically pull it out as taught by Many Horses; physically or mentally smudging around the person as well as inside them; visualize sucking it out as Michael does with a blue flame or vacuum; visualize or throwing Holy water on them, obviously you can't go around doing this if you don't have their permission, but I found I can di it with my mind.

You can create your own Holy water by asking Jesus to bless it or get some from your church easily done at Catholic ones. You should also put some on your own personal alter. I also like to visualize joining a person's hands to Jesus. I've also had success using a tecnique of asking that a person be surrounded by 3 angels and i ask Jesus to complete the circle by standing behind and above the person and together with the help of Michael, i ask that all negative energies and spirits be sucked out of them. Dowsing can also be a good technique for trying to remove something that's non-beneficial. (this was a method that I was shown by Raymon Grace) Only if i feel this doesn't work should i contain their energy with one of the methods of surrounding them with light. I visualize a gold bird cage, with a glass dome, filled with gold sunlight light could also use white light. I used to do the gold bird cage as told to me by a psychic advisor and if this didn't work add a glass dome as well. I have witnessed this on a number of occasions to cause a release. If it doesn't, i wonder if the person desires to have this energy with them, perhaps it makes them feel powerful, i don't know. If i feel it stills continues, sometimes i feel that i have to visualize cutting a cord that attaches to the top of their heads, before surrounding them in light. Sometimes i will also mentally put crosses or crucifixes around this enclosure. I have found recently that just mentally putting a white cross between myself and the person that the negative energy was coming from caused the person to leave immediately. I also found that this happened when i privately pulled an Archangel Michael card out of my pocket. I didn't even have to read the invocation. Of course, learning to tell where the energy is coming from, when it comes at me does takesome practice and awareness. I just go to the people around me or the 'usual suspects' with my mind and put light around them or a cross and see if i can feel a change. It gets easier and if you happen to put light around someone by mistake, you're doing them a favour. Believers of Christ have the ability and there is nothing to fear.

Again, putting protection around yourself regularly is important. Keeping yourself grounded and surrounded mentally with a ball of white or sun light. I also find saying the Lord's prayer and the 23rd Psalm and reading scripture works wonderfully in clearing yourself. Drinking water helps as well, as is being in sunlight. The Divine Mercy card is very good to read, repeat the last part 3 times. Since going to the Catholic Church i now find i am crossing myself on a regular basis. I will also go up to the white light, or surround myself with a white dome, usually i use a sun-filled one. Doreen Virtue talks on her Angel c.d. about using a pink tube or putting white walls around you. See what is the most effective for you and sometimes you may find that different techniques work better on different occasions. Lately, i have found myself mentally putting on armour. This past weekend, i took a course and found out in that course that there is a passage in the Bible that talks about putting on the 'armour of God', i found that very helpful to know and will get more into that in a minute. I like to physically smudge but know that you can also mentally smudge yourself and your home, or like i said another person. I like to see myself using a smudge pot that you see them using at the Vatican. I don't know, but i imagine it might contain frankincense and myrrh. Lately, when I smudge my house, I will use sage or an incense called frankenmyrrh. It was suggested to me to use a bell as it can be helpful in clearing, and i think Spirit told me to use Lysol as well. I use the one that eliminates bacteria and find that in many cases this is the same negative energy that is being sent and frequently works.

I'm sure i have mentioned this before, but it happened to me again where having a Michael card where he is depicted standing on top of a demon to actually allow a negative energy to be present. I've had a problem also in the past with certain figurines. I've found that it's best for me not to use those ones or at least not to leave them out but just to have them in a plastic bag or i have a brown bag full of sage and to pull them out only for short periods when needed.

The crucifix is invaluable tool and weapon against evil, i believe if you stand in your faith with it nothing can stand up against it. It's good to hold one when commanding negative to leave.You don't have to be present with the person your doing this to, just your intention is good enough. While holding it or visualizing holding one you can with the mind throw holy water on a person in a cross manner as you bless them or command evil to leave.

I recently took a course that i felt i was guided to take. It's called Healing Rooms by an organization known as International Association of Healing Rooms from Myrrh Ministries. I would strongly recommend this course for Christians who are interested in healing or for those battling negative energies. The course encourages and helps you to connect to the Father's energy as well as that of the Holy Spirit. The course encourages you as well to go to Jesus and hold His hand while doing healings. I know also that by the Bible talking about using "God's armour," it also verifies that becoming Christian can frequently involve doing battle against the enemy of God, but don't let it prevent you because that's what the enemy wants is fear. I feel that this is a very significant course for me. While i was driving to it and was very close, there were about 100 hawks directly in front of my. After the first night of the 2-day course, i got home and i heard Jesus say to me, "we will do great things together." I swear to God! This i feel was a life changing event.

Prior to this course, during meditation and just afterwards, i connected with Jesus and i felt that He directed me to the Father i felt like i have had conversations directly with God. Jesus says that only he can take you to God and i can tell you that i experienced this happening to me personally.

Recently, while under attack, i was guided to open up the Bible and face it outwards. This seemed very effective. The Bible has power, no doubt it's from God.

Recently, i keep hearing Jesus refer to "His Father's house." I'm pretty sure that He is referring to the Sun, and He's telling me to go there for protection.(mentally and spiritually)

I really believe that through giving you receive. An interesting thing has happened lately that i feel shows this. I received some Christmas cards in the mail from the Society of the Little Flower of Jesus (St. Therese). I donated some money, which i am fortunate to be able to do. I had a wonderful feeling of love come over me from these cards or when i sent the money, i can't remember exactly when. I've been hearing lately in my head that "everything is coming up roses". It says on the brochure that "I let fall a shower of roses on you from Heaven." I don't think that is a coincidence.

I have a c.d. by Doreen Virtue to manifest your destiny with help from the angels. It is really amazing as you go into meditation you are taken a year into the future and shown your life, or at least the potential of your life, if you keep your focus on love. The only problem i had was that i started to become attached to what i saw. I started to want. I became afraid of losing it. I was told, and it's true, that the harder i try the more what i want eludes me, and when i don't try things seem to fall into place. When you start wanting, you give your energy away and become needy. You become an energy taker and this repels people and situations i find. The Buddhists talk about attachment causes suffering. The Lord's Prayer mentions about not wanting. I heard the phrase i think it was from Jesus, "keep your gaze upon Heaven." It's a tightrope sometimes. Fill up with

the sun. Be of service to Jesus. Ask what can i do for others. Stay in a place of love and service. Coincidentally, as we stay in this place of power and love, we will draw people and situations to us. People will be drawn to our energy. We all want love, but we have to be love. In this way, we walk in peace, spreading light rather than looking for energy or things for ourselves. Remember, we never really own anything anyways we just borrow things for a while. Appreciate what you have. Share the Father's love and focus on what you can do for others, even it it's just showing interest. In doing this, you're giving energy and love to someone and helping them to feel better, which is the greatest reward anyways. At the same time, the Father will reward you with what you need, and just be open to receive while glorifying Him by showing your appreciation for the many small miracles that come your way. That song "Count Your Blessings" is so true. "Count your blessings, name them one by one. Count your blessings, see what God hath done." Song by Johnson Oatman. I've been guided to do a daily devotional, in which i talk to the Father and tell him how grateful i am for everything that He has done in my life, especially for allowing me to feel His loving presence with me and i will ask Him to let me know His will and what He wants me to do with my life. I ask that His will be mine and i ask that i can serve Him as much as possible. I ask Him to help me to let others feel the unbelievable loving presence of Himself, Jesus, and the Holy mother, and also the Holy Spirit. I feel Him wrap me in His arms and i can't help but cry with gratitude for His love. All i want is for others to experience this because this is all that matters.

It's amazing when you think about all the little blessings and some big ones that God does for you. I mean, some seem so small and yet you know it was exactly what you needed, and you think why would God care about such little things unless He loves me so much that he cares about all the little details of my life. I also found that if my energy is down i can fill myself up just by thinking about the things i have been given rather than what i want. I'm not saying get attached to our material goods, but more the realization and trust that God works little miracles for us all the time and trust that He will provide what we need. It is by the grace of the Father that we are provided for, according to His will. Be humbled by what he provides.

I was starting to miss my parents and i was one day directed somewhere to a grocery store where i bought a bag of groceries that were set on the table for a local food bank. My grief was transformed by service and i dedicated the deed to the well-being of my parents. I heard a faint "thank you."

I got something in the mail from a local mission. It had the sign of Jesus on it and, although i had already purchased some tickets to pay for some people to go to their Christmas dinner, i felt Jesus was asking me to do more. I donated a little bit of money, the smallest on their list of suggested offerings. On the back, it asked if this was in anyone's memory or honour, so i put down my parents' names. Then, i heard Jesus say "they will be invited to the banquet." This blew me away and i was brought to tears again. Jesus is present and directing me and the good deeds that i do can help my loved ones on the other side. Thank you, Jesus. If you need a reason to help out those less fortunate there it is, you can help them receive blessings from Jesus and the Father, when you dedicate it for their benefit. The reward for me is an overwhelming feeling of love that i get; usually, lately, it brings me to tears. I am reminded that all i need is Jesus and that all i want to do is help him by focusing on love and service.

At the cemetery where my parents are they have a yearly Remembrance Day service that is also a memorial service for your loved ones. My Brother and i like to attend, especially since they passed a few weeks after Remembrance Day (Nov. 11) This year we didn't get an invitation, so i dropped by the office and asked about it. After registering to attend the service, the woman asked if we would like any names included in the service and i gave my parents' names. I then had a vision of my Mother thanking me with her hands held together in prayer. At the service, as names were called, we each went and lit a white candle. As i sat there, i called up the Father, Jesus, the Holy Spirit, and the Holy Mother to take any souls here into the light. With my eyes closed, i saw a long procession of people walking down the aisle towards the lighted candles.

Another thing that i have done in the past and now feel to do whenever i get the opportunity is when i am out in public and see children, elderly people, handicapped, or just those in need, i visualize taking them by their hands and holding their palms up and asking Jesus to take their hands, bless them and take them into the light. Sometimes, i will visualize holding up an infant to Jesus. I know it works because i have seen Jesus taking them into his arms. When there's so many i kind of see myself just touching them on their backs or surrounding them with my arms and corralling them towards Jesus.

I have been guided to do a daily devotional to the Father, where i spend time praising Him and thanking Him for all the blessings he has brought into my life. I have had Him take me into His arms and hold me. I mean literally being held in the arms of the Father. I have looked directly into the Father's eyes and felt such a deep pool of love. I made a commitment to God and Jesus to serve in any way they want in this life and forever after. A girl at the Spiritualist church said she saw the spiritual pathway i was on and saw it lined with oak trees and that it went on forever. In this devotional that this first happened, i was having a conversation with Jesus first and he was telling me to keep my focus on Him not on negative energies. He sat on my lap and basically told me to just keep looking at Him. HE then took me to meet the Holy Spirit, and together we all went to the Father and that's when the Father first took me into his arms and cradled me. After a while, after soaking in His love, i asked for some things for my parents, brothers, Earth, the animals and nature. I asked that the people on Earth just be kind and caring and i asked for blessings for all my teachers and others who have showed me kindness and love. I didn't want to ask for anything for myself, but He told me to "go ahead" and i asked to have children if it was his will. I confirmed that with everything in my life, His will be mine. I've been hearing lately "keep your eyes on the prize." They are the prize. This is the greatest reward and blessing that i could ever receive.

The other night, i felt Mother Mary holding me in her arms. I have been given so much love i don't know exactly what i have done to deserve it, but i know that i don't ever want to lose what i have found. Aside from my parents, (i always have to mention them) this is the best thing that has ever happened to me or can every happen to me, and this was even confirmed by a new friend of mine and pastor, who saw both Jesus and the Holy Mother doing their healing work through me. The people that are getting the healings in most cases will thank me afterwards and tell me how powerful it was. It's a nice confirmation, but i know it's much more powerful lately as i can feel this intense energy passing through me and i will usually shake. I feel the main reason for this is my regular attendance at a Catholic mass on Saturday and going to a Baptist church on Sunday. The experiences or curses of the negative energies have led me to have these blessings. When i am in their loving presence, i feel what more do i need?

I have been trying hard to not do anything to lose their presence or be less deserving of their attention. I keep hearing "pure as the driven snow." It's not easy, but i keep reminding myself of the benefits of their love and remembering what i heard before: "keep your eyes on the prize." Being devoted to this path i am frequently finding myself in feelings of rapture, walking in bliss. Sometimes i see people looking at me. There was one little girl in particular, and i think they're seeing 'them' through me. Part of me feels like i am going through a rebirth, i am wanting to recapture that innocence of being a child. Part of me sometimes is afraid of losing my identity. That's just my ego. I tell myself to give over and trust. "Have faith and believe", i am being told.

One of the principles of Spiritualism, and i know that it's true, is that "the path of reformation is open to every human soul, here or hereafter".

While doing my devotional meditation and prayer on Remembrance Day, (in case people don't know, that's the day when Canadians remember those that gave their lives in the fight for freedom; the date is Nov. 11, at the 11th hour, which is11/11. This year is 2011. I saw my Grandfather Williamson standing there in his uniform saluting me. He was a WWI veteran. I also had a vision of a friend of my parents. He is a veteran of WWII. He was sitting in a chair by a window at a table in a hotel room in Virginia Beach, which is where we all used to travel to together. I was looking at him and behind him the Sun was coming up over the Atlantic Ocean. Earlier that morning i had lit a large white candle and i was instructed to leave it burning all morning. I visualized taking him by the hand and we flew across the water into the sun. Later, i took out my Grandfather's picture of him in uniform, which happened to be in the drawer in the front room and i took him by the hand as well and took him into the sun. I saw him walking away into the sun. Bagpipes were playing on the service on t.v.; my Grandfather is Scottish, of course. I had a vision of a bagpiper lately and i couldn't help think of a Pink Floyd album called Piper at the Gates of Dawn.

Cassino's To Cardinals Part 2

The time when Jesus appeared to me so clearly, i was having a conversation with spirit and they showed me a blind man with a cane. I had just started doing spiritual work with my friend who is a medium and i wasn't witnessing spirit. I concluded that i wasn't witnessing much because of what i have seen in the past. I had experienced a lot of very negative and bad things and again Jesus appeared before me he came and literally sat on my lap and he said, "i want you to look at me not at them." He was referring to the dark energies that had haunted my past. I know he was saying that they cannot harm you when you when i am around and when you stay focused on me you don't give your energy to them all they have is fear and if you don't give them your energy and your fear they have no power over you.

The first time i witnessed mother Mary's presence with me was when i was returning home from the Catholic Church after mass. I started going there to get relief from very intense negative energy that was being sent to me, i knew the source and there were at least two. They were both making it hard for me so i went there to get help and it came to me by the way of Mother Mary. She is very dear to me now. I remember getting into my car and driving home after mass and on the way home i would just start bawling because i could feel this embrace of this loving, warming nurturing spirit holding me. I kept hearing "lying in the arms of Mary." Even when i got home at night i could feel her lying next to me holding me nurturing me and keeping me safe. I even felt that my spirit was wanting to suck its thumb and i felt that she was nurturing me in the way that a mother nurtures a child. During this time i also witnessed a priest looking at me as if he could sense her energy and spirit with me. I told my friend who was working with me doing prayer work about what was going through and she told me she was going through the exact same thing.

I remember a book called living Buddha living Christ by Thik Knat Thay. I didn't read much of it but what I remember him saying, to ask yourself what would the Buddha or Jesus do? Again with all due respect to other teachings i have personally experienced a number of times when Jesus took me to the father directly. More about the book, i think that it's important to use Buddha and Jesus as guides and walk through life to emulate them they are examples for us to follow. More important then knowing everything, thinking that we are wise we need to be loving and giving and operate from the heart. When we think we know everything we are in trouble. We can never know everything. This attitude creates intolerance for others it puts up walls instead of building bridges. When you look at how the native people have been treated in the name of Christianity ask yourself is that what Jesus would have done? When you find it you want to share it with the world but not for my arrogance but from love. You want others to experience it because it's so wonderful. I know that i have some friends who kind of snicker behind my back thinking they're so wise. I want to say to them to ask themselves honestly if they can, is your way of operating in the world working for you? It's just you there be honest with yourself, are you happy? Because there are times lately when i found myself walking in the state of bliss, there are times when i have felt so much love it causes me to weep with joy and gratitude.

Jesus said to me "cast your eyes away from Satan and set your gaze upon me." I reach out my hands and i take his hands in mine instead of focusing upon where the attack is coming from. I concentrate my attention more on the one who i know will protect me from all evil. I need to remind myself of this time and time again because it's so easy to give my energy away by focusing on where the trouble is coming from. It's better for me to give and receive my energy to Jesus and the Father and the Holy Spirit and the holy mother, not to the evil ones. That is my strength and my salvation and nothing can never hurt me again as long as i build and keep that connection strong. This is the dawning of a new day and i will never look back. Jesus sent me up to the Father and i looked into his eyes. I know that i have hurt him with sinful acts and i will try never to do anything again to shame myself in his presents and i am going to remain always in his presence.

I keep hearing it said about the power of the word, and it is the best way to resist Satan, as Satan has no choice but to heed the Fathers word. I'm focusing now on prayers and learning more about 'the word.'

That it is healing and protection from everything. I try to remove everything within me that is not of light so the divine light can shine through me. I will meditate on them so i can hear their words directly and know the truth and know their will in my regard. I think of stairway to heaven by Led Zeppelin"...and a new day will dawn for those who stand long and the forests will echo with laughter." They were very spiritual and in some of their music.

Just an example of what i am talking about just happened yet again. I'm out of town for a few days to relax and meditate and go out for a few meals and a show. I went up the street to Value Village as i found some great things there last time i was in town and it felt like the right thing to do. I found a 6 cd set called the Freedom series by Peter Horrobin, the first session is, setting the captives free, (freedom from the enemy), there are 11 different sessions. I feel this is exactly what God wanted me to have at this time it's amazing. If anyone is interested to know more about this series contact Ellel ministries, USA. Their email: info.usa@ellelministries.org, www.ellelministries. org / USA. I also found the audio cassette of talking to heaven by James Van Praagh and a certain figurine that when i walked by i could just feel the joy from it and i feel it's going to help bring even more of that energy into my life. As i am paying for it at the cashier my Mom's favorite song comes on the radio, Four strong winds by Neil Young, and i know that she helped lead me to these things which i know they're going to be very helpful to me thank you God thank you Mom.

When seeking guidance from the Father and Jesus i just asked them sometimes just to show me the next step i don't necessarily need to see where everything is heading but if i focus just on one step at a time and trust that it will lead me to where i need to be. I feel that this is the easiest way to follow God's guidance and it keeps you focused on the present and not the future leaving this in the divine hands of God.

Even though i am out of town and not attending my usual mass today i decided to return to my room and say the Hail Mary's and other prayers at the time that they do at my church, just prior to starting i heard the words "beam me up." Holding my rosary and little prayer book saying the prayers while kneeling my hands started vibrating just like to do when i am at service. I think water is probably one of the most valuable tools. I'm just starting to appreciate it more and more. When doing clearing work on my brother in the past, i would visualize throwing water on him in a cross pattern after i had blessed it. Now i am calling on the Father, Jesus and Holy Spirit and also Holy Mother to clear him. But in regards to water someone mentioned to me about the 'Living Waters', as reference to The Lord and i also picked up a book entitled that. My friend mentioned that it's good protection to put a glass of water next to your bed. My teacher Jean always said to bless your water. One reason of going away was so i could relax in the whirlpool and swimming pool. The value of water for protection is something to explore. I also have not been calling upon Michael as much, like i said i am trying to call upon the Trinity and Holy Mother more. One thing i found i have to be very careful with is figurines of Saint Michael with a demon under him. I felt that numerous times i could feel the energy coming from the demon and i have often removed these figurines and even gone to the point of taking a hammer and trying to smash them out. What i tend to do is put them away in a safe place and if i need them bring them out. I just find it's important to pay attention and if you get that negative feeling from it then it's not worth having out. I do have many St Michael figurines without the demon and there is never a problem with them although like i said sometimes the other ones were needed. I sometimes found this with crucifixes as well, they are the most useful tool, but again sometimes you have to be careful and it may not always be best to display or hang on the wall as sometimes you can take on the energy and you become the one being crucified, as my teacher gene has verified to me before. Crosses are much safer. Just i know that many times when getting attacked putting a crucifix away seemed to alleviate the attack. Anyways just something to be aware of. When i have in the past had to deal with a very negative energy demanding that negative energy to leave with the crucifix in my hand was the most effective tool, this also could be done just in my mind visualizing a crucifix there. Again i don't know if i will need to do this as much as in the past because of my stronger connection to the Father, Jesus the Holy Mother and Holy Spirit and knowing relying on prayer more to deal with it. Negative energy is attached to many people and it's usually when they don't feel good about themselves and that seems to create an opening for the negative energy to come in, or it's a result of behavior that people choose to do because they want to feel better about themselves but it isn't in the light. I can't say enough about reciting the Lord's prayer and the 23rd Psalm which to me work well together to protect and energize.

I find so much inspiration from music i really feel that God often works through certain artists. Listening again to an old rush album Farewell to Kings some of the lyrics go"...cities full of hatred, fear and lies withered hearts and cruel tormented eyes. Scheming demons dressed in kingly guise... beating down the multitudes and scoffing at the wise. Can't we raise our eyes and make a start, can't we find the minds to lead us closer to the heart." To me it speaks loudly to the times we are living in today and it was so prophetic, showing that so many powerful individuals are under Satan's command.

Although i have been learning to pray and calling upon their help i know that i still need to continue doing work to remove negative energy as well from myself, home, and someone close, etc. As i mentioned before i feel that Jesus refered to the Sun as his Father's house, i feel that he often tells me to go there for protection, to put myself there 'energetically' staying connected to the Father, i hear him say. In this way i am using his energy and hearing his voice in my dealings was Satan. I have been getting attacked at the back of my head and Jesus guided me to join my hands, holding the two forefingers on my right hand in my left. Also joining my hands together with my fingers interlocked.

Lately i keep seeing myself in ways i can only describe as regressing to childhood and it's come to my attention after something that happened with the father that i have been leading up to a rebirthing. During this time i began felt mother Mary lying beside me holding me. I've also been told basically they want me to remain celibate even if i am involved with somebody. They want me to respect the sacredness of the marriage bond and i keep hearing "marital bliss." Jesus has been told telling me that He "will set me free." I was about to start to listen to that cd set i mentioned earlier called the freedom series when about 50 crows appeared in front of my house and neighborhood. I know that something significant was occurring as crows represent magic from Animal Speak by Ted Andrews. The freedom series includes topics like setting the captives free from the enemy slaying the Goliaths in our lives, ungodly soul ties and more. As i listen to the c.d., particularly to the ungodly soul ties i could feel releasing from the side of my head and solar plexus this is basically releasing ties or psychic chords to people who we have had a connection with in the past and still do energetically have some control over you. It's also gives me confirmation about the importance of marital sex only and explains how we make soul ties with people that we are intimate with and that those ties remain. The c.d.'s also talks about following God's guidance one step at a time. It was also a reminder to bolster my faith and if there was any fear or doubt my faith needed to be stronger. This c.d. is a very valuable tool and moving towards freedom and Irecommended strongly if it can be found.

Today is November 20th, 2011 and i believe that this is the day that i have been saved. Last week at a local thrift store, where else, i bought a Jesus figurine with two sheep but i felt that i was supposed to give it to the pastor at the Baptist church that i go to, along with the Catholic one. So i went there and on that day they were doing baptisms. Prior to starting i asked Jesus to take my Brother spiritually into the water and baptize him and then afterwards i asked for myself. I did this with our minds and spirits and i feel that it was achieved. I have been having some troubles with negative energy and i felt cleared and and much more removed from its grasp. After watching the first child be put under the water i heard "another soul saved." I definitely believe that this is a very important step in the life of a Christian and i feel that even doing it my way will make an enormous difference in my life and certainly my soul. Freedom means being saved from the enemy by Christ. I'm glad that i did it the way i did because i believe that i was baptized by Jesus himself and personally don't want any intermediaries. No offense to any ministers or even saints but i want a direct connection with Jesus and the Father and the Holy Spirit. I respect all those were helping others to make that connection to Jesus and they are great guides and i welcome their help guidance and prayers but once that connection is made i don't want to take a step backwards. The night prior to this happening i felt guided to let go of an eagle Father that i had been given, it was very difficult to do and no offense to the Native American people or teachings but i am quite sure i had to do this. I feel it was significant for me to show Jesus of my loyalty to him and through him to the Father is the route i want to travel and keep as pure as possible. In my experience i feel that it is true that Jesus is the only way to the Father. I hear Jesus say "when you honor me i give you peace." It may have to do also with releasing myself from a past-life connection and maybe the connection with the person wasn't too pure. Yes it sometimes gets confusing when following a life of spiritual development but i really felt it was needed to break that attachment and maybe also a connection to a past life where i was abused as a Native American person. I didn't want to continue bringing that past into my present life. I think also I had to let go of some of my Native American guides also and focus on the greatest guide one can imagine, the Lord. The next day i kept hearing in my head "what a difference a day makes." As i was going shopping i found a picture of three crosses that was entitled A New Day. It states, "I am the light… Follow me to a sunny place where dawns bright new day." As i hung it up in my meditation room the Sun came out. I want to state that I still honour them in my heart and i still respect them.

On November 22nd the 4th anniversary of my Mother's passing, i was hearing "grateful for life unseen" and "mass intentions for the grave." I also pulled the angel card that stated "eternally yours." I knew these were messages for my parents expressing their gratitude for the things i had done here and dedicated to their benefit. I know they had received many good things on the other side of life. I feel that giving money to the society of The Little Flower for them to say a permanent mass for my parents was what they were referring to by "mass intentions for the grave." I heard from spirit that i was granted three wishes. I immediately responded and my first wish was for a special blessing for my parents. I clearly saw my Mother receiving a very powerful blessing and could see her afterwards just beaming. I felt that i should go to a store to buy flowers. I first thought about pink and then it didn't feel right so i knew the red roses were required. I grabbed the nicest bunch that i saw, two dozen as my fathers anniversary was on the following day. As i was paying for them I noticed they were called 'freedom roses.' I feel they were telling me that they were free. I said some prayers to the Jesus statue and i heard "saved", i also said prayers to the mother Mary statue and Archangel Michael one as well. The next day i did the same for my father when i prayed to the Jesus statue i heard "what you ask for in my name believe that you have received it and it will be given unto you." I know this a quote from the Bible but he said it to me also.

You must believe in him, you must have unshakable faith, like it is said belief can create miracles. On the way home a hawk flew over my car. In my meditation / devotional time that evening with the Father i heard him say "welcome home son." I asked for a special blessing for my father and I saw him standing there with his favorite jacket on and this cap, a bright white energy was at his side, together they turned and walked into the golden light.

When doing healing work i call upon Jesus in the Holy Mother as well as the Father and the Holy Spirit, angels and guides. A few weeks back during my first meeting with a new teacher and friend, she said she saw my hands going from a male's back and forth to a female's. She said she thought it was Jesus and the Holy Mother's energties working with me. While doing healing work at a Spiritualist Church which i was eventually led away from, the girl that I worked on a number of times commented afterwards "has your energy ever change" and gave me two thumbs up. The president of the Church sat in my healing chair and after the service she came to me and said that she sat there because she saw Jesus standing beside me. This was shortly after i had taken a course that called upon the Holy Trinity for doing healing work. This was offered by Myrrh ministries or the Healing Rooms of Hamilton. In meditation at the end of this week Jesus told me that "we will accompolish great things together."

During a few meditations in the recent past i felt that i connected with John the Baptist. I felt a nice energy sitting in me and we talked, actually he did the talking. Just recently, i thought that Jesus sat inside me and talked to me. At church yesterday the priest was talking about John the Baptist and how he comes first prepare for the Lord, and i couldn't help but pay attention to this as i feel is a confirmation that want to experience was indeed genuine, i hear the words now "believe."

I went to a Christmas service at Bethel Gospel Church which i love to do. Near the end of the service the minister comes on and gives an inspirational talk and then says if we'd like to accept Jesus to follow his prayer, i have done this before but i will never miss another opportunity, so i shared the prayer and like a year ago i saw Jesus with me this time holding my hands i felt that he wanted me to do it again to really take it to heart and to walk knowing he is with me. Thank God that i did it again i heard Jesus say bring my Brother there next time the following weekend. I took my Brother and i asked if i could mentally say the prayer for him since he often doesn't do for himself and i saw his soul then accept Jesus. During that week i was talking to a friend at work about the old days and how difficult things were for labour and the battles on the picket lines and i brought up some stories about my Father fighting on the picket lines and then started to say how tough he was and that it was his Mother's Scottish upbringing that made him that way. She was very tough on him and i know that my Father thought she didn't love him but i do believe that by talking about this made him realize that his Mother had prepared him to deal with a tough life and i think it helped him realize even though he's in spirit, that his Mother did love him and it was his choice that he chose his parents to prepare him for the life that he had to lead, just as we all choose. A few days later i was having a dream, i heard my Father's voice and i went looking for him. His friend, actually his cousin Jimmy, was leaning against an old car and i asked where my Father was and he pointed without saying anything. I saw my Father walking up a long grassy pathway that reminded me of a path of a golf course going up to a club house. There was a barn of sometype or structure on the left. My Father had on his cap and as i ran to him a voice said "don't stop him." As i stopped an energy came and wisked him away, i became very emotional as i could feel my loss and i lay down on the ground. Instinctively i knew however that my Father had gone into the light. He had made a significant crossing, i heard him say to me "carry on." I felt that the realization he had a few days earlier about his Mother's love helped him to move on. It was holding him back but the biggest factor though was that when my Brother and i both accepted Jesus my Father was with us and he accepted him as well and right now i hear "that sealed the deal." I know my Father as well has accepted Jesus as his Savior, beautiful stuff. Instead of grieving my loss i realize i was privileged to witness something very sacred. It sounds like my Mom's voice but i keep hearing the song "It is well with my soul", by Horatio Spafford. I felt that she had already made that crossing. I was aware that my Father had been following me to churches for a while and he was learning about the Lord, a few days later i was watching a Wonderful Life on t.v., (as im typing this i just got something in the mail about the show a wonderful life in july) This is a show that my Dad and i have watched many times and was very emotional for me. At the end of the movie when they showed the inside of the book where it was written "no man is no failure who has friends", i again thought of my Dad. I knew he saw himself as a failure but nobody had more friends then he did and they had great respect for him and for a very good reason. He was a leader and he was tough and honest and intelligent, he ran everything the poker games, fishing trip, golf tournament, coached the baseball team, came to him for advice, etc. I decided that i needed to send my parents energy at this time and as i did so i called upon the Holy Trinity and i saw both of my parents walking hand in hand over a rainbow, i saw them going through whitish clouds and i saw them step onto a beautiful green landscape, as soon as they got there i saw my Father toss his cap far into the air which was very surprising because my Father wasn't overly demonstrative. I then realized this was another issue that was holding my father back, feeling that he was a failure. The realization that he was far from that set him free to take the next step on their journey together and i believe reach true freedom. Like spiritualism states the path of reformation is open to every human soul both here and hereafter. It also shows how our behaviour, actions and prayers can help our loved ones on the other side as well as helping ourselves. It is a wonderful life!

I also want to give credit to my Father that when things have gotten tough for me is often the lesson of his toughness and integrity than i thought about. My Mother, i draw on her strengths of nurturing, decency, mental toughness and inner strength and humbleness. I know i chose my parents to bring me the qualities that i would need in this lifetime and hopefully my Father realizes he chose his Mother to prepare him for his life. I also had the realization that much like my Grandmother's 'tough love' made me think that my Father in heaven, God was doing the same thing to me to make me tougher to face the challenges on the road ahead. There were many times when i wish i was as tough as my Father and as pure as my Mother. The Celestine Prophecy experiential guide by James Redfield and Carol Adrienne talk about this and this is where i heard about it first but i feel that i had a knowing of this as when because it just rang true, that's how we know our truth is when it just rings true to us.

I wanted to mention that i first had the realization that my Mother and Father were maybe not at the same level was while i was listening to a cd by the Montreal gospel choir as i was getting ready for church,the song was Glory Train. I had a vision of my Mother clapping her hands and dancing to the song…"going to catch that glory train…" I wondered why i didn't see my Father then i thought i heard him say to me "you really caught the bug haven't you." I was in the spirit and i told my Father that was the only train worth catching and that he had better jump on board because it was leaving soon, as the song ended i had a very clear mental picture of my father jumping onto the back of the caboose.

I'm about to start writing about my recent connection with Mother Mary and swear to God the song on the radio is Let it be by the Beatles…"Mother Mary comes to me there will be an answer let it be…" I feel that she has come to me often holding me, comforting me, nurturing me and protecting me. I heard her say "you are my child in heaven." There were very negative energies around and i was shown to use a white candle. I removed the blue candles that i had been using to draw Michael's energy they changed and they felt very negative at that time. I put them in a plastic bag to contain any negative energy but i still kept them. I bought a number of tall white candles and it did seem to help. As i was laying down to try to sleep before going to work i clearly saw Mother Mary at the end of my bed praying, as soon as she did i saw a procession come into my bedroom through the back wall, they were led by a man with a long beard, hat and gown holding a crucifix on a long stuff there were others that came with him, i saw someone dressed the same and he had what looked like a smudge pot and they walked around my room clearing the negative energy away. I believe it must have been frankincense. When Mother Mary prays for you she gets an answer immediately.

I also wanted to mention that when i accepted Jesus again i heard him say "you are invited to the feast" and after my Brother accepted him i heard him say "I make things new." He said this to me, i also heard him say it in the movie, Passion Of Christ, by Mel Gibson. I feel that i am being led to places to do his service. I like to visualize joining peoples' hands to his, particularly the elderly or handicapped. With my mind i take their wrists and hold them out and i ask that he takes their hands bless them and take them into the light. With children i imagine picking them up and handing them to him and ask him that he take them in his arms, bless them and take them into the light. It can get a little frantic sometimes especially at a mall when there's all kinds of them. I do believe it does some good i even try to do this with those that attack me. I don't know if i would recommend this. I have found myself again being held in the arms of the Holy Mother, she wants to hold us and care for us and give us a nurturing like a child.

Recently i gave a donation to the Princess Margret Hope campaign after this inmeditation i saw a white dove landing on my shoulder around the same time i pulled the angel cards by Doreen Virtue archangels, that said gifts from God. As i opened my arms to receive i felt my arms being moved to cross my chest and a white peaceful energy descended. I'm realizing that Jesus is aside from many other things becoming my best friend just like he was when i was a child. I've always been looking for a best friend but they all seem to betray me one way or another just like partners have. Besides my parents and 2 or 3 they are the only ones that have shown love for me. I only ever wanted love but i always seem to get attacked instead. Also i never really felt accepted or that i fit in. I have found a best friend in Jesus someone i can talk to about anything and not be judged or condemned. Someone who always loves me and will never ever betray me, someone who will give me the best possible advice and guidance without him i am nothing with him i need nothing else.

I want to tell about my most holy Christmas. On Christmas morning i awoke and i knew Mother Mary spirit was lying beside me and she was holding a baby. I couldn't believe it, at first i thought i was being shown the baby Jesus but i realize it was my own rebirthing. But being born again with the blessing of the Holy Mother being right there with you on Christmas morning... unbelievable.

My friend and i get together regularly and send prayers and healing to people and situations and we observe spirit in action. We are seeing blessings happen and it brings an overwhelming feeling of gratitude and love, devotion and life purpose. When i am doing this i leave all worries and fears and i find the true love i have always been seeking. I want to jump head first into service, i want to lose myself in it, to lose all the pain and suffering, disappointment, disillusionment, resentment and hurt. I put it all behind me and be with God. None of it matters anymore. I'm able to let go of my mind, ego and desires and have a single mindedness of helping, serving and loving. What piece it brings.

I can't believe all the help i am getting from God. I'm moving out to a place close by so i could live on my own but still be close enough to support my brother, who needs assistance. I'm finding all the furniture i need and everything i buy new is on an icredible sale. A bed, couch, t.v.,d.v.d.

player. I have one small older dresser that my Mother bought me, reddish brown in color with a mirror. Something told me to go to Value Village and as i walked around i found a few things and then i stepped out into the aisle to leave and i saw a large tall dresser being wheeled on the floor, it was reddish brown in color and excellent shape and an antique. It has the dovetail or tongue and groove joints inside the drawers, it is solid maple and is made by the Krugg brothers a well known company in the area, it was $14.99. It was perfect getting it home was another story, it wouldn't fit into my car so i had to put it on a hand cart covered in plastic because it was raining hard on New Years Day and wheel it all the way home, but it was worth it . I previously founded a solid cherry night stand with dovetail joints at another Value Village that was $5. It has a few marks on it but no big deal. A week later i was talking to a friend and i heard someone in my head say "Salvation Army." I went and found a really old funky chair for my meditation room which i was thinking that i needed, it was $35 but when i went to pay for it i was told that the furniture that day was 50 percent off. Also i found a stereo cabinet previouly for my Brother for $7. He had an old stereo in the basement that henever listensed to, but i felt he was enjoying listening to mine that was in the spare room, only thing that he really listened to was his little ghetto blaster. I felt this is one way that made him feel lesser, that he didn't have quality things. I took my street apart and brought his up one night and being upstairs the receiver got better reception and with fixing a few connections and pushing a few buttons his stereo sounded great. The first song on the radio was sweet child of mine. Obviously it was from Jesus and he's telling me i was on the right track i was guided to buy him a tall cd tower at a specific place for $5 and you should have seen the look on his face when i bought it into the room. For his birthday i bought him a good blue ray player on sale of course, to play c.d.'s on and now he has great music if he wants it and he doesn't have to feel lesser by sitting in the basement listening to his ghetto blaster. I really feel that this helps along with him being the owner of his own home now to instill some pride and self worth that he really needs. In any event i know that God was guiding me to do this so it has to be helpful. Again i can't believe all the things i am being led to, it's not just at the one place were it started but other thrift stores as well and I finding it's stuff that i need. Thank you. It's simply amazing! What really amazes me some of the things aren't even things i realized i need them until i find them. I was told by spirit to enjoy the ride and that's what happens when you give yourself to service to God. He takes care of you.

I was thinking about how when was a child i used to lie in bed talking to Jesus. This was also the time that I had a crush on this girl for 3 years. It was more than a crush, when she moved away a part of me died and i realize now that's why i stopped talking to Jesus as well, i was 12 years old. A teacher of mine J during a reading told me that something happened when i was 12 and it's almost like i stopped living. It took me 6 months to figure out what she was talking about because i forgot about it. I talked to my friend and mentor Many Horses, who is a shaman, and he told me that my soul left me then and my grandparents who were in spirit have been taking care of me from that point on. It wasn't just that she moved it was the circumstances. She seem to be avoiding me, not talking or looking at me and i was going home on the last day of school and her cousin came up to me and invited me to her birthday party. I don't know if it was because i was mad at her or hurt or but she's seemed to avoid me or because she didn't ask me herself or because of my incredible shyness and fear of dancing but i said no. As i walked away i felt like dying and i guess part of me did. I also knew or heard later that it hurt her that i didn't go. Just recently i decided to send her some prayers and healing and i saw a pink heart in the middle of her chest surrouded by waves and waves of rainbow energy and i knew that any pain I caused her was being healed. A few days later i sent her energy again, this time more focused and i told her mentally why i did what i did, how much she meant to me and what happened afterwards. At the time i was watching a Neil Young d.v.d. that a friend loaned me and i felt that she and i danced to the song Helpless..."And in my mind i still need a place to go, all my changes were there." When the song ended and Neil left the stage, the music from the stage that was being played was…"this, this is Christ The King..." Once again i knew that Jesus had orchestrated this whole healing. The song Christ The King is written by William Chatterton Dix.

Having some psychic attacks going on i pulled a Michael Archangel card, by Doreen Virtue, that said, "guarded and protected", as i closed my eyes i saw him standing there and i was in the midst of a hell scene, as i followed him we went through a door he closed it after we walked through then he took me upwards and walked me to Jesus. I had a dream that a man came into a room he closed the door he handed me a cup of water (which i refer to now is a cup of the Lord after this experience)…i knew i had a negative energy attached to me at the time. As i was drank it i witnessed my spirit rolling around the floor wretching. I knew i was shown the way to rid myself and others of a demon or negative energy if it is within you. In my mind i have tried to doing this with others i feel are possessed, initially there's a lot of resistance then after i have seen reactions similar to mine, i have also send them hissing like a serpent, but as i keep pouring it into them (again this is mentally), eventually they accept it and it feels similar to a baby holding a bottle when they are being healed and nurtured. I usually see the person sort of crack and disintegrate like an egg and on the inside comes out this wonderful light like the Sun. I feel this helps a person to be reborn it doesn't mean the persons totally healed but definitely helps a lot. This could be done as many times as necessary and i am sure that it will eventually release them. I'm reminded that sometimes we need to experience the negative to appreciate the positive. I also believe that this is why i am put through so many things and that's to learn first hand experience. I have also been praying the Lord's Prayer to help the deliver a person from evil. I think i got this idea from the Freedom series c.d.'s by Peter Horrobin, (beautiful stuff), when i got to the part that refers to "delivering", i will stop and call upon the Father, Son, Holy Spirit and Holy Mother and sometimes also call upon the archangels and saints to deliver that specific person from evil. I usually find saying it three times to be effective before continuing the prayer. Seeing it as many times as needed as long as there is negative energy there. Of course i am doing this mentally or through prayer work so it's affecting the person's spirit. When someone is sending me negative energy Jesus has instructed me to say "I receive it not", as i hold up the two fore fingers on my hand.

To me the connection with the Holy Mother is invaluble not only for her prayers but for her wonderful nurturing presence. When saying prayers and sending energy to people i know that Mother Mary is involved when i see the person spirit regressing to childhood. My friend and i often see them sucking their thumbs and will see Mother Mary come in caring a baby. She seems to be bringing about a rebirthing or new beginning. I feel she did this for me and my Brother. One time while doing some energy work with my friend, my Grandfather showed up and was just sitting there watching. My friend had said to me "who is Sam?" Sam is my Grandfather and then i saw him sitting there eating a big stick of pink rock candy which is a treat he used to get when we went to Niagara Falls. Near the end my dad showed up from behind her, from behind me Mother Mary came in holding a baby. I remember seeing my Grandfather's mouth hanging wide open as he witnessed her in disbelief. My Father and Grandfather then went together. I know what a blessing mother Mary has brought to my father. The process never stops, not even on the other side and it's amazing how much we can help our loved ones when we progress spiritually and also when we send our prayers and intentions for their healing and well being and then sometimes miracles like that just happens according to God's will. I have since decided to become Catholic and am currently enrolled in classes which will allow me to be accepted into the faith on Easter weekend. I can't wait for this wonderful moment, i know it will be very powerful and profound.

Again i have found when really up against it the crucifix to be much more powerful than a cross. Nothing can withstand the power of the Holy Trinity. There have been a few occasions when a white cross seem to be what was needed. I have to use the discernment or trial and experiment to see what works for a given situation. I feel though the power of these items i am sure are greatly influenced by your own faith or dedication to your religion. I have been shifting lately from just trying to contain people's negative energies to trying to deliver them. I have gone this route before but didn't seem to have much success but i feel guided it to do it now as perhaps because of my stronger convictions and connection to Jesus and the Father i have more access to their power. I know that it is well within our abilities to use the power that is given direct from them that we can command the darkness to leave anyone.

Sometimes visualizing large white crosses or crucifixes around the person or even placing one directly between me and the person i have found effective. The same can be true for putting protection around yourself your home or somebody else, but face the crucifix outwards. Jesus also showed me how to best give help to my Brother he show me that just using my mind to hold his left hand and with my right hand to mentally place my left hand on his forehead, this is especially for clearing. I was also shown to mentally place of golden halo over his head. It really helps to meditate regularly so we can open ourselves up to guidance from spirit and follow their instruction. I also want to mention that one day i was having a social cigarette and a negative energy attached itself to me. I feel this energy was attached to the person i was with but i know this is not the first time this has happened to me while having a cigarette. When a demon gets attached to me i get fearful. Then i ask for Jesus to step into me and remind myself that i have been held in the Father's arms, i have looked into the wonderful eyes of God (it's like a bottomless sea of love). I have been nurtured by the Holy Mother, i have talked to Jesus and he has held my hand, there is no more fear when i think of these things.

I have been guided and continue in my desire to give myself fully to God. There is no turning back. Again i find it extremely helpful to spend time daily in devotional to God and to express my gratitude for his wonderful works in my life. I know he's hard at work for me and my family and the least i could do is be appreciative enough to take a few moments to let him know that i know that he's doing his miracles in my life and i am so grateful to him. I know this means a tremendous amount to him. I'm reminded about how the majority of the world is about seeking pleasure rather than seeking God. I to have been guilty of this and sometimes still fall into self indulgence. I'm reminded that you have to look to the Lord above and trust what he provides, not the other way around of the world first because it corrupts us. We become wanters and needers, selfish and unfulfilled and not receivers from the divine.

Just tonight i was thinking about a number of jobs i wanted to get done and was getting frustrated and agitated and even went so far as to express anger towards Jesus for leading me to that place that needed so much done. I know it's ludicrous. I started feeling better when i walked away from the whole situation, look at my priorities, made a list, change my perspective by looking at the positive things about the place i liked and just positive things we're happening in my life. And what really made me feel better what's to do donate a small amount of money to the local mission and dedicated for the well being of my parents. It takes work sometimes to stay positive but it's important to do what you have to do to get there and doing something for others seems to be the best remedy. The reality is to that i was starting to get too attached to my material world as well and i need to walk away from it to get a renewed perspective.

I think i mentioned before that many people feel that religion is a way of control and it has definately been used that in the past, but i am finding that church especially the Catholic Church for me is leading me to freedom and liberation from the dark side or the devil if you will. I read this quote from Pope Benedict XV1 and I agree with it very much, "the church proposes her moral teaching as a message not of constraint, but liberation." I recently had some changes in my life that seemed like they were going to bring me into contact with certain individuals who i have had a lot of trouble with in the past, energetically and spiritually. This also includes the individual who did much to harm to my parents in there later years. For awhile i thought that after being attacked lately by them i engaged in a psychic battle with them and i felt that i had won. I feel now that i am much more powerful than i was before not to say that the power is mine but is working through me. I am careful to only engage in battle when directed to or given permission to. This lasted for a fairly brief period of time and then i thought i was guided to refrain from war like behavior and to focus on attempts to redeem and deliver the enemy, or at least attempt to as i was given clear guidance i would be lifted out of the path of any harm. I didn't know exactly how this would happen but i put my trust in Jesus and the Father and they delivered as promised. I do not fear the enemy because i know that they can no longer harm me and instead of thinking about them, i will focus on the positive loving presence of God and the guidance of Jesus to them i give my power into noone else. I have to be careful sometimes to not to want to fight the enemy too much for my desire sometimes is to do so. I know God wants the enemy, the lost souls to repent and return to Him.

During this whole process i was reminded of the importance of staying positive and to keep a positive image in my mind. On Valentimes day i took flowers to the cemetery, later that night on my way to work i had a vision of my mother standing there with flowers in her arms. While working an insert from Bradford Exchange fell out of a magazine, there was a poem that i once gave to my aunt in a card, it was called i am with you still. I knew it was from my parents and loved ones. When i occasionally still have regrets about them i think about how they're doing now and that's far more important because it involves their souls development and it's permanent. I was reminded by a spiritual partner and friend that my parents are benefiting from my own spiritual advancement, my prayers and i also believe from donations dedicated to them. I've been hearing lately "You raise me up." By Rolf Lovland, and Brendan Graham of Secret Garden.

I arrived home one morning and had a message a good friend of mine and at one time a teacher had passed away. As i sat there wondering what happened i felt her come to me, made a comment about her size and pointed to her heart. We continued to have a conversation and she mentioned that my parents were doing well. I could see that she seemed happy and i kept hearing her say "don't cry for me Argentina", just like her. This song written by Andrew Lioyd Webber. The next day i had to go somewhere and i felt guided to go into the thrift store next to where i had to go. I heard "Blue Jay hat" and sure enough i found one there, then i heard book. As a flipped through a book i found a passage that come to my mind earlier that day when her husband said he would ask people to come forward if they wanted to speak at the service. This is what my Mom also had in her kitchen embroidered by her Mother, it was the King's Message from 1939, "I said to a man who stood at the gate of the year…he said, put your hand into the hand of God, etc." This was King George 11 Christmas message.

I want to Toronto for a, raise Jesus higher rally, the energy was awesome especially when during the procession. I went to the washroom a few minutes early before the final break and i as i walked down the hall Cardinal Collins was walking towards me with a small group of people. There was only myself and one other guest in the hall. The Cardinal and i nodded to each other and i was thrilled i knew this was not a chance meeting but a special blessing and as i walked out of the washroom still beaming from our meeting i ran into him again in the hallway and this time it was only him and i and we said hi to each other. By the way he was just made a Cardinal two weeks prior at the Vatican. He is such a nice person he seems like a regular guy, very friendly and down to earth. I was especially inspired by his talk as he was saying that there are many ways to serve God. He mentioned that when priests were ordained in the past they would say "arch tome" which is Latin apparently meaning, "Here i am lord." He continued by saying that service to God should come with a proclamation "Here i am Lord lead me." He said that the most important part of service to the Lord was being present. But as he said "standing on the mountain top and making that proclamation is one thing but you had to take it down into the valley with you and do your service." He confirmed what i had recently found, but admittedly had gotten away from was the importance of daily devotional work to God. This also confirmed what i had seen in a few books that we should just ask for the Father's will, the Lord's will for your life to be revealed to you. But all you really need to know is, what is the next step for you to take, because if you just focus on the next step you will follow the path they have designed for you and you will wind up at your destination. Cardinal Collins reminds us that just showing up is what is important because they do the work for us. I felt the Cardinal Collins energy and my own on we're connected for a few days.

Lesson's From The Light Part 1

One lesson i am being taught again is to not strive. The more i try to make something happen, the more i seem to push it away. When I don't try, it seems to come to me. I've especially noticed this with my attractiveness to women, but it seems to apply to many things.

Some things have been going wrong and i have lost my patience and my temper, and get all upset and two or three times this week, this happened only to reveal to me later that the so called 'negative' thing that happened led to something i didn't see at the time. These events later showed themselves to be blessings. I realize now even more that i have to just give over and trust God. I've been hearing before "enjoy the ride." I have to try harder to remember this.

What seems to happen to me is that when i am focussed on being and doing energy work, and staying connected with God and on path, your energy is high and this draws a lot of things and people to you.

When you become attached to someone or something, it's like you change from being a giver of energy to a taker of energy, and this seems to repel people. When cut off from the source, you become needy. This leads into striving behaviour rather than allowing. Stay connected is the cure.

A lot of people in religious circles talk about Reiki as being an occult practice. I don't believe that's the case. I feel it's again the same intolerance that so many religious have towards other teachings. I feel that i was led to Reiki like i was led to spiritual healing, and led to a Christian based spiritual healing. I feel it was God that led me, and each one was an important and helpful step. I know that i was led to do healing work and, at least lately, it was Jesus that guided me there and is working with me, as is his wonderful Mother.

Many people have problems with me going to the Catholic faith. To me, His Mother has been invaluable also, to my Father and my Brother, and to people we send healing to. Also, when she prays for you, it gets answered. I don't feel that my connection with Mother Mary has lessened my connection with Jesus but enhanced it. I go to a catholic Mass on Saturday and a Baptist church on Sunday, and i feel that they are both very beneficial for me; and i plan on continuing to go to both.

I was lying in bed partly asleep and in my mind, i went to the Father and was lying at his feet. I saw a bag of batteries being poured onto the ground and saw them being put into me, especially my wrists and hands. I think this was done to raise my energy level, as well as i have been having some carpal tunnel symptoms from work.

There are times when i get into feeling sorry for myself, thinking, why does that guy have the perfect life? The wife with three kids, a successful business, musically gifted. What do i have? Then i also wonder, is this girl interested in me or not? What happens if i am with her and she loses interest, or becomes more attracted to someone else? Then i saw a show on t.v. about kids baseball and how the Ugandan baseball team was not allowed to participate in the little league world series; eventually the team from Canada went over and it was very heart warming. They also showed the unbelievably horrendous conditions these kids had to live in and i decided to send energy to this situation. As i was doing so, i apologized to the Lord for being selfish. I realize that my life is meaningless. What i mean is that the conditions of my life don't matter whether or not this girl like me or cheats on me. What matters is that the suffering in the world needs to stop. I'm only here for a short while, then i go somewhere else. The details aren't important. If i can't help to change things for the better, then my coming down here was fruitless. I feel that i have too much as it is. I have too many clothes and too many books!

I pray that those who have the ability to help change the conditions of these people, and others like them, will be touched by the Lord's love; and open up their hearts with compassion for their suffering; and to think less about their own needs and realize that it's pointless to have more than we need, especially when others don't have enough.

People, including myself sometimes, have bought into a false world. It reminds me of, the movie the Matrix, where it's all an illusion. Our focus is all about greed, fulfilling our own needs. We are slaves to this system. Think about who must be behind this system that is run again by greed, corruption, control, poverty, misery, and torture. The rich are getting richer at the expense of everyone else's suffering. Is this the world that God created or has it been manufactured by men who are under the control of the enemy? People are slaves to the master. They sell their souls for a piece of candy. It might bring temporary happiness but like this life, it is only temporary. Like i heard someone at church say, "I've been to a lot of funerals before and he's never seen a hearse pulling a U-Haul trailer behind it!" We are worshipping a false God!

Last week, as i was buying a lottery ticket, i heard in my head, your treasures are in heaven. Jesus is the path to freedom from Satan. Who else but Satan would want or allow people to suffer so much. Only the sickest of minds would propagate such a system. I also think about the hurt i have endured at the hands of others and yes, i was hurt but i think now that really no one can hurt me because i love myself. My hurts are temporary. I have myself and needless to say, i have Jesus and the Father. People who have hurt me have really just hurt themselves because they are no longer a part of my life. I forgive them but i state to the universe that, i break all bonds with them. They are no longer welcome in my energy. I only let those in my sacred space that come with love.

I was watching, The Passion of Christ, which i do often and i paid attention this time to what

Jesus said about the helper. Jesus says in movie, The Passion Of Christ, "watch for the helper." Our heavenly Father will always send help to us because he loves us so dearly. He watches over us.

Sometimes things take a while to dawn on me. I realize that Jesus sent me to the Catholic Church, Scared Heart of Jesus. In meditation, i was begging Jesus for mercy from the attacks i was under, and i saw him raise his right hand and hold his two forefingers up. This statue is above the door of this church and many times, i found myself standing in front of this church when having difficulties, i felt this blocked the attacks.

When in the process of joining the Catholic faith, i was told that we should choose a Saint. It came to me that St. Joseph was the one i was supposed to have because of my closeness with Mother Mary. Now it makes sense to me what i heard Mary saying to me that "you're the new Joseph!"

My confirmation was a beautiful ceremony, as it was held on Holy Saturday evening during the Easter Vigil Mass. They turn the lights out in the church, light a fire outside and light a large candle from the flame, then bring it into the church. We then light our small candles. When they turn the lights back on, starting from back to front, i could really feel his presence come in. I keep hearing from the spirit that i am being "ordained."

I know that my parents are getting spiritual benefits from my own spiritual developments, so it makes it even more special and significant. On Easter evening, i had some dreams involving my parents about boxes containing ashes (remains). I remembered that i kept a small portion of their ashes and had them in boxes under an altar at their home. I felt they were clearly telling me to release these ashes. I guess that having them has also held them here to some degree but i also feel that they received a lot of spiritual benefits from remaining for a while. Now, it is time to let them go and give them complete freedom. I got up immediately after the dream, dressed, collected their ashes, as well as a prayer book, and headed down to the waterfront, as the sun was still low on its horizon. Canadian geese flew over my parked car, honking, to the natives they often represent, going home. After the prayers and releasing, i got back to the car and two geese flew from my direction out over the water towards the sun. I knew this was a sign that they were heading home.

A few days prior to my confirmation, i had to do confession, or reconciliation. I found it to be a very powerful experience, i felt alot was released and i really felt that my soul was made clean again. It was like a weight was released, especially in talking to the priest about what had transpired with my parents. I said to him that it must sound crazy what i was saying to him about my experiences with demons and such and he said "no, not at all", as he sat with his arms folded over his solar plexus. This is a natural way to protect oneself as is crossing your legs. I was quite relieved to share it with him and not being chastized for it. I guess for them it is more common than we realize.

I realize now that this may sound kind of morbid but after my parents passed, i asked the funeral people for a clipping of their hair to keep. I forgot about it until the other day and decided that it best i release this as well, in case it was holding them back at all. I felt guided to go to a favourite spot in nature that i had a memory of being there with my parents. I remembered one trail where my Mom and i were looking at plants and i was telling her about this edible plant wild carrot. My Mom surprised herself as she recognized it as 'Queen Ann's Lace.' As i left the clipping there, i heard crows off in the distance, they became increasingly louder and louder. Shortly thereafter, a hawk flew by being chased by about seven crows. I felt it was a significant sign but a good one. I walked down the path and spotted two dear in the woods lying quietly in a shady area very peacefully watching me. I viewed this as a wonderful sign and know that the releasing i am doing is helping to set them free.

The flow of prosperity from the Father continues to amaze me in regards to finding exactly what i need for my place; and it's usually at thrift shops. The items i find, and i know when to go, are so specifically perfect, it's hard to fathom how this can be. I feel like they (upstairs) are making it personally and placing it there for me to have as rewards for my service.

The things that i have been led to lately include a table that is perfect for the space. For example, a very narrow table with three rows high to put beside the bed and the wall to put my c.d. player and a few other items on (so i can listen to my angel c.d.'s); and a small wicker stand to put my angel cards on. I found another to go into my meditation room so i could read prayers and do healing work and meditation on a regular basis. I was also led somewere shopping where i found a steam cleaner. I have been having trouble getting the upstairs hallway rug clean. I've cleaned it four times, with a rental and twice with a small hand steam cleaning machine. Also, i have used Carpet Fresh, as well as Fabreeze carpet powder on it. Then, i found this, and it works great, it's easy to use, all for $14.99. Oh and by the way, it was made by Hoover, where my Dad used to work. When i saw that, i knew it would work and that it was definately from him, in conjunction with God. By the way, i also told my brother previously i would steam clean his carpets and now i won't have to rent one, fantastic gift. The latest one was a nice looking little lamp and shade for next to my bed. But the interesting thing about it is that it's white and in the design there are four crosses in it facing in each direction, and i know this was meant to help give me protection as i sleep.

It sounds like i am bragging and i am thrilled to receive these things. It's simply when you're in service to the Lord they provide for your needs, you are looked after. You have nothing to worry about they take care of you. It's wonderful. You just have to pay attention and listen for guidance and trust what they tell you. I'm not just talking about in receiving the things you need but also what steps to take in your development or with every day decisions, as well as big decisions.

I don't think I mentioned about what happened after i gave my confession or reconciliation with the priest. After he absolved me of my sins, i truly felt relieved and felt that my soul was unblemished, that i never felt so clean and light, spiritually. I went back to my parents' house and the light was coming in from the window in the front door, and it created this wonderful rainbow on the fridge and seemed to illuminate my parents'picture. There was a wonderful energy there that i knew came from the other side, as rainbows are bridges from the spiritual to the material world. I knew my parents were happy and relieved, and i felt they received many blessings from my atonement or from my devotion to God expressed through the process that i was undertaking through confirmation. During the ceremony, a few days later on Holy Saturday was very special to me. I definitely felt a very powerful energy present, as i was being confirmed. My body was shaking from this presence.

Aside from being in service to the Lord, i also have been making quite a few donations, some to benefit my parents by donating to the Society of the Little Flower and requesting prayers or Mass intentions be said for them. I have also been given to the local missions, one has the Jesus fish as its symbol and the other called the Good Shepherd. I felt i was guided to do this by Jesus. I am fortunate enough to have what i need so i know that He wants me to help out those in most need. What would He do? I also support a child through Christian Children's Fund. All these things i do, i ask that my parents receive the blessings that they be protected and provided for, and lifted up and given blessings. I know for a fact it works.

Basically, there are givers of energy and takers of energy. Not surprisingly, people who are cheap are takers of energy, usually. I've had experience in dealing with people like this who attach themselves to your energy and i have to keep removing them (usually through dowsing) or cut the psychic cords that they attach to me.

I find that when i am sending energy to the earth, i can feel a lot of people attracted to me. This isn't a bad thing because it's God's force energy that they're really drawn to, not me. When doing this type of work, you draw a lot of people to you sometimes. Like my friend says, "things happen when i don't put any effort forth." This is because i am connected to God's energy. When i attempt to try to bring something to me, i cut myself off from this energy and try to draw that energy from someone else, which repels them. A healthy relationship is when both people are givers of energy and when both people are connected to the Father's energy or at least operate from the heart. I remember reading somewhere in the Bible that there are lovers of themselves and lovers of God. Doing high vibrational work does draw the other side as well that wants to steal or intetfere.

I went to see the play, To Kill A Mockingbird. It still remains my favourite book. I especially relate to Atticus and feel that this is a wonderful guide on how to live. I think that i figured out why i felt so much love for his daughter, Scout. I'm pretty sure that their connection and her spirit reminds me of my own daughter from a past life when i was a Viking. We actually connected in this life and it as a very difficult experience, but remembering the love i had for that girl's spirit has allowed me to forgive the girl from what she did and to send prayers asking that she be healed. It's an amazing world and our love never dies.

I just have to mention another gift that proves the Father provides. I noticed that i didn't have any vacuum bags left, which i never had to worry about because there were always plenty of them, since my Dad worked at Hoover. I wrote down the type i needed and was just wondering where to go. Different events led me out of town and i stopped into a thrift store and saw some hanging there. I couldn't remember what type i needed but bought them anyway. Sure enough, they were the ones i needed. It still blows me away and there's plenty of incidents like that which I don't mention. My place is filled with blessings from 'The One'. I am telling you when you do for others and serve the Lord, you're taken care of, period. It's not so much what your given but that your needs are meet and its so specific it amazes me.

Love… the overflowing elixir of life, filling and refilling the voids and cracks in space, ever-present, everywhere. It makes the bees buzz and the flowers open, the grass grow, sustaining all that allows it to enter them, fuelling them with abundant energy and inspiration. Indescribable feelings of fullfilment. Thank you, God, for the bounty of your love. Keep me in your good graces and bless all life. Teach all life to love and respect each other so that there may be peace and kindness in the world. Every day, i turn to you and ask that you show me the way to express your love like it was meant to be done. Let me be a channel for this wonderful warmth that is the only real thing in the universe, and i wish that everyone finds this truth. Forgive my obsolescence and indulgences on pettiness and perversions of this pure love….i had written this a while ago but it seemed necessary to add it here at this point.

I love attending church and find it very important to do it regularly. Unfortunately, i am dismayed at some of the individuals that i talk with in afterwards to find this intolerance they have for not only other religions and teachings but also for different denominations of the same faith. Is it just me or is that ludicrous? There is only one God with so many expressions. It's really about building bridges and finding commonalities, not focussing on exclusivity. Service brings many rewards but the real reward is in the experience itself. To be following your soul's purpose, to help the world to be a better place, to be more filled with its love.

The main thing is that you keep going and you don't quit. You fill up and go again. Acquiescence is not acceptable and you don't let them tell you what is what, no matter what position they hold. Their truth is not y ours. You fight to the death, if necessary, for your ideals. Ideology is what makes you meet the dawn and it is your birth right to be free to find your truth.

Another old writing of mine i found: All God's Children are we, although some seem to have lost any realization to this fact. It matters not to hem who they hurt or what actions are taken to further their own interests. They belittle the sacred things and torment the gentle spirits. Those things that they do kill the kindness in the world through fear-mongering tactics and episodes of absurd coldness weaken the heart of the righteous spirit. All good things come to those that wait. Perceive the truth, and bound yourself with good graces and loving thoughts to drive away the tempests and turmoil. Loving and kindness defeats any ill wishes you are a loved gentle one precious in the eyes of the Almighty Spirit. You will be cared for and your wishes kept dearly. Bless the ground you step on for it welcomes your touch. Love is the way, the truth and the only thing worthwhile in the whole of creation. Spread love, not bile, even when you feel rankled by their ill intentions.

I found a c.d. series at a thrift store called Desiring God, by John Piper. The one thing i got from it so far was when he talked about suffering and perhaps suffering is necessary to get into heaven. This has helped me come to terms somewhat with some of the suffering my parents had to go through. I know in my own life, the suffering or difficult times has pushed me in directions i needed to go. They also provided lessons and have created in me a stronger desire to serve the light and destroy the darkness in the world. Tough lessons from the Father, resembling tough love.

I feel that I may be entering a new phase of my life. I have come to a place where i am willing to forgive the people for what they have done. I also understand what their motive was and the pain that they felt, at least in terms of one person, i know that we cared for each other like Brothers at one point. We have to also understand that they too are victims of the enemy. Like Jesus says, to forgive is what he wants for us. Hatred only destroys yourself. It's just best to enjoy your life the best you can. God always forgives that's why he sent his son. Remember he is Father to all of us.

I'm reminded of how everything in life seems to have parallels. As i was steam cleaning the basement stairs, it occurred to me that i was cleaning my past. As i steam cleaned my stairs leading upstairs, i was helping to clean a path for my future. I know that i need to focus more on trying to clear the people that attack me and trying not to engage in spiritual battles, if at all possible. Certainly, sometimes it comes to a point where that is necessary but even then, its best to let the spirit world deal with it. I'm finding more and more that doing prayer work is the best solution.

One of the ways i have been doing clearing lately is again placing the person in a gold cage, putting a glass case over it and then filling it right to the top with holy water. Also, i find myself wearing a white hat often in public. I feel it helps to keep white energy around your crown and sides of head. My friend told me that a Native American person had told her that regular salt is more effective than sea salt, so i am trying that out. It seems to have a much higher energy.

I have to tell this story about a spider that's been in my house lately. I have a lot of respect for spiders. The Medicine cards by Sams, Carson. It refers to them as being "weavers of the web." I feel that they help to create your destiny. The Native American people also believe, i think, that the universe was created by a spider. I was meditating in my meditation room and the spider was dangling about the same height as my altar. I was sending energy and prayers to my parents to help raise them up higher. I swear to you that as i did this, the spider made his way upwards to the ceiling. There were a few other instances. Once i was trying the decide whether to go to a play, i was tired but decided to push myself and got into the shower. The spider was in there. Another time, i came home with a picture and, trying to decide where it needed to go, the spider was on the wall on an empty space, i believe showing me where to put it, for energetic reasons i am sure. I asked and was told that he was sent by the Father!

There is a prospect of a relationship and, although i know that i shouldn't put too much emphasis on it, i did anyways and got myself off balance. It's easy to say and not so easy to do sometimes. I guess that's part of being human, we get attached to the physical and to outcomes. I think the important thing is knowing when and how to get your balance back. I find, though, what happens is that i lose the focus on love and faith, and become fearful and needy. In doing so, i cut myself off from the source and lose power. I become someone who is looking to take rather than staying connected to the source of God and being a giver of energy and love. In doing what i did, i feel it can repel people. When i decide to stay in that love and power and decide to be happy with whatever comes into my life, i remain centred and in control, and my higher energy and joyful demeanor will draw good things into my life. I finally went into prayer and asked Jesus for help and opened the Bible. I feel that on almost all occassions this works for me. It's like it's speaking right to me, pertains to my life and situation, it's very profound. Some people can do this with cards (medicine or angel), i find this works the same way. But it also has the power of God to cure and clear which i have experienced countless times, especially when the going gets rough.

Let his word bring you up. It's power! I was focusing too much on control and physicality and lust. I apologized to Jesus for losing my focus of him and i asked Him to write His name on my heart first and foremost above all others. He wrote it with His finger and He wrote it backwards so the letters were facing me, and He said, "This is so you can read it." He reminded me that our connection is eternal. Then i saw a white skull cap on my head and as i leaned forward, someone put a white scarf around my neck with a Jewish design and insignia on it then i heard the words, "Shalom, peace be with you." I did this after watching the Passion of Christ again and becoming emotional for the feeling that i forgot him. Anyways, He told one that He "helped make it", meaning the movie, that i thought was so cool.

In regards to this relationship possibility, Jesus told me that it was "written in Heaven", and i have been hearning the words "Divine Union."

I was putting some salt around my house by my front door and i got hit on the head by droppings from a pigeon. Thanks God. At least it got me laughing and i needed that. But i also took it as a blessing, something to do with my home, because i think of homing pigeons. The next i heard the song He sends down his pure sweet love on the wings of a Snow White Dove, by Bob Miller. Animal Speak by Ted Andrews talks about the close relation between pigeons and doves. I asked what the song meant i heard "peace!" The day after that, i noticed i had a pimple on the same spot which i got constantly when someone is sending we negative energy. I feel the pigeon was getting rid of an energy that was attached to me.

I bought two pairs of new shoes, one for work and one for daily use and like i said about metaphors, i feel that this has made me ready for new beginnings. To begin a 'new walk!' Everything seems to happen for a reason and has spiritual value, in everyday life there is the spirit of God. I feel that was Saint John Paul 11 who just spoke through me, amazing!

I went to a special Mass today for the crowning of Mother Mary. I went there to pay homage to her because of everything She has done in my life and because i love her with all of my heart. I also feel there was more significance for my personal life and i couldn't help notice a rainbow close by me on the floor as we are singing during the ceremony. (I feel the rainbow is the bridge from the divine life to the physical). The morning sun (new beginnings) was on my left side and was coming through a glassed in solarium which contained a large statue of many and prayer, candle, one of which i had lit.

After the Mass of the crowning of Mother Mary, later that evening, i was watching the movie Joan of Arc. I found her story incredibly inspiring and i love her heart and courage and devotion, then i felt the gift of her presence with me. Earlier after the Mass, i kept hearing St. Catharine. Since i was driving to Niagara Falls and the City of St. Catharines on the way, i thought it was being suggested that i would stop there for some reason but i didn't. I also heard St. Margaret and Mary. I thought it was being suggested that i got to this church which was previously recommended to me by a new friend for the reason of connecting to someone who is in charge of healing groups in the Catholic Church. It was later while watching the movie that i realised that St. Catharine was Joan of Arc's patron saint and the main one that communicated with her. At her trial, she also mentioned St. Margaret and Mary also talked with her, as did St. Michael. This blew me away. In any event, i felt that watching the movie and connecting with these energies helped me a great deal in raising any discouragement i was feeling and helping to raise my desire to carry on with 'the cause' at all costs. These Saints are still here as well as Joan of Arc who was Canonized 500 years after her death, and they are helping as still to our service to God. The key is to listen and to follow God's guidance.

I feel that i was told that my fear is based on my lack of faith in the power of God. This beautiful young woman had such incredible courage because of her unbending devotion and faith in God. Let her be an inspiration to all of us, especially those willing to dedicate their lives to service.

I think back and i see how i have felt hated and mistreated by life. So know your in good company as Jesus too was hated, and know were the despised nature comes from, the enemy of course. It doesn't matter what people say or do, they can't touch your soul if your focus is on God, Jesus and the Holy Spirit. The Holy realm is were we need to place our emphasis to do service and be protected. Where do you place your emphasis? Which world is more important? I believe Jesus said to me "that this world is like sandcastles you put all your focus on building it and then the tide comes in and then were will ye be."

People do what they do for whatever reasons they do it, shouldn't worry about it or take it too personal like Carlos Castranda says, "We shouldn't be offended by the actions of others, they just do what they do." Why give your power to them by getting upset why give your power to the world, unless it's to help soneone in need. We need to be less of this world, but more of the other one.

I remind myself again that i get everything i need from the Father. I trust that he is in control. "He's got the whole world in his hands." Written by Edward Boatner from Spiritual Triumphant. He provides everything i need according to his Plan, not mine. Give God glory and trust him with all your heart. It's a walk in faith and don't let anyone shake you from that. Think about the life eternal and believe that the Lord truly is your Shepherd. I'm turning up the volume on God and turning down the volume on the world. I've been hearing lately "Your God walk starts now." It's good company.

I did some things around my home that I feel were significant in helping to bring into my life things i felt 'inspired' to do to help manifest in my life the type of relationship that i need and deserve, but especially the one that 'He' has chosen for me. I've been hearing lately that, "my path is laid in stone." Anyways after i did these things (I was told to keep the details secret), i noticed a spider climbing up the stairway in my home. I feel that this is a very significant sign that my manifesting was helpful with sign that my manifesting was helpful as the spider represents Creator energy; symbolished through weaving and your stairway going upstairs represents your future path. In a previous meditation, i saw Jesus at the top of the stairs and He was beckoning a certain individual to come up them. The next morning, the 2

Angel cards I pulled, one from Karmic Angels by Helene Sattarnic, says "infuses hearts with the desire for great love and passion that totally absorbs." The Doreen Virtue/Archangel Michael card says "new beginnings and a fresh start." I opened up my door to welcome in the morning sun and the promises of a new day and standing on my fence looking right at me was a squirrel, preparedness (Animal Speak, Andrews) and noticed that there was a large spider web built at the opening of my gate.

When we walk with Jesus and touch the Face of God, we remember our own divinity, or own perfect selves that we are created by God. We forget who we are and we forget why we were created. Walking with God helps us to remember those things and to reconnect with the who we are.

In a meditation and prayer session, i saw Cardinals, Saints and Angels throwing seeds on the ground. They were planting seeds of Christ. I saw as dove of peace descending which i feel was the Holy Spirit. People are hungry and there is only one thing that can truly fulfill their hunger and thirst, and that is the Love of God. I saw a rainbow bridge and saw Jesus walking across it, coming down. He is here. We need to open up our hearts and minds to receive Him. The King of Kings is here. The Father is here as well open up to his promised love and promises of peace. Turn to Him for guidance to follow your destined path. God has a plan for you. He's beautiful. He has an answer for every problem. Follow your path that you were meant to follow when you came down here. Turn to Him for guidance to follow your destined path. God has a plan for you. Turn to Him to show you to way. Pray. Jesus reminds us that the world is like sand castles, temporary, to be washed away back into the sea. The Kingdom of Heaven is external. The temporary things of the world are gifts that have been given to us to use for a short time and then placed down and left behind when we make our journey back to the Holy Trinity. What fools we are when we make our whole life out of these things. The Holy Trinity is the only thing we can be sure of we can be with forever. We can be with them now. You can be on your 'God Walk'now. Heaven on Earth, the bridge has been built and they have crossed it. "Open up your hearts to receive the Lord, The Kingdom of Heaven is at Hand."

I was at the store and i heard the song Somewhere Over the Rainbow. I was thinking about my Mother and i knew the song was from them. I wondered again about their wishes that i have children so they could reincarnate as them and i know that these plans have changed and they're fine that they are way up there. They're very happy and as much as they love me, they don't want to or need to come back. They made it. I know that i helped them through my connection to Jesus and Mary. God bless them for what they have done for them. My parents, i know, are fine with everything. They acknowledge the price i have paid for their freedom. I hear my Mom saying "it's so beautiful up here." She tells me to "just keep centred, to keep my face in the sun, and focus on service, and keep it going." I do know that my Mother had strong spiritual beliefs from her Mother and good friend from work and no doubt was going to get 'there' based on her own goodness and inward faith of Jesus.

I know that sending energy to the earth and sending blessings and healing to people keeps me centred and focussed and detached from life's melodramas. Jesus acknowledges that there has been great success. I hear the words, "a life worth lived", in regards to my parents. I feel that i as well have accomplished some wonderful things already and everything else is just icing on top of the cake.

In a situation i felt the other person was not following what i though was 'the plan', i have just remind myself to stay focussed on what i do, how i can serve and trust that God's will, will be done.

The other day, i stopped at my Brother's home before i went to the beach. He came out of his room and asked if i wanted to do something together. This was a small miracle. My Brother rarely wants to do anything. He came to the beach with me and as i lay there and told him how i showed this local spot to my parents and they liked it, i had a vision of my Mother there with a sun hat on and sunglasses. That same day, or the next, i bought a beach blanket for him and i heard my Mother say, "you're a good kid." I found it a thrift store along with a red roots sweatshirt. I knew it was a birthday present from my parents because my Mother had bought me one very similar and it's now pretty beaten up, but I couldn't let it go. The week before, i was having trouble waking up to go to work and i heard someone say, "Let's go, Ace." That's something my Father used to call me.

For some reason, i was remembering the movie, Chariots of Fire. I remember the impression that the Scottish runner had made on me. He was such a pure person with beautiful character who, even though it was the Olympics, refused to run because it was 'The Lord's Day'and against his faith to compete on Sunday. I need to get this movie. I remember him running and saying "I run for His glory." This is another individual that i would like to be more like. The joy he had when he ran, the pureness of his devotion he had, his strong character, it's beautiful. This movie i saw a number of times years ago and i think that even then, it was put in my path to make an impression on me. God truly works in amazing ways.

Another inspiring person was this 21 year old girl who just had a double lung transplant. When i see Prime Minister Harper pinning a medal on her, i could tell she got to them. That was opening up his heart. This girl has been on Ellen DeGeneres'show and will be again, and i really feel that she is serving God through this journey that she's on by opening up the hearts of everyone who sees her. She is such a beautiful spirit you can't help but be affected by her. I know she affected me and when i mentioned her to a friend of mine at work, she said she cries every time she sees her. I need to remember her name. Is it Helena?

I realized that in a certain situation that i was giving my energy away to this particular girl. It seems to me that that is really what she wants, my energy. I realized i wasn't getting any back. When you're losing power in a relationship, something's wrong. It's about giving and taking, and mutual respect. I talked to another girl at work that seems to be interested in me and when i got home, there were two doves sitting on my stoop. I had noticed these two doves sitting on my fence the morning before. I believe they've come to tell me something. Interesting enough, i had lost a pair of glasses that i was using, even though they were all scratched up, and i went out and ordered a new pair. This is telling me that i wasn't seeing a certain situation clearly and now i have 'new eyes' to see with. It's beautiful how the metaphors in life are always telling you something.

I spent some time in Europe and i really loved it. I just felt they had a richer experience of living. What's the French expression 'je ne c'est quoi.' Enjoying the quality of life rather than quantity. Enjoying the things of the world in the right measure. It kind of makes me think of maybe that's what they refer to when they say the 'art of living'. It's touching the world with our senses but not to the point where we get attached and off-balance, slowing down at bit, that's my goal. It's not about owning, but being.

I keep thinking about Jesus' metaphor about sand castles. I think this must also be what the Buddhist's talk about in the movie Little Buddha by Bernardo Bertolucci, where they say "form is emptiness and emptiness is form." Things are opposite to appearances, the material world, in essence, is unreal because it is temporary but the unseen world, the spiritual world, is the permanent one.

My Brother bought me a birthday cake and i put some candles on it, made some wishes and went to blow out the candles one at a time. Just as i was taking a breath to blow out the third one, someone else blew it out and it wasn't my Brother.

I just noticed that with a particular friend who started to do more service work for God, it just struck me that she seemed to be feeling good about herself that that when you're following your Divine purpose, your inner light starts to glow.

I occasionally come to the realization that i really don't know anything. I just see a small part of what's really going on. But i like returning to this state of being where you are humble. There is no ego. I feel like a child, unspoiled by self-importance. I love coming back to that place of wonder and awe of mystery of it all. I'm hearing a song now in my head, "I hope you never lose your sense of wonder"... "I hope you dance." This song is from Mark D.Sanders and Tia Sillers. I knew this is from my parents sending me their well wishes on my birthday. It's the same song i heard at the doctor's office when my Mom was in the hospital and knew then it was her.

Speaking of inspiration, and i was just reading about the Holy Spirit. Filled with the spirit, is this what happens when we are inspired, are touched by the spirit, is this when we get a sense of Him that we are filled with this awe and wonder of the mystery, the beauty and the power that moves in all things. As if to add an exclamation point, the sun just popped up shining the first rays of the morning into my meditation room.

I have just been thinking more and more that it's really about building bridges. I feel that love is that bridge and i am not just talking about different denominations or churches of the same faith, but amongst all faiths and races. Shouldn't we just focus on the common goals that we should all have? For example, when i am doing healing work, my goals are to help raise consciousness by bringing in love and peace through prayer, healing for the earth and animals, stopping the suffering. Say for working with the animals, i will always call upon the Holy trinity first and St. Frances but certainly, the fairie realm works closely with the earth and the Native Americans. If anyone can help and comes from the light, i welcome them. To me, it's about the cause, affecting a change. It's about the result, not who or how it gets done. I get help from a lot of different realms. I'm sure that i am not aware of a lot of them. Why can't we operate in society to come together in some way to affect positive change in the world through our common love of humankind, the earth and the animals.

Anytime i am feeling down or sorry for myself, i am guided to help others or i see the suffering of others. I'm moved by having compassion for the suffering of others. Maybe that is how i have responded to the suffering i have had in my life. My fixation on my own life and problems pales and fades away. I feel this is an example of how 'the spirit' works with me.

I opened my door and there was a raccoon on the neighbour's fence, and we just looked at each other. I knew he had a message for me which i looked up in Animal Speaks (Andrews). I feel that he came to me to help me because i always say prayers for the animals i see killed on the roads. I said some further prayers for that species asking that they somehow are taught to avoid roads or ask that the angels or nature guides help them.

It's amazing when you feel the love of animals, the earth, nature, certainly the father, Jesus, the Holy Spirit, the faerie realm, the Angels, the Saints. It's so overwhelming sometimes, the gratitude i feel being sent my way when i send prayers and healing for them. I do it because i care, because I don't like the way a lot of things are in the world, because i don't like to see pain. I feel it makes a difference. My reward is the feeling of love, gratitude and friendship i get from them. Some think it doesn't help but it sure doesn't hurt to try, and i believe our prayers are heard. One thing i learned from Grandfather (through Tom Brown Jr.'s books) is that it's our responsibility to try. I just heard from Grandfather, "tears are not enough."

It is not uncommon for other Ascended Masters/Angels/guides to make an appearance as when i am doing healing work. I don't know exactly why but some are better at certain things. They're all welcome.

I went for a bike ride today out of town, along the Toronto Lakeshore, harbour front and across on the ferry to Toronto Island to ride around there and spend some time on the beach. It was a super-hot day but this has been one of the great joys in my life for the longest time. Before i left, i had a vision of my Father with a bicycle helmet on. On the drive there, i was reminiscing about all the trips we used to take together to Toronto, especially in his last few years. Sometimes, my Mom would come too and it was wonderful to share time with them. They loved going on outings. On the way back to the car i heard my Father say "what an awesome day." I don't know if he ever rode a bike before. As crazy as it sounds i think Jesus even took them for a sailboat ride to make up for one time when i paid for one for them and it was lousy, it got cut short because of sail trouble and my poor Mother felt jipped.

One thing that i have been doing quite a bit when i am out is blessing children and handicapped people. I'm not sure what good it does but i felt that Jesus is working with me alot i have to try to use my time as much as possible in service. I visualize picking up the child and handing him to Jesus, asking Him to bless the child and take them into the light. Today, i received a confirmation from Him that it was working. After spending much of the day doing this, i heard Him say, "splendid" and i knew He was commenting on my efforts. I had seen Him holding the children in the past but sometimes, i still wonder how much i am imagining. But now, i know that He had been wanting me to do this. With handicapped or elderly people, i hold their wrists and ask Jesus to take them by the hands, bless them and take them into the light. For a while now, as soon as my energy takes their left wrists, it moves to their heart chakra (middle of their chest). This is a common reaction to 'His' presence. Of course this is with my mind, but we can amazing things with our thoughts.

I'm still reminding myself how not to give energy away to others. For example, as i am trying to get my writing published and getting letters of rejection, it's hard not to get down because i have put my heart and soul into this. I can't give my power to them to decide whether it's worthy or whether or not i am worthy. I realize my self-worth is too connected to my writing. I can't let them dictate my self-worth. I know i am worthy and i believe the writing is good. At least the messages being delivered through me are good. I have to remember to take an action and let go of the consequences. If it doesn't produce a result, then i focus on what action i take next. For every situation or problem, there is a solution. Again, i have to focus on responding, not reacting. Responding requires a decision and an action. A reaction is emotional and mental and may be spiritual and physical as well. It's a giving away of energy and power. Once again, stay away from the wanting or craving. Pray. Ask for guidance, meditate and what step is next. Then, after you act, let it go. In any given moment, we choose to walk in power or give it away.

I'm hearing again on a t.v. show about the power of manifesting your desires and positive visualization, and i know there's truth in it. But i just believe that focussing too much on this is just what Jesus warned about, remember that it's just 'sand castles', and i should put the focus on Him and the father, and the serving. The other sounds a bit too much like self-gratification, i am not saying it's wrong to have dreams and hopes and wishes but let God control it. You know let go and let God, and trust His plan and not worry.

I thought if this is something that i should be doing more of but i think i want to focus on God's will and being confident that his will, will be done. I just feel better about this approach to life. Believe! I'll let go of my feelings or unworthiness and if He wants my writing to be made public, He will make it happen. I have to be able to recognize where i am being led. I'll knock on the door He tells me to knock on. If it opens, i will walk through it. I'm going to focus more on faith and the power of prayer. My prayers, though, can't be self-serving, but more a request to know His will and how i can serve better.

I do object to comments about an 'impersonal creative force.' This is totally not at all what i have experienced. I have met with the Father often (although not as often as i should) and i have talked with Him. His love is so vast and deep that to call him impersonal is ludicrous. I can only assume that those who say that have not met Him. I suggest you find out for yourself. The way i have found to the Father is through Jesus. There are times that i lose heart, get discouraged, fell unworthy, slip back into old ways a bit. It is His presence that brings me out of it and all i can do is feel foolish for my lesser ways of being. I feel, though, that i am being guided to hold an intention that my dreams will be made manifest, to expect it, to feel that it is already there. As long as my dreams and desires are what the Father wants me for and they are based on love and service.

I've been feeling that i have become too obsessive about my clothes and i told the Father this. He responded that by saying "you appreciate them." This made me realize how just how understanding and supportive he was of me. I expected to be condemned for this attachment. I also want to say that lately, i have been finding things again (usually but not always the same place that happens to be in front of a large white cross). But these were things that i had no intention of finding. Once i saw them, i knew that's why i was led there and yes, they are things i needed and were perfect. It just shows how it is not my intention being manifested but a caring, benevolent Father who knows my needs even better than i know them. And He provides these things that i need without even my asking. It also shows how observant and aware He is of the details of my life. He loves me so much that He goes to the trouble of making sure i have what i need. This is the way He works miracles in my life. They are small miracles, but miracles none the less because of how it all comes about. I mean, sometimes i am led to different towns to find things and it's made pretty clear of where i have to go in or where i have to stop and also, sometimes, who i have to talk to. This is why i have to trust in the Father and his love, and know that He provides for me; and in doing so, He shows His love and appreciation for my efforts to serve and i in turn want to serve him more.

I find it difficult to walk a spiritual life when you're single. I'm trying, not always successfully, to not give my power and energy away to the physical world, i.e. attractive women. I find that when i focus on service, that it just fades away. Jesus did suggest to me "to acknowledge it and then let it go." It reminds me of the Buddhist meditation of observing your thoughts. He also stated that, "on the road of life, there are many obstacles. It's important to keep a focus. Do what is pleasing to the Father and you will have a happy life." The minister at church mentioned about staying on your road and i had a vision of a roadway with cement barriers on each side. I'm trying to rechannel my sexual energy by keeping busy in blessing children when out in public rather than looking at woman (for example) to focus on love rather than lust, but exercising or working out just a bit on my own, sit-ups, stretching, push-ups, etc., jogging, bike riding, certainly doing chores and errands as well. To try to keep busy. But when i am not actively busy, to spend time in prayer, reading the Bible, writing helps, listening to music or transformation c.d.'s and meditation.

On Father's Day, I feel that my father was around, as i had a funny thought that came to mind while we were out for dinner. It seemed to happen just after talking to some other people about how my Dad and i used to go to baseball games together, even when he was in a wheelchair. The humorous thought was just so much like my Dad and when i acknowledged it in my mind, i had a clear vision of my Mother and she was killing herself laughing. He's such a comedian. There's no ill will attached to it but I dare not speak because it may seem like an offense to some. But i know my dad well and it's just his dry sense of humour and witt to notice and make a comment of certain 'nationalities' in the restaurant that you normally don't witness eating Italian food. You know, i think i needed a good laugh. It's without any harm or judgement just a comical approach he had in life to notice stuff and witness life that most of us didn't but he mostly always had a little comedy in him that cracked us up and that's what i miss the most. Without humour were in trouble, it's healing! More proof of their presence because i heard this first from spirit before i noticed it.

I've been having a lot of dealings with negative energy lately but Jesus, told me, "Don't let it distract you from your path." The power of the enemy is fear. You overcome the enemy by not fearing it, stand up to it, ignore it, focus on building and strengthening your path. I believe also that the most effective tool is prayer. Faith and prayer can remove all obstacles and accomplish all things. Also with meditation, we create a strong connection so we can clearly receive guidance as to what actions we need to take to defeat the enemy. I don't believe in standing behind the cross but standing in front of it, knowing it's there to support me but i am willing to do what i need to do instead of just relying on having it done for me. By taking actions, i feel they will give me even more help because i am not being lazy or powerless. I want to be a warrior of Christ. I'm wanting to find the balance between my own masculine and feminine, the warrior and the nurturer. Both are necessary.

I've become aware in the past year that the problems i am having with a group of individuals stems back to at least two past lives. I've been focussing my prayers lately towards removing these past life conditions, 'closing the book on it', so to speak, closing or removing the openings that allow these conditions to be brought forward into this life. When i say closing the book, i mean it figuratively and literally, as in going and asking that your helpers go into your Akashic records and close the book, cut the ties and do whatever needs to be done to put an end to these situations. I'm also paying close attention to the things i do and havein terms of possessions or practices or beliefs i have that may be opening this vortex. For example, i released alot of Native American belongings.

I had seen myself as a Native American chief being chased and persecuted by a cavallary. The other life i am currently working on is where i see a white knight and a black one battling. This by the way does not meen i don't honour who i was, that stays with me and is part of me. Just another note on this, i felt while praying to God he told me that "i would not die by the sword." It's amazing how people come to you to help you on a spiritual level and most have no idea that they are doing it. Their spirits are aware of whats going on and i know they are sent from the Father. I know these people are coming to me as i can sense their energies but it's also a confirmation i am doing something right to get their help. It shows me Im on the right path and it gives me motivation.

Just like i can usually sense when another person's energy is around me, i find that i can also talk with other people's 'higher selves.' I do it quite frequently. I find that it is helpful when doing healing on people (saying prayers) to have discussions with them.

One time, i was thinking about Deepak Chopra and then i felt we had a conversation. I'm quite sure i didn't imagine this. I feel he ended by saying "remarkable journey, isn't it." By the way, i found an old tape i had of his and on it, he was talking about 100 monkeys experiment that i mentioned earlier,which refers to a mass or collective consciousness and gives hope to me that by raising it can effect change throughout humankind.

The synchronicities are really quite amazing. I was complaining about how i constantly have to deal with negative energy. At church today, July 8th, there was a reading from scripture and just talking about how difficulties lead to strength from above. It's really quite profound but definately saying that our suffering has a purpose. I believe Jesus said to me, "persecution is making me perfect."

A few days prior, i was outside barbequing and i talked to the Father and expressed my gratitude for all the ways that i was aware of how he was sending me help. I confirmed that i knew and trusted in his plan for me but admitted that i sometimes was getting confused over what action he wanted me to take. I confessed that i knew i wasn't meditating enough and this was the only way to receive his direction. Just then, out of a mostly sunny sky, rain began to fall, and even though i was looking forward a hug drop landed right between my eyes. I don't know if it was a blessing or a confirmation that he was telling me. Of course, use your inner vision.

I keep telling people about this prayer that i found most helpful in connecting to Jesus in meditation. I may have mentioned it but here it is again. It's in the Good shepherd Prayer Book (Pocket Edition) by Devon trading Corp., N.J., 2001. It's called Prayer to listen to our Lord. If you're going to connect with spirit for guidance, then you might as well get it from the top; not all guidance is at the same level.

I felt a great deal of sadness the other night after talking with someone and seeing their suffering, yet when presented with a path, i feel is guaranteed to help them, they don't like it. I sometimes feel there's just too much sadness in this world and sometimes it's just too hard to take and i wish i didn't have to see it. I often want to rush into a situation and try to rescue the person and i know that's not healthy either and i think that's a pattern for me. The best way to help someone is to point them to Jesus and pray that they will turn to Him in their suffering when they are ready. When i think about it, it was my own suffering that pushed me to Him and thank God for that!

On the lighter side, i was on my way to the library which is in the complex with the YMCA. There was a car directly in front of me as I pulled in with the licence plate that consisted of both of my two Grandfather's first names. I thought that was pretty amazing. The library was closed so i know they must have been pointing me to the YMCA. I feel that i need to join this in the fall and winter and just maybe my Brother might come along. After leaving, i had a clear vision of both of them, as well as my Mother.

My guardian angel and totem of mine are around a lot today too but i feel that's more to do with warnings of negative energy around. God bless them all. (It turns out that is were i end up frequently now typing my book and by the way it was guidance from one of them, if not both, to write.)

In a meditation, i was being carried by Jesus across a river, i saw him stepping on stones (this may represent a time period regarding some aspect of my path), he placed me on the other side of the river upon the bank and then he faded back into the river and began to sink down into it. I asked him, Jesus, where are you going? And he said, "I am the water." Jesus may also have carried me across because i may have, in his eyes, reached a new level or a new realization. I was thinking of how i was acting towards a certain person that i was trying to avoid her sort of because I didn't want to encourage a possible relationship, and i just started thinking that i was being silly, that i needed to send loving energy to everyone. Also, i needed to keep sending loving energy without needing to receive, to spread love to the world. To keep the 'tap' turned on, to allow the 'the living waters' to flow through me to the world. Jesus gives to me and i give to the world.

I've been thinking lately about how the 'new science', quantum physics and how they discovered that our thoughts are energy and effect the outside world. Then i thought what's so 'new'about that. Jesus always talks about the power of faith.

In the past, i easily stopped. I lost faith easily. I lost motivation. I didn't have confidence. Now, i have confidence in what the father and Jesus tell me, so i will never quit. I'll just keep taking steps. If things aren't working or i get confused, i will just try harder to understand what steps i should take thorough daily devotional time. But keep taking steps and putting forth the effort is important to me. I feel that if i keep waking the path, will reveal itself, the works thing for me is inaction. I feel actions are empowering and freeing and it helps me to face my fears and to let myself be known. I also feel that you show the spirit world that you are serious about your desire to develop and implement the play they have for you and i believe this encourages more support and guidance. It also gives the negative energies a clear message about this time i will not be stopped.

I was guided to meet with a Deacon who directed me to a particular church, that's name was related to Mary. I found a cubical to kneel in front of a Mary statue and as i was in prayer, i saw her and she told me that, "I am a divine child of God, and that the Father loves me very much." She told me to look up and i looked into her radiant face and loving eyes.

It was July 1ˢᵗ and i went to Mass to meet the new priest (new beginnings?). Then i went to the Baptist church where i felt a beautiful uplifting energy as the music was playing. It was a perfect warm summer morning and i had a clear sense of my Mother dancing. Even my Brother was standing and singing. I went to a park, it was Canada Day. A marching band walked by me, a band that my parents i had seen numerous times at football games. I felt a lot of emotion also because there were many times spent at this park with my parents as well. I felt they were both with me. I realize that i still miss them very much and that my heart still needs healing and maybe this has prevented me lately from operating from the heart and thinking too much about the physical.

A week later, i saw my mother at a Catholic church walking down the aisle with the altar boy behind her, carrying the Crucifix. I sensed a bright light as i felt a vortex opened coming from the Jesus painted above the altar. At Value Village, i found a 45 record, Just a Closer Walk With Thee by Pat Boone.(first known recording is by Selah Jubilee Singers) There was also a Maple Leaf's sweater lying on the floor which i knew was a gift for my brother. That evening, i was sending energy and my guardian angel told me that my mother loves me. I kept hearing her favourite song, Four Strong Winds, by Neil Young "... if the good times are gone, i'm bound for moving on, i will look for you, if i'm ever back this way ..." I played the song and lit a Mother Mary candle. I felt that she danced to the song, then she asked if "I was sure this is what i wanted." She told me, "Jesus was waiting for her outside the gate of my yard." I walked her out of my house and then opened my gate. I heard, "She's gone! Gone from my sight. That is all." From the poem by Henry Van Dyke. As i write this, i heard, "a fitting end."

In doing healing work lately, i have been seeing a rainbow coming down from the heavens, like a bridge, and i see Jesus walking on it. I believe it is truly a bridging of heaven on earth. Is this what they are referring to as the second coming?

I was reading about the rewards of a path of service and i quickly lost interest. First, i had heard them tell me that "my rewards are in heaven." Besides, it's up to them to decide what i deserve and when i am not worried about that, that's their department. I'm not doing it for rewards. I'm doing it because it feels good, because i have compassion for the suffering of others, because i see a lot of things wrong in the world and i want to see them changed. I want to be part of the solution and not part of the problem. Also, i do service because He wants me to. My rewards are being in his presence and Him telling me that He is proud of me. What could be better than that? My desire is to not to try to want, to be content with my life and what the Father gives me; to enjoy the simple pleasures and to focus more on the things of God rather than of man-made things; to feel the presence of God and his helpers in my walk through life; to walk in His glory and presence, and to make Him proud of me by doing good things and trying to refrain from my old ways that bring shame to myself and don't make Him proud. When i think about Him, and pray and meditate, and also work in His service, i know He is there. I want to keep walking forward and to not look back with regret or longing at my past, time to let it go.

I am always amazed at His presence, so easy going, and patient with me; so light and benevolent. The more i am with Him, the more i will know what He wants me to do. He tells me to "fight the urge."I know He's referring to lustful thinking. I've been hearing again a lot of talk about manifesting abilities and i know there's a lot of truth to it. I probably already mentioned this but i feel the focus should be on what he wants and trying to connect with him to understand that. When i am feeling down or a little lost, it's helpful to me to read some scripture or an inspiring book, or say prayers, or do some service for others. I need to keep fed with inspiring things of God. When my thoughts are too much on the physical, i will take my two forefingers of my left hand and draw a line from my navel to my heart, energetically and intentionally raising my focus from the sacral or sexual charka to the heart chakra. I believe that our sexual energy is kind of like the fuel for the engine but we must are you focus or direct this energy.

I was told by my former teacher, J., that i have a Brother in spirit, that my mother had a miscarriage, and by the way, he's helping me. This just proves that the fetus has a spirit and is a human being.

Lately, there has been a lot of negative energy around. It seems like witchcraft and i found it coming through the mirrors. I got rid of a lot of mirrors and mirror-balls, and i have sealed the mirrors in my home and my Brother's home by putting a white cross over them, using my intention and drawing it with my right palm.

I find that my physical and energetic life are full of metaphors. For example, i was getting rid of a lot of clothing and things that i don't need and upgrading some things. This seems to be the same for me spiritually and life-wise. I want to use what i have, i.e. my gifts, and get rid of things i am not using. I want to bring things into life rather than leaving my 'good things' hanging in the closet. Time to use my gifts and step forward; time to let go of behaviour, thoughts or energy i don't need. I feel like i am getting ready for forward movement and, like i said before, i am going to move forward, to keep walking. Knowing that as long as i am moving forward i will eventually get where i am supposed to be. They will guide me and i may go down a few dead ends or wrong turns but eventually, i will be guided in the right direction. The worst thing for me is indecision and inaction. When things aren't clear, ask the Father and Jesus, and only them, for direction. Let them be my g.p.s. If something doesn't work out, not regret, just what's the next step. I'm not attached to results.

Also, when i feel the need for something external, i find that since the Father has given me everything, i need to change my focus of gratitude and appreciation for the things i have. For a while, i was getting too attached to the searching and finding the gifts from the Father. Now i am also focussing on enjoying my own physicality, as well by using my good things but it also encourages me to take better care of myself, the way i look, and to exercise a lot more, and to start watching what i eat. One thing just seems to lead to the other and i am getting better at balancing the physical and the spiritual. It's always something that i need to consciously do. I ask myself, what part of me have been depriving lately? In this way too, i feel like i am giving to myself, appreciating myself and taking care of myself. I find it makes me feel strong and not needy. It doesn't matter if someone else doesn't like the way i look or what i do. I like the way i look and what i do.

I have just been noticing more and more about a person's body type, posture, movement, voice, etc. and their energy or way of operating in the world. I feel we can learn a lot about people by observing them. For example if a person's voice is really high, it's like they have a really high energy but they're ungrounded. They're living way up there and someone who has a really deep voice is very grounded and seems to be operating more from the root or base chakra. I just find that people who are very obese are hoarders of energy and certainly of food and often times, money. I'm not judging i just find it interesting. Maybe if we want to change our physicality, we need to change our outlook on life; we need to be aware of our own energy. When i am struggling and sometimes i feel ashamed because of certain thoughts i might be having or maybe i find it embarrassing or that i shouldn't be thinking that i should have done something above or beyond that. These are times when i need to stay connected to the Father and Jesus. Don't turn away and run from God. These are especially the times that i need to talk to them, to let them know what i am feeling or experiencing. Instead of feeling unworthy of their presence, or if that's how it makes me feel, then express it. Only by doing this can they help you to move beyond or to shift thoughts and behaviour. They will see you through the other side. Besides, they know you and i better than we know ourselves. What's the point of trying to hide anything from them or ourselves for that matter? It's important to be honest and authentic and to keep the doors of communication open at all times. I find that i need and desire to stay connected to the higher powers more and more, whether it's in service doing healing work through prayers and sending energy, writing about the events of my life and connection, reading something inspirational, or listening to transformational c.d.'s, or sitting in devotional time with the Father. I also want to say that more and more i want to expand this time and both through meditation, prayers, and in my daily walk through life. I want to talk to them, reflect, and one thing i need to work more on is to listen. When is say listen, i don't necessarily mean clairaudience because for me, i don't always know if i can trust that. For me, it's listening with the heart, which i think is more clairsentience or feeling. Also, i am learning more to develop claircognizance, or the recognition of thoughts that are not my own but are from spirit and are answers for guidance, a knowing. I am also working on furthering the development of my seeing, or inner vision, or clairvoyance. I seem to trust all of these things more than my hearing but that's just me. Everyone has to learn which of these methods works best for them. I feel that when i go too long without feeling the presence of God and his helpers, my life seems boring and empty. When i am connected with them, i never feel alone and life seems magical and on purpose. I also need this connect to feel inspired (in spirit). I feel that this is what drives my life force energy. In devotional time this morning, when talking to 'The One' (as Van Morrison sings about in the song, Have I Told You Lately That I Love You), the Father acknowledged what i was saying by telling me that "He gives inspiration."

I also want to mention some of the helpers that have come into my life. I felt that i have had communication with Joan of Arc, which i talked about before. She talked to me after i watched a movie about her that i 'found', or more likely was guided to. In some of our healing work, i witnessed Pope John Paul11 had come to help with a specific task (he would use a staff and knock away negative attachments to peoples energy). Shortly afterwards, i 'found' a movie about him. I was guided to buy something for a friend of mine and i thought it was Michael that guided me. On the way home from this particular outing, i felt guided to stop at the usual thrift place and i 'found' his movie. After watching it, Michael spoke to me and gave me some very helpful and specific guidance on how to recognize the girl i am meant to be with ("watch for the light in her eyes to be on"). It's amazing the help that comes and i get so overwhelmed with gratitude for their love but i know i need to thank them more than i do. Bless them all for their kindness. It spurns me on to do more good deeds. I have to be honest, though, and i feel that joining the Catholic Faith has opened a doorway to receive these beautiful blessings. There have been helpers that have come that are not of this faith as well and they certainly are most welcome also but the core of my help comes from this connection.

When i do healing work, i connect to the ones that i feel strongly connected with. As a friend in spirit says "dance with the ones that brought you." I also leave it open though, that anyone is welcome to assist, as long as they come from light and come with the permission of Jesus and the Mother Mary, who i believe are the main ones that are with me. I often pray during healing sessions (especially when doing healing on the earth), that we all come together to put aside our differences and join together with a common goal, and to defeat a common enemy. Together, we are strong and will win the fight. Building bridges is the key to saving the earth and raising the consciousness of humanity and helping to bring forth a new age of light that is based on love, compassion and healing.

In reading about Grandfather from Tom Brown Jr.'s books and i remember how he said, "that the world can no longer be healed physically, only spiritually." He also said that "when you set on a spiritual path for yourself, it's self-indulgent but when you do it for a higher purpose that power will be given to you." I also read in a prayer book lately something that said something similar, it said to ask God to give you the power. The point is, is that our prayers can and do help and Grandfather inspired me very much to at least try. I feel that as long as i try, i can be at peace in my soul that when i go back to the Father, i will be able to look him into the eyes and both of us will know that i did what i came down here to do.

I'm dealing with negative energies but i know that Jesus and Michael help me. Jesus advises me to cut their throats (with my mind using a sword). I feel that this separates them from a negative spirit that's attached. Jesus says "It removes a ghost." Time to time, i attempt to point the way to them and i have tried clearing them. It is true that the path of redemption is open to every human soul but if they choose to attack and interfere with me, even after i have forgiven them for what they have done in the past, then Jesus, the King of mercy, directs me how to best deal with them. But His mercy has limits and they will be moved out of my way so i may serve. I did have concerns still about the well-being of my parents and whether they were safely in the light. I thought i heard "seventh heaven." Mother Mary told me after praying to her that "they are in heaven child." Don't the Buddhist's believe there are seven realms on the other side? Again in dealing with negative energies you have to know that they are weak and i found it helpful to point this out to them spiritually. They are weak because they don't have self-love. If they did they would not be focussed on destruction and causing pain and suffering. They probably don't have self- love because their own Mothers didn't love them. There weakness is their self-hatred and contempt for themselves. It's like there backbone is weak and ready to turn to dust. Their hatred destroys themselves it eats them away from the inside out like rust or cancer. I think it's helpful to point this out to them, to hold a mirror and then offer them a path of salvation to the one that loves them will see to it they are destroyed if they continue on doing harm to Godly or gentle people.I think back to when i was hurt as a child and i knew it was my spirit that left me, not my soul. I know when your spirit is not present than another spirit can take control and that's why i do try to do clearing work on those doing evil first.

Jesus has been working with me on opening my heart. He told me to "remember your Mother." I acknowledged how much i missed her and my Father. I went to Value Village and i found a lot of Rod Stewart c.d.'s, which were my mom's favourites. I also found a cd soundtrack from the movie Four Weddings and a Funeral. I knew this was significant because the poem that was read during the funeral meant a great deal for my Mother, "Stop the clocks…" I feel it expressed her feelings when her brother died and i guess it sort of expressed mine too with my parent's deaths. I knew that my Mother was with me' for sure. I remember a poem that i gave my Mother about death where basically that said the person's "gone from my sight that's all"… and "there are other eyes watching her coming."(Henry Van Dyke) I hoped it gave my Mom some comfort and now i need to be comforted by this knowing that her reunion with her Brother and all those that she thought she lost had occurred. To think about what a wonderful happy occasion that must have been for her and my Father as well. I should think about their joy not my own suffering.

I was then directed to go to the beach and while there, i saw a teenage girl with an ill-fitting bathing suit and i felt sorry for her. She reminded me of the girl i knew when i was young because she was quite poor, living in what we referred to as the 'wartime shacks.' I remembered that someone had told me that she cried at her birthday party, i believe, because i didn't go. Although i had sent energy to her and connected with her spiritually a few years ago, i still felt very bad for the pain i had caused her to suffer. So my pain was double, one from her leaving and for hurting her. I decided that i needed to send her prayers again but to direct them to her at the time of her birthday party so long ago. I did so and i told her exactly why i didn't go and that i regretted it. I told her how much i loved her. I saw her receiving my prayers and message, and i saw her happiness. As i was doing this, there was a freighter (in real life) coming in and it was going to go through the lift bridge. I felt it was a message 'that my ship had come in.' It was also significant because my Uncle Alec had helped to build that bridge and i knew that for my Mom, seeing a boat pass under the bridge had been a sign for her from her Brother. So again, i know my Mother was at work. I also thought that this girl that i had a crush on as a child who moved because her Mother got remarried and they were leaving to go to Ottawa, that if i loved her, then i should be thinking about how this was a wonderful blessing for her to have a real family and certainly a better life. I thanked the Father for blessing her. It reminds me that instead of thinking of myself, which causes me to suffer. I am healed when i thing about the happiness of others. Thinking of their happiness gives my heart peace.

If you love someone, their happiness is what's important. I also thanked the Father for blessing the girl and my parents because i know that i blamed Him for the things that happened. Now i feel that that i am free. I feel that i am freed of my spirits so that i can move forward with my life in the way that way God wants me to.

The Father has been leading me to inspirational movies. For example, Rob Roy (directed by Michael Caton-Jones) Troy (written by David Benioff) and The First Knight (directed by Jerry Zucker) during a time when he was encouraging me to take up the sword (spiritually) and kick butt meaning involved in fighting fiercely against the enemy. Then Chariots of Fire. To me, no one is more inspiring than Eric Liddell. Of course being of Scottish descent, i can relate to him even more. Eric Liddell says "God made me Fast and when i run i am feel his pleasure!" I want to do what the Father made me to do and make Him proud.

I find in order to do this i have to be more like John the Baptist, as he felt he needed to become less so Christ could become more. I want to do this by trying to move myself out of the way and letting him work through me in a greater way. I want to become part of the solution rather than part of the problem. I hear the words 'development class'and i feel he is now speaking through me:

"Make way for the Lord. He is coming and you better be prepared. This is a dark time we are living in and, as they say, it is always darkest before the dawn. The dawning of a new day is upon us. The beginning of the house of David. Lights come on beginning above people's heads, they begin to look around and see with new eyes. Their hearts open and they truly receive the gift of rebirth. Light a candle in the window and ask the Lord to enter the dwelling place of your soul. Put a log in the hearth and stoke the fire of your hearts. Rekindle your joy for all things good and decent. Man of gentle hearts will be the rulers of the new Kingdom. Take your best glasses down from the cupboard and pour a glass of your best sherry or wine, for this is the time of celebration. The light is coming into the world and the dark has nowhere to go. Perish he will at the feet of his conqueror. Crushed for all our iniquities. Don't tarry and be late for the feast of the Lamb."

I'm at home with a cold now but i feel that it's His will that i spend a couple of days on writing and meditation and an inspirational d.v.d. The important point in this is that through connection to spirit they can be helpful in leading you to remedies. Like i said before, that the Father had an answer for every problem you face but you must take the time and effort to connect with him regularly so you can understand his direction. Even then, caution must always be used in case you are misunderstanding of His guidance or you have interference from another entity.

Maybe sometimes, you have to ask the Father to bring blessings and a miracle in your life. I guess i was feeling that our focus should be in the things of heaven first and i am sure that's how it's supposed to be. But we have to keep talking to the Father and asking Him for the type of life that would bring us happiness as well. I heard, "it's okay to prosper."

Acts of kindness bring great rewards but the rewards that are stored for you in heaven are what's really matters. "There's a light at the end of the tunnel. The day is coming when you will see the Son of Man come down on a rainbow from heaven above." He says to me, "Many times you have heard the knocking on your door and you have yet to answer. Just keep walking and the Faith will build bridges to the islands of your dreams. The time is coming when all men will see your light shining as it once did." I felt that Jesus just spoke through me about my life and dreams.

Again about manifesting your dreams, i think it's about giving your dreams and the power to make them a reality to God and opening up to receive, having faith that He is at work in your life. But belief and faith have to be there. The only positive thinking you need to work on is trusting that He will provide for you.

"Know that the path opens up for those that have faith that the Father is at work in their lives. Belief is the key, the gift of life is in His hands, the giver of life. He has the power to make or destroy anything He wishes. My Father wishes that everyone opens up their eyes for the Kingdom of Heaven and all its glory are there, waiting to be bestowed upon those that come before Him and praise His glory. That is the promise that He makes to all His believers. Have faith children for the Father is not cheap with his loved ones. He wants to give freely His blessings to bring forth His abundance and place it in your laps."

The smiles on your face and the tears in your eyes when you feel His love brings great joy to His heart. He says, "Look, the Kingdom of heaven is yours for the asking, are you ready to receive?" The key is to believe that the Father is real and conscious of you and involved in all of the details of your life. He loves to touch you in little ways that gives you signs of His presence. The details are important to Him. You are significant.

"Wants are the destructive force in the universe begging and pleadings only causes you to lose sight of what's the real issue is. What are you seeking to fulfill, the emptiness you feel in your soul? The abundant love of God is the only peace your soul requires, everything else is icing on the cake. Make your mind one with God and you will see the light in his eyes and you will know that He is the one that created you and the one that provides for you. Come into his loving arms and you will be filled with such peace, your belly will be filled with His warm loving sunlight. If you want a taste of His love just look at the sun and feel it. Feel it's warmth touching you but feel the love filling you as well. This is the Creator source, this is the Fathers house, i think. Feel how the earth feels first thing in the morning as it stretches it's welcoming arms to the warming rays of the sun and the light of the new day dawning brings the promise of new beginnings."

It's now time to let the flow of God work through me. First, i need to tell you that i am trying to get out of the way and let the words come. "Mine eyes have seen the glory of the coming of the Lord! Praise be to God and His son Jesus Christ for bringing me this for that I may be partaker in this righteous experience."...For now let's just say i am learning to channel the higher power, be it not my place to pass judgement on what is said or by who. I feel it's The Spirit.

"It won't be long before the contented walk the earth. My followers will see the beauty of the heavenly kingdom as it is brought down from on high. The animals need their maker more now to stay alive. They are partakers in this great time of light that cometh forth like a rainbow from the sky. My God on my left, my children at my feet. I'll keep the council of His host with my eyes upon the brightest day to dawn upon this wonderful planet. In due time, the darkness will rise like a vaporous fog and in its place, the heavenly host will bring forth the peace of the Kingdom of heaven. Do not smite the forces of evil, they are child's play for the one that is entering into this realm like a cannonball shot from up on high. The blast will destroy the stronghold of the enemy and send them scampering like rats fleeing a sinking vessel; and sink it will at the Lord's command. The Host with nets will scoop up the prey and devour them at the Father's will. Lord have mercy on those who have stood long against the righteous, born of virtue and gentle hearts will cry no more tears when this day will come. The light of the world is coming. Raise up your hearts, open your eyes and behold this beautiful day. The coming of the King of Jerusalem!"

"Keep your house clean of all negative things what are destructive to your mind and hearts. Don't let evil into your life by poor choice of habits. Confess your sins if you want redemption, don't tarry for the time is nigh. We beseech you to give your monies, made tithes and offerings to the poor. There are many in need in desperation and in suffering. Don't turn a blind eye to your brothers. In wanting, we all suffer. Life is everlasting. Time here is short in comparison to the life that is waiting. Don't worry or fear but live to the fullest in love and peace. Don't dwell on past mistakes. The time is nigh to walk fully onto the path, to live to the fullest, to manifest fully the dream that lies fulfilled before you. Give your worries and fears to God, you are but a mere stone's throw away from opening up the gates of the heavenly blessings that He has in store for your future beginnings. Life awaits you at the next corner and your faith has brought you to this place so now is the time to remain full of the faith in the 'One', the Almighty, the one that has the power to create anything He wishes to make the flowers grow and the birds sing. They sing his praises every morning and you should to."

While doing our healing work, there are many that have come to love their skills and expertise.

It's amazing and touching to get so much help and blessings from the presence of all these wonderful beings. Lately, we have had the honour of Pope John Paul helping us, certainly Rafael and St. Theresa. Just recently, there was a Native American medicine man who has blessed our prayers as well as a Chi-Gong master. It truly is amazing. It just seems that whoever can help the most comes in. I'm sure there's others that i am not aware of yet.

I feel that Jesus is speaking to me. "Now is the time to put the past to rest and listen to your heart. You'll manifest gold in abundance if you stay still and listen to your heart, your smile will bring glory to God for the world to see. Rest you weary gentleman for life awaits in all the Lord's splendour. The time is upon you to see the glory of God at work in your life. You deserve the best and it is brought to your door. My Father enjoys your smile and some of your antics give him cause to laugh. Your mind is a refreshing change of pace. You do try hard, i will give you credit for that. Be still and be at peace and feel the love flow in your direction. The winds of change are with you."

One of the things i have been doing lately was to go through my parents'/grandparents' old jewellery to get rid of broken things, to decide what to keep, hopefully for my future wife who i believe is coming into the picture soon. I sold some broken gold for $80.00. One day shortly afterwards, i was driving and i pulled over because an ambulance was wailing up the other way with a siren. As i was stopped, i looked over and there was a thrift store that donates Bibles. I had heard about it but didn't know where it was located. I decided there was something going on and went in. I saw an upholstered rocking chair that i was drawn to. As i stopped there, i had a vision of a woman sitting there nursing a baby and i knew that i had to buy it. Also with the jewellery, there were many broken watches. I decided to either fix them or get rid of them. I felt that this was somehow significant in regards to the time being now for my life to get going. We received a letter in the mail from Revenue Canada addressed to my Father, almost five years since his passing. It was a credit of over $1,000.00. I felt it was a gift from the other side. I decided to use my portion to fix my Grandfather's watch.l immediately saw him with me with his chest puffed out.

I was at the mall and i had felt a slight attack and since i had been working on this stuff a lot lately, i just asked for more protection. I felt 'them' doing something to my energy (you always wonder how much is real and how much you imagine) but as i felt this going on, a woman walked by with a young boy under her arm and he was looking directly at what they were working on with wide-eyed amazement. He then looked at me with astonishment and a huge smile. He saw it all right.

I went to Lillydale, NY, the largest spiritualist centre in North America, for a course in Spiritual Development. I was nervous about going but the people there were so loving and supportive, it was beautiful, loving energy. I felt like i was part of a family. These are the people i have been looking for my entire life. I was very emotional because of all the love and acceptance i experienced. Part of me was somewhat hesitant in going as well because it isn't really known as a Christian establishment, but with no disrespect towards anyone, i need to talk about one experience. On the last day, i prayed at break time because i wasn't feeling that i was getting it like i wanted, so i asked for help. After that, we were broken up into groups again to work and the mentor that was placed with us i seemed to have a great connection with, even though we only talked on a few occasions. But she was even more supportive, understanding and helpful than anyone else. She was exactly what i, and i am sure the others in the group, needed. In giving her a message, i saw Jesus standing beside her with his hand on her shoulder and He was telling me that He brought her to us. It turns out that even though she's a spiritualist minister, she is very close to Jesus as well. She and i really connected because of our love for him. Without giving away any of the message i gave to her, it was very obvious that Jesus holds her in very high esteem. So you can certainly be a Spiritualist and a Christian. There is no need to be conflicted. In fact to me, i am other things as well but a Christian first and foremost.

Even though there may be some difference in beliefs with some people, we still have love for each other. In that place of love, the differences fade but we can share with each other our unique experiences and beliefs and allow them to bring us closer to each other by being loving and accepting rather than being judgmental and moving us further apart. We have to build a bridge not a wall.

"The time is at hand for people to stop hating, to stop waging war and attacking each other. To recognize that they have the Christ and a piece of God within them and to bring it into being. To give life to this part of yourself. To enjoy helping one another instead of finding pleasure in hurting and destroying. For truly one cannot do this if you love yourself, when you are doing this you are hurting yourself as well as we are the same under the skin. We all have feelings, want love and all are made of the same stuff. We were all created by the same Father." "It's time to heal yourself with The Lord's love, find the Christ within and let it come into the world. Only by doing this can the world be healed. Only through this self-healing, by allowing Christ to heal us can the world be saved. Jesus calls to you now to join Him for this purpose to bring peace and love into the world. He calls to His lost sheep and wants you to come to Him now for it is time. Change is coming and it is time for you to come to him and board His ship. He is the saviour; hear Him calling you, feel His love asking your heart. Are you ready, for it is time."

In watched a video of Dr. Wayne Dyer manifesting your destiny where he talks about how you can view the world as a friendly place or a hostile place. Our belief expands and we can create a friendlier reality. That reminds me of how Jesus told me to put my focus on Him, not the ones in darkness. I went to Lillydale a few days after seeing that video and i feel that the experience profoundly changed me. This really struck home as we held hands at the end in a circle and they played, What a Wonderful World, by Louis Armstrong. I've never felt such love and support before from a group. It was a beautiful experience, just being in the Spiritual Insight Training class for this alone made it worthwhile.

I woke up one morning and I told Him very emotionally that i am tired of experiencing all the garbage in life and now i want to experience love. I can't believe how much love i am experiencing and feeling from so many people. The other day at work, i was having some troubles spiritually from someone and all of a sudden, all these people showed up and I could feel their love and support on a soul or energetic level. They didn't even realize why they were there but i knew they were sent by the Father. I had a vision of my light surrounded with numerous other lights. I have seen this happen many times when i am in trouble help just appears and i am always amazed with His touch of Love and concern for me especially in times of need.

Around this same time, i felt guided to go out of town to go to Cambridge. I went to a thrift store and found a floor cleaner for wood floors which happened to be made by Hoover where my Dad had worked.

I then knew i had to go to the Outlet Stores where i often went with my parents and while having a coffee, i heard bag pipers playing outside. I became very emotional as i knew my relatives were with me during this challenging time telling me to take heart and have courage and that they were supporting me, that i wasn't alone. I was involved in some spiritual battles and they were telling me to remember who i was and to inspire me as the bagpipes would inspire the troops when they went to war. In the mall was a British store and i knew Braveheart (Mel Gibson) was a movie i needed to see again. I took my Father to see that movie at the Cinesphere in Toronto. It also reminds me of a past life as a Viking when my Father and i were together. On the drive home, i felt spirit painting my face and sharpening my sword getting ready to deal with the enemy show have been for a long time interfering in my life. I feel victory is assured. Over the next few weeks, which included some battling, some deliverance, and lots of prayer work, i heard Mel Gibson cry "Freedom."

I've been dealing with a lot of negative energies over the last while. I saw in my print out from Mass that another church was having a special Mass the next weekend honouring Mother Mary. It was to pray for more vocations but i also read somewhere also at work that that day was a feast day for Mother Mary to implore for protection. I knew i had to go, divine timing or what. I wrote down a few petitions which were to be burned after a procession following Mass. While i was getting ready earlier in the afternoon, because i wasn't coming back to the house before going to church, i felt her presence. She sat beside me while i was getting ready and told me that i needed to add more petitions to the list i had. I went downstairs and got my list and she listed for me what needed to be added. She stayed with me that whole afternoon and all the way down to the church. I've never been to that church before. After a short while the priest came out and it was the Father who did my confirmation at Sacred Heart. I had no idea he was involved with that church. Anytime i have any significant ceremony at the church that same Father is there. And just as i was the last one to get communion from him at Sacred Heart, i was the last one again and it was totally unplanned. I don't always understand the significance of events but i sure know that they are orchestrating things. It's too unbelievable sometimes to really grasp it. I feel that i need to lie down and just let the holiness of her presence sink in.

Mother Mary, i felt, was beside me at night and i felt that she was pregnant.Very pregnant. The next day i was guided to clean my basement stairs, which meant my past. I knew that the underlying condition of any problems i was having now had to do with my past and that they needed to be released and i feel i did so through prayers. That evening, i was guided to get a bath which is located at the top of my stairs. The bath represent new beginnings, i think because it's like being in the Mother's womb. Before lighting the white candle and adding epson salts and blessing the water, i noticed a spider at the bottom of my staircase. As i got into in the tub, i saw the spirit of my future partner brought in and i saw Mother Mary come into the bathroom carrying a baby and handed it to her (i believe representing new beginnings, a divine and sacred union and partnership inspired by God). As i left the tub, i saw the spider mostly all the way at the top of the stairs, representing the weaver of webs. The next day, i was guided to say some prayers for deliverance from the book Power Prayers by Donna K. Maltese, and then i watched a movie called Saul and David, directed by Marcillo Balde. David with his faith defeated Goliath. It is through my faith that i can release the past and overcome the Goliaths that have been put before me. Amen.

"Don't spoil the mystery allow it to unfold with divine magic like the unfolding of a flower, a pedal at a time. Don't try to understand the workings of the divine plan just go with God's love and trust His path. It's like a beautifully interwoven masterpiece that i am being allowed to read a paragraph at a time."

I don't want to know the ending until it's time i need to know. With God, all things are possible. It's an exciting journey that has begun. I don't know why i was chosen but i am not going to question it: i am just going along for a beautiful ride, inspired and enlightened as i walk this path in every waking moment, feeling the touch and grace of God.

On this day Kateri Tekakwitha (Lily of the Mohawks) was canonized by the Catholic Church and made a saint, the first time a Native American person has been honoured on this way. I see this as a very significant occasion, not only in my own personal life and belief system, but in the realizing of the potential that this offers in building bridges between teaching and belief systems. I feel that we need bridges if there is to be any real changes in the world. Only through love, sharing, understanding, common grounds and common goals, can we come together as one people.

I feel that i am being guided to pray for peace when faced with conflicts in my own life from people who are under the influence of negative spirits. I also feel that i am being guided to help the person rather than engage in battles by attempting to deliver them. I'm not recommending this. I know that it takes a strong conviction and a knowing that you have sufficient protection. You have to be clear in following your own guidance, in the name of Jesus.

I felt that Mother Mary told me that, "My Son and i are with you as i journey through the Hell realms." Jesus said, "You have done well to listen to my Father to work from your heart."

I was told to not engage negative people with my thoughts, meaning do not even think of them because this seems to allow them to connect to me but to keep my focus on Jesus, service and love, and other positive things. Jesus also told me in the past this same thing and He also told me to say,

"In the name of Jesus, i receive it not," (three times) when i feel negative energy coming to me. I found that crossing my arms, in reality or in my mind helps me to be protected as i say it. It also helps to hold up my right hand with the two forefingers together and the thumb over the smallest two effective as we often see Jesus depicted this way. I am also reminded of the importance of purposely filling and surrounding myself with God's love, light and protection. Putting on God's full armour mentally and with prayer.

I'm faced with having to learn how to use some of the new technology and, although i know it has many benefits, i feel that technology has become almost like the new God in people's lives. Obviously, a false God created by people who want your money by creating a world where you need or think you need these things. It seems to me that it keeps people distracted rather than taking time for peace and to listen to the voice of God. They don't want us to do that. Remember when children learning how to communicate relate and develop leadership skills through involvement in unstructured activities. Now, they're at home playing violent video games, becoming obese and communicating through texting rather than talking. They are also becoming, i believe, more indifferent to the conditions of the natural world, as everybody seems to be, as we are more removed from it. Which world is real? Which is God's world? And which is created by man? Why are there animals all over the world in danger of becoming extinct if this is a good thing? "... and a new day will dawn for those who stand long, and the forests will echo with laughter." Staircase to Heaven (by Led Zeppelin) I believe the staircase is being built which will bring Heaven unto Earth. Amen.

"Develop a bond with God that is everlasting. Give Him your will and a light will appear in your life that will truly lead you on a path that your wildest dreams could never have imagined." The song Bless the Lord my Soul. This is actually derived from Psam 103:1. "He needs people to allow him to reach into their hearts and change them, and make them his children to change the processes of the destructive one who is at work in this man's world that has led to the downfall of the characters of people who cheat and lie and deceive one another for profit and gain, not loving their neighbours but fornicating with their neighbours wives. Cruel and evil has this world become under the siege of the enemy. Men's hearts have turned to stone and their lives are meaningful only in terms of profit and loss. Their cares arranged neatly on how to achieve their endless need to fulfill all their cravings, wants and desires, scoffing at the Godly few who want to live a pure life, enriched with Godly wisdom. It is enough to have your needs met but to stuff your pockets to overflowing as your neighbours barely have food to feed their families. This is a sin. Love one another. Forgive your debtors and you will be forgiven, feed your fellow man and you will be fed. This is God's law. The law of abundance through providing for those in need... i see an old man weighed down with a bundle on his back. Instead of granting some of his excessive portion to others in need and trusting that he will be provided for further down the road. The need to trust God as the one who provides, needs to be restored in men's hearts, minds and souls." "... dear lady did you know your stairway lies on the whispering wind." Stairway to heaven, Led Zeppelin The most recent difficulties in dealing with people under the influence of the enemy, i continue to be amazed at how the Heavenly Father Almighty always sends the help or advice that is sufficient to help me. At church today, the song Amazing grace was sung and they used the line "... my chains are gone i have been set free, my savour has ransomed me ... Amazing God, Amazing love." This song is written by John Newton. Also during our Catholic service, one prayer is, "... Lord, i am not worthy for you to enter under my roof, but only say the word and my soul will be healed." I found that i was often saying this automatically as a means of clearing negative energy from me.

Aside from this, i also became aware of some things that i still had that had some ties with people to the past, and it was helpful to achieve freedom. I'll do just what I have to to keep aware of what i am being directed to do and am always asking, is there anything i need to release? Just a few examples of things i have guided to do is to spray Lysol around my house to smudge (especially stairs, mirrors, crucifixes, animal figurines) with Frankmyrrh by Jabon. It's a combination of Frankincense and Myrrh. Also pouring bleach down basement drains, purchasing more Jesus and Angel figurines, occasionally lighting white candles (the taller the better) certainly prayers. Lately, i have been led to the Prayer of St. Francis, as well as the Catholic prayers, especially, "... Lord, i am not worthy ..." (previously quoted); reading scripture, reading prayers from prayer books, i.e. power prayers, having baths and soaking feet in salt water. I also make sure i am aware of the energy that is around and figure out where any negative energy is coming from, and then acting appropriately, which frequently means getting rid of things, or putting them away for the time being, or moving them. It really helps to just be aware and to keep connected to your guidance. Most of all, i don't allow myself to get or stay discouraged for very long. I stay positive and i never give up. I know that I'm making progress and i know that even the difficult things and maybe mostly them are important. When i look back, i realize that recent problems i have had with a few individuals lately (over the last year) have led me to some very, very important life changes. I wouldn't have gone to the Baptist or Catholic Churches, which has led me to Mary, resulted in me joining the Catholic faith, close relationships with a pastor and a Father, has led me to some beautiful prayers, has helped me to build a stronger relationship with Jesus, the Father, and the saints. It was very significant in my development spiritually and to leading me closer to my divine path, my god walk. So obviously, all of it was divinely guided. It's all part of His plan so how can i doubt that everything will not eventually work out beautifully? I also know when my life is on 'purpose' when i see parallels happening that gives me confirmations that i am divinely guided. For example, when the church services i attend frequently parallel what i am going through at present. I even notice parallels from religious articles that the Bradford exchange has on its cover. Sometimes, it's all a magical experience. Without God, there is no purpose, no magic, no power, no life, no hope, no inspiration, no depth or meaning, no heart, no love, no faith, no guidance, no blessings. Therefore, i will follow His plan for my life, no matter what He asks because i know His plan is always perfect. He removes all obstacles and brings miracles to those who trust Him.

I was thinking about whether or not a particular girl i have feelings for is the one i am waiting for and i just acknowledged to God that i couldn't deny the feelings that I had for her, and that i would wait for her and try if it was an alignment with His plan for me. I immediately had a vision of my floating around the statue of Christ the Redeemer and on his right palm, i saw the vision a ship coming in and i knew that this was a clear sign that my ship was coming in and it is the plan He has for my life.

Speaking of visions, i was at work by myself sorting mail and i had a vision of Jesus walking towards me, and i have never seen him before in such clarity. He was smiling and his long hair was blowing in the wind. I tell you, there's nothing that can compare to some of these beautiful experiences. I saw beautiful rainbow like colours around him, more of the paler, lighter colours. This relationship that i was led to did not go according to what i believed it was supposed to be but it did bring myself and Jesus very close also with Michael. I still believe it was God led. I can't go into many details but i believe it was service, as well as serving myself by recapturing some light from a past life situation. My teacher J. picked up on this as well. Alot of significant things happened to verify this. Anyhow it was purposeful.

I've been noticing that there has been a correlation between my parents' spiritual path on the other side and my own and today is All Souls ceremony. I feel the prayers and my own new found freedom has benefits to them as well.

"Forward on i march, hand in hand with my master, Jesus, forever at my side. No longer need i fear the creatures of the night for in his light, they wither and turn to dust. Like smoke being blowing away by a mighy wind. Hand in hand ever higher we reach in the ultimate journey to freedom, within and forever ; light returning to light, like drops of water returning to the everlasting sea. Pure and clean like it was in the beginning of time. That is how it as like and now is returning to be. The immortal life of the soul everlasting at peace and at home in the heart of God. The peace of the Lord be with you. Amen."

Once again, the topic at a Baptist church was about Jesus breaking the chains and setting you free. I believe that Jesus has set me free from those who have persecuted me spiritually for a very long time, in that life time and probably from past lifetimes. "No more", he says, as i see Him break the chain. Another topic at the church was on being still. The previous evening, i was writing some notes on this regard. I was writing that instead of worshipping God, much of our society worships science and technology. I guess we could include sex, money and sports as well. My main thought was how all this stuff keeps our minds filled with mostly useless or meaningless activities or thoughts. It's all man created and for the most part is a waste of time. It takes us further from God. Instead of entering into the silence and knowing God personally, we are constantly needing to be occupied, maybe it makes us feel important. Maybe keeping us from knowing God is the true reason behind it and who would be behind that, but the one who doesn't want you to know the love of the Heavenly Father who created you. Turn off your cell phones, iPad, computers, laptops, tabs your text messages and go for a walk in nature before it's all gone for another subdivision. Who cares, as long as you have the latest iPhone and 3D.t.v. Sorry if that's a little harsh but it seems like everyone's absorbed into this false world almost like the movie the Matrix. When the simplicity and beauty of nature is being destroyed, the noise keeps us distracted so we don't take the time for silent prayer and meditation and just being still. It seems we, as a society, have bought into a completely false world.

I was watching a show about the potential of various asteroids hitting the earth and how some are devising ways of preventing this from happening. Basically there's a lot of fear and concern over it. I feel that these things are all in God's control and he deems it or any other 'act of God' necessary then there must be a reason for it. Why should i fear anything that comes from the father who created me and loves me. Science worships itself, worships the mind and ego of man. It might happen, leave it in his hands for i believe he knows best since he is the one who created the earth and everything in the universe. That's right. Science doesn't believe in God because it's 'too busy' to take the time to enter the silence and know Him. Who am i or anyone else to question His decisions or worry about it. To live in fear of God is silly. Only if you are full of sin or don't know Him. Is He something to be feared? Pray to Him. Show Him your love, your faith, your service to him and then you would not be so afraid. If something happened and you were taken back to Him, is that so bad? It's going to happen sooner or later anyways. Do you think it would happen randomly? There are much more important things to worry about than our deaths you best start thinking about what will happen with your soul when that inevitable day comes.

Though i am still trying to clear the negative energies in my life and express my frustration to God over them still being allowed to sometimes attach to me and interfere with my life, i ask Him why it is allowed. I watch the movie about Pope John Paul 11.(screenplay by Francesco Arlanch and Francesco Contaldo) i am reminded of what these people suffered at the hands of the Nazi's during the second world war. My own suffering and focus on the evil energies interfering with me and i take a larger focus on the evil energy that causes all the suffering. I change my fear to anger at this spirit and send my prayers to removing this energy that delights in the suffering of all souls, not just my own personal battles. So maybe that is why the Almighty Father has allowed me to continue to experience these things to encourage me to take up the fight on a larger scale; to continue to experience these things; to continue to be a warier for Christ; to overcome my own fears and to use my faith to help destroy the evil and help to end the suffering. With God's help, this will be accomplished. I have already been told numerous times that i will not die by the 'sword.' So i trust that everything that happens in my life is purposeful to direct my focus as i have promised my service.

I found a Dr. Dyer c.d. at the thrift store and i usually find him inspiring and i think that while there must be something on here i need to here right now. Even if i feel i know it, it shows me where to put my focus. The four d.v.d. set Experiencing the Miraculous and the part that i feel i needed to hear is that i need to firmly state, "I am free" of all negative energies and spirits. Because the next day, i was watching a sermon on Sunday morning on the show the pastor was saying the same thing, you need to state, "I am choosing to be free of Satan. I am choosing to be free of negative spirits. I am choosing to be free of sickness." As i was stating this, i heard in my head my teacher Jean say, "That's right." I guess she was keeping an eye on me. This is similar to what Jesus told me before when he told me to say, "I receive it not." It's firmly stating this and repeating it.

I have a sore on my left big toe and i have been trying to heal it for some time. I know that it is a releasing that i am doing, as i saw the energy leaving my body and not the other way around. The left big toe on the left side corresponds to the left side of my head where i have had lumps for a long time, and i felt it had to do with the presence of people attaching themselves to my energy. Just as an interesting side note, i was sending prayers while my foot was in the bucket of water and i asked that all the water in the world be blessed. I immediately got a jolt, more proof that prayer works.

I was also coming back from Toronto on the train and said prayers that the lake be blessed and purified. In my mind's eye, i saw a spaceship rising out of the water and leaving, much to my surprise. Obviously, they weren't very friendly, as i don't think they liked being in holy water. Blessing the waters works, it makes it holy.

One more comment on what the reverend on t.v. said was, "Jesus rose you up to heavenly places." You go where Jesus went when you become saved so know this and empower yourself in the name of Jesus. I've been getting this a lot lately in different ways. It's about claiming your divine right for freedom in His name. A friend told me to claim it in the blood of the Lord, Jesus Christ. I claim my freedom and the freedom of my family in the blood of the Lord, Jesus Christ. There is power in His name to break any chains. He paid for our sins with His blood and because of that, we are free and no one can harm us or contain us. Know this and claim your place in His kingdom.

It was the fifth anniversary of my Mother's death (my Father's being the following day). I found myself at work to be in a situation where i was close to my new supervisor. It seems she is somewhat open to spiritual matters so i had some conversations with her about things and mentioned to her about this prayer i have recited. I felt this prayer was significant in helping me hear His words of guidance for me in my meditations. She mentioned, "If you build it, we will come", which is the first message my parents gave me five years ago shortly after their passing. This is from the movie Field of Dreams by Phil Alden Robinson adapted from W. P. Kinsella's novel. As i was writing about this, i saw the statue of liberty on t.v., which is a confirmation for me. In a meditation in which Jesus first came to me he showed the statue of liberty, which to me represents freedom.

When i visited the cemetery, i went inside to pray to the various statues of Jesus and Mother Mary and St. Michael. As i was praying to Mother Mary, i saw her pull out a scroll and was looking at it. I felt she was checking to see if my parents' names were on it. I heard her say, "They made it". The other day, i was overcome with grief and sadness, not so much for my own suffering and loss but through the suffering and loss of my loved ones. I felt such desire and passion and sadness for the suffering of all. As i ate the bread and drank the wine (juice) the following morning, i gave myself to Him with a renewed desire that He just take over my life and use me in any way possible to bring an end to the needless suffering, not just of people but of the earth, nature and the animals.

I have mentioned lately to a few people the movie 2001 Space Odyssey and the message of the monolith. "Remember, you're just the tenants, you're not the landlord." Is this what is beginning to take place? These devastating storms are so called 'Acts of God' for a reason. They all must be purposeful. I feel that these storms are in some manner a clensing of sorts on an energetic level, to clense certain areas of the planet. Im not saying certain people deserved to die, i just feel we will witness heaven on earth but the earth needs to be purified and made ready for the second coming of the Lord, Jesus Christ. "The Saviour is coming to claim His throne as ruler of the earth. Those both near and far heed the call to make ready for the day is at hand. Be steadfast in your devotion to your fellow man in these great times of change. Delve into your funds, your own reserves, to feed those in need, for we are all our brother's keepers. Help each other to find comfort in the coming months. It is not the end times but the beginning of a new age of the Christ consciousness. Behold. The coming of the Lord and make way. Sturdy be your loins and prepare for the light of the world to make His presence known. Glory be to God in the highest."

Just recently storms hit the east coast in Hurricane Sandy (two storms within a week). I wonder about this and found it interesting too that the Statue of Liberty, although damaged, still remains in take the symbol of freedom. But it too was cleanse and on the news, it was said that it was closed to the public. I felt a parallel in my own life, as i too am being cleansed and purified, that i am too in the final stages to attain my own freedom, and the freedom of my family. I too have to do this by the removal of other energies entering into my own being or space. I've had an issue within my left side for a long time. I've had lumps on the left side of my head. Then, i got this large infected lump on my foot which corresponds to the left side of my head. I saw a psychic cord attached to the front of my toe but i felt the energy was leaving me and not coming in. I've been trying diligently to heal and remove this for about a month. Actually, for much longer but know it is time to remove these negative energies and spirits that somehow have managed to attach themselves to my soul or energy. I have to remind myself to check all 'spiritual' doors, which sometimes mean close relatives and friends. I have been soaking my foot in salt water, putting Tinactin on it, as well as boil-ease, and these have helped. (Of course, i blessed the water.) But it seemed to make the most progress when i soaked it in vinegar and salt. I also cleaned my toe with rubbing alcohol a few times and then later, put castor oil on it. I also constantly wore white socks. The toes represent the head in reflexology. One other thing i found helpful was to pour bleach down my basement drains because it seemed energies were using this as an access point as well. Always remember to pay attention to the energy of your home because it can metaphorically and energetically correspond to your body and your life. I also spend a lot of time going through things and riding myself of past energies that were either attached or were no longer suitable. I've done lots of upgrading to my wardrobe. Good things to pay attention to are old shoes (old paths). I also spent a lot of time smudging and cleaning the basement stairs (meaning past) and my upstairs stairs and hallway (future). As well i paid attention to releasing things that belonged to my parents. I felt by using my gut feeling or clairsentience, to determine what needed to be released for their sake. Certainly, i also feel that prayers have helped a great deal, as have donations with the intention of it going to benefit the souls of my loved ones have done wonders. I've also been paying close attention to the guidance given from spirit over what i needed to release or attain and what actions i needed to procure a great release. I paid attention also to my dreams as this is a way that they can get you information that is helpful. Also, i had a dream during the most difficult time of both of my Grandfather's, one with his chest puffed out showing me his pride in me and the other, playing the bagpipes to give me encouragement to fight and continue on. They both gave me a great deal of encouragement and the knowingness i am not alone and am supported.

I took the train to Toronto again and during the 45 minute trip, i kept praying, i plead the blood of the Lord Jesus Christ for many intentions but mostly for the removal of negative energies and spirits. Eventually, i saw a type of cocoon that looked almost like a seashell (lengthwise) and i saw myself coming out of the opening of this, as i turned in a counter-clockwise direction.

I have just been feeling more and more the desire to help remove the suffering of the world. I won't deny that it feels good to receive some nice thing or to have a good meal or drink but i find the more i focus on others' needs, the less i suffer whenever i focus on myself. I have a bit of a self-indulgent feeling unless it's something i know that I need. This is why i am sure that when i buy something, i like to release something in that way, i am not being a hoarder but am upgrading and in return passing on something to someone else. It also helps out a charity. Everyone benefits. There are just so many people who are in need of things and i have been fortunate enough in my life of late to have rarely gone without.

I have been doing everything i can to release myself from the past and from the attachments that many others have made to my soul or energy. One way has been through intensive prayer. Another is through releasing items i am guided to let go of and some of these things were not easy. This has been a long process but I feel i am almost there. It seems i am removing one person at a time. I had a dream of a former co-worker living in my house so i knew his energy was tied to me still so i concentrated my prayers on him, after already focussing on at least 20 others. One thing came to mind to get rid of and this was leather jacket that i had picked up just a few years ago at a Salvation Army. It as a beautiful coat and i had debated getting rid of it in the past. I just heard, "the time has come." It reminds me of a gangster type coat and for whatever reasons i needed to let go of it. It somehow had negative affiliations. I felt i saw snakes or some kind of creepy spirit slithering out of it when i threw it outside.

Over the past few days, i have a lot of help from the likes of St. Joseph, Mary and St. Michael, and another saint that i am told not to share. As i watch a movie about them or read about them, it brings their spirit and their help and we converse. Just as an example, i read about St. Joseph in a book about saints and then i saw and felt his energy appear at my doorway. He came with the brightness of the sun and it just happened to be dawn. The sun was rising in that direction. He gave me some advice and encouraging prophecies for my future.

Michael told me he will put an end, to "the reign of terror" in my life. He said it persisted for so long because "I needed the practice" (I assume he meant in fighting them). I heard him say "bold new beginnings." He told me to "leave it with me." He said "because i help others, that's why i get helped so much." He said also "that he loves to help the innocent fight evil." I'm telling you there is nothing better in the world than hanging out with Jesus, the Archangels and Saints and your loved ones.

Also when i was driving on the weekend and talking to the Father, i heard Him tell me "that He was proud of me because i have persevered." I've persisted in fighting for my goals towards achieving freedom and independence. He says again, "I'm proud of you, my son, you have achieved much and you lighten the path. I bless you and welcome you into the land of the living. You need not fear any evil for your path is laid in heaven."

For quite a while now, i had been given a vision from spirit. It was of Dorothy skipping down the yellow brick road with her three friends. I felt spirit was telling me a number of things with this vision: the yellow brick road representing God's path that is laid down before me; also, the three travelling down the road with me i feel Jesus and Michael are two of them (the third i feel i need to keep to myself).

When i heard the play the Wizard of Oz was coming to Toronto, i knew its appearance had significance for me and i was determined to see it. The fact that the show began December 20, 2012, the day before the Mayan calendar ends, blew me away, as i saw this date as representing a new age in the world. The appearance of the Wizard of Oz (produced originally by Mervyn LeRoy), meant to me a personal message signifying a new beginning for me as well as i saw it as becoming a time where obstacles on my 'God walk' were going to be removed, at least i hoped this is true. The fact that it also dealt with the overcoming of evil 'witches' also struck a personal chord with me. Prior to going to the show, i visited St. Michael's Cathedral. I had been hearing things all day, like "significant journey" and lately "protected path."

When i awoke Christmas morning, the first words i heard from spirit was "Ding, dong, the witch is dead."(from Wizard of Oz) When i was at the Cathedral, i could see the presence of Cardinal Collins. I also wanted to mention when i went to the cemetery on Christmas morning to place flowers on my parents' grave, i heard, "It's a joyous occasion. We're with the Lord on His birthday." The energy and feeling of His divine love and presence was so intense all day, it was almost too much to take. I felt watching the movie, "The Nativity Story" written by Wyck, Godfrey, and Marty Bowen, really helped to bring this intense energy. It's a beautiful movie that goes into a lot of detail of the lives and journey of Mary and Joseph.

I've been telling people that to me, the end of the Mayan calendar really, i feel, represents not the ending but the beginning of a new age. An age of light. Like the song. This is the Dawning of the Age of Aquarius/Let the Sunshine In, by The Fifth Dimension. I feel that December 21, 2012 is a significant date in regards to this spiritual shift. I also feel that January 1st, 2013 to be significant because of a new year, new energy. I was at my Brother's house on New Years Day watching a movie with Steve Carroll, The 40

Year old Virgin on t.v. At the end of the movie after he marries a woman and has sex for the first time he starts singing the song This Is The Age Of Aquarius. It blew my mind because to me this was a message from The Father that i was right. Hearing that song on New Years Day was no mistake. It was God talking. I also feel it was a message about my own love life, not that im a virgin but let's just say i might as well be, sort of joking but not really. I also feel it is a clear message about the Father's desire for me and everyone to have sex within a committed relationship especially after they have made that commitment by becoming joined in marriage. In the presence of God with His blessings. It's truly is then a sacred bond, a sacred union, the joining of two souls that shouldn't be taken lightly. It's true i believe, the way it should be.

Lesson's From The Light Part 2

January 2013

I was working with this guy at work and talking about some spiritual things. I've had a few conversations with him and in his presence in the past and i felt he might be taking in some of the things i was talking about. Not trying to push anything but trying to plant seeds of light and truth. At one point i thought this guy's a lost cause, immediately i heard Jesus say "nobody's a lost cause." I was humbled but also a little shocked because i didn't even realize Jesus was present. One point that we touched on was how our government is really uncaring towards the common man and how they're also attempting to take away our freedom and rights. It's really about control and certainly greed.

A lot of people feel that religion is about control and in reality what Jesus offers is the ultimate freedom. Freedom from control of the enemy. Truth is also freedom and i told this gentleman that it was very significant for me to grow up in a home that was not religious and i was able to explore and learn from other teachings prior to returning to a Christ centred belief. But to me i was not confined by any one teaching of just one belief system but allowed the freedom to experience truths on my own. Seeing is believing. I mentioned to my friend about a Buddhist phrase i heard i think from the movie, Little Buddha, by Bernardo Bertalucci, "Even in a prison cell your mind can be free." That evening i found the movie Stigmata by Tom Lazarus, and it felt like i was supposed to see it, it did in some aspects reminded me of my own life sometimes. I wouldn't recommend it. I got a little freaked out as i was watching it and i asked continually if it was something i was supposed to watch, i was tired and i heard a voice "don't fall asleep there is something at the end for you to see." At the end, the camera showed the sun which to me meant that this was a message coming from the Father. And then it talked about the Gospel of St. Thomas which were as some claimed direct teachings of Jesus that were basically disclaimed by the Catholic Church. I don't know for sure if they are but to me it certainly does no harm in reading them and considering them. Like i say all that matters is the truth, that's all that God wants for us is to know is the truth. I feel that this was something that i was supposed to read and i am. Don't worry i am still going to mass, i am still a

Christian, and always will be. Nothing can separate me from Jesus. But my relationship is with him and God first and foremost, and i believe in getting the guidance and direction straight from them.

As i am writing this i am sitting on a park bench outside in Niagara Falls in January. It's a cool but beautifully sunny day and as i write i can feel the intensity from the sun, and i get a sense of the energy coming from the sun particularly when i am writing about a critical point. I feel the Father is letting me know his energy is behind me. This is just another way that we can all experience him first hand, being outside in nature or alone in the quiet, it's about experiencing him and Jesus first hand.

I felt like going for a walk since we had an incredibly unseasonably warm day in January. I had the impression of downtown Burlington, an upscale neighbouring town and its funny because i was also thinking back to how i used to like going downtown in the 70's and buying records. I had just bought a turntable on Boxing Day and have been playing my old records.

I was walking and something told me to turn right and a few doors down was a used record place. I went in not really sure of what to look for and sitting in plain sight was an album by the Fifth Dimension and yes the first song is Aquarius/Let the Sunshine In.

I really feel that God is always communicating with us. I know also when i am doing something good or important i will see a lot of crows usually flying across my path and to me it's a confirmation that i am doing the right thing. Like i said i just have had my interest in music rejuvenated again and even my car radio started to work and it hasn't for years. I had been having some troubles this week with negative energies and it has gotten me down because i thought this stuff was over. When i had the radio blasting and the song by Kansas came on "Carry on my Wayward Son, There'll be Peace When you are done, Lay your weary head to rest, don't you cry no more." Song from Kansas, written by Livgren. I'm sure it was something my heavenly Father sent my way to boost my spirits and assure me that i have to keep on fighting and never give up when you give up, become frightened, lose faith or motivation that's when the enemy wins. Just keep fighting eventually the war will be won. If nothing eventually the war will be won.

If nothing else it's not letting them defeat your spirit. If my life is not going quite like i hoped or things don't seem to be happening then maybe i made some wrong choices or the timing isn't quite right yet. In any event the only thing i can do is to focus on connecting with the Father in devotional time, meditate and talk with Jesus as well and ask for direction and certainly pray. I've gotten away from the listening part lately so i have got no one to blame but me. Also i know that if i do my part (i.e. service) then they'll take care of the rest. I heard "You do your part and we'll do ours."

It's amazing how God works. You never know where he's going to lead you and it's fascinating when become aware of a direction or pattern that your being guided upon.

Lately i have noticed that i am being exposed to some of the Jewish faith. It's started with someone mentioned Schindler's list, it was that same person that i was with when Jesus said "noone is a lost cause." i felt a need to watch it and say prayers. I feel those prayers have been recognised and lately i found a couple of d.v.d.'s that i think i needed to see. One is the Daily Devotional Journal by Clyde Williamson. This d.v.d.'s series takes us on a prayer journey through the tabernacle and shows us God's model for getting closer to Him in our devotional life. Then the second one is Chicago Spiritual Warfare Conference - Wage and Win Spiritual War by Morris Cerullo. He is an evangelist but i feel it was helpful for me at this time in hoping putting an end to some of the spiritual battles i have had for years. Invoking the Holy Spirit. I've felt the presence of Jewish spirits in my home as a result of this new direction and its very profound. I was also lead to a religious based thrift store and as i walked in i saw a spirit pointing me towards the books, lying on top of them face up was a book entitled 10 minute Kabbalah, by Shoshanna Cohen. It made a good read.

I was also dealing with another negative spirit one that seems to be attached to mould. I remembered before that my mentor Many Horses told me tea tree oil was good for this, as an external use oil, as i am sure they all are. I felt they guided me to put a dab behind my ear. Also i found some dead sea salts and i bought some that had tea tree oil essential oil in it and i have been soaking my foot in it. I had a flair up of an issue with my left big toe which corresponds to the left side of my head, according to reflexology teachings, and i know there has been in energy or spirit there that's been attached for a long time that needs to be released. I also have a lump on the left side of my head that i felt was connected to this problem. Tonight i put my two fingers there and i prayed that all negative energies, entities, spirits, demons, connected souls, dark side influences etc. be removed. I felt a healing and the lump is greatly reduced.

Last week i was writing a letter and i mentioned how i believe that everything that happened to me and my parents was God's will, just at the same time on t.v. they talked about how some people thought that Mother Mary's features were found on a grilled cheese sandwich. This was something that happened in the past and i remember it well. I was doing some dowsing on this person that i have had a lot of trouble with trying to depossess him, just then i got a phone call from my Mother saying she got into a car accident. Then i called my teacher Jean and as i was talking to her she mentioned just then on t.v. they were talking about how Mother Mary's image was seen on a grilled cheese sandwich. At the time i felt that i was being told that Mother Mary was the one that was coming to us to help, i wasn't Catholic on even a church goer at the time.

I've been in a down mood lately, seemingly because i have been impatient about things developing in my life that i had believed they would at this point. I've also have still been involved in some spiritual battles. Something clearly led me to a small book on the Kabbalah. I feel that i just need to learn more about some aspects of the Jewish beliefs. At least i feel this is where God has led me. I'll just say this right now, i don't care what anyone says. Jesus Christ is the Messiah and nothing could ever change my mind and heart regarding that. As i was standing in line a girl ahead of me was buying a couple of c.d.'s and a small figurine and she didn't have enough money. She was obviously developmentally delayed. I volunteered to make up the difference and this act got me out of my self-pitying funk. What right did i have to feel sorry for myself when this poor girl and so many others don't have hardly anything. I apologized to God for my own immaturity and selfishness and i know he placed that girl in my path for a reason. I once again dedicated myself to helping others not helping myself to have everything that i can think of. I am provided for and i need to help the less fortunate. Sometimes it's so easy to forget this. It turns out that it was this girl's Mother's birthday the following day.

I was still having some problems with certain individuals from my past. There were a number of them. I could feel myself being attacked and then i had a dream of two of them. I feel that i am always given guidance as to how to deal with them and spirit had directed me frequently on how to fight them and i feel that they have provided me with the power to defeat them or any other of the enemy of the dark side.

I was guided to go to Toronto, and i usually go on Saturday's as a result of the weather conditions and paying attention to what i was being told i went Sunday instead. I was tempted to fight what i heard but i listened instead and i am glad of it. I decided this was the perfect opportunity to attend mass at a wonderful cathedral in downtown Toronto, St. Michael's. I also drew the card from Doreen Virtue's Angel Card, to ask Archangel Michael for help with this situation. So what better place to do it then his cathedrals. I said numerous prayers for help for spirit release while there so i can put more focus and have more success in other areas of my 'God walk.' I had a tremendous release and I felt that my prayers for me and my family have finally worked.

I have been looking at my own ability to not be afraid to keep learning from other teachings. I know that so many people hold onto their beliefs and teachings so tight that they cannot learn from anything else. They are closed off. What are they afraid of? I find that many become cliquish or almost 'cultish' in there exclusivity. I believe in sharing and exploring. I am proud of my ability to read or study something and take from it what is right or good for me while still keeping my core beliefs intact. My faith is strong enough that i am not afraid of looking at new learning. I feel that we should always be open to learning, growing and expanding and to consider new or different ideas.

My conviction that Jesus is the Saviour is unbreakable but i feel that God continues to show me more teachings to increase my understanding to expand my mind once more important my consciousness. After all we are all from the one God. When we believe we have separate God's it is easier to harm others in God's name. If we harm someone else, we are harming his child, his creation and therefore harming him. We have to be Godlike ourselves, loving and understanding, not exclusive. How else can this world continue to exist.

I was listening to some tapes i found the other day by Kenneth Copeland and one thing that stuck out is when he said the devil likes division and i believe this is exactly what i am saying. We are all God's children and when we realize that we can put aside our differences and stop the wars and focus on what's really important. Creating a beautiful world that we all can live in and share. Together we can overcome all the problems in the world with i do believe are the work of the enemy.

The musical group The Who are coming to town and my brother bought me a ticket. They are playing Quadrophonia which way one of my favourite albums growing up, it's also a movie. It's basically about a misfit, alienated youth named Jimmy. He was into drugs a lot, music, and acting like he was tough. I kind of related to that growing up, not feeling that i fit in. It isn't necessarily a bad thing because you look around the world and what are you supposed to buy into, the world that man has created is a mess. It's all about greed and corruption, selfishness and despair, everyone for themselves. I believe it's a good thing not to fit into that. It's important to think for yourself and decide for yourself what's right and wrong. Also, i felt that drugs although kind of an escape and also feel that getting high was a way of getting the feeling of elation, like touching the divine. Also expanding the mind or experiencing a different reality. I wouldn't recommend it though. It's just too dangerous, especially now, because i think it's not good to open oneselves spirit up in this day and age because of all the dark energies around. Now i can get the feeling of touching God and it's for real, it's cheap, it's easy, and it's safe. In fact, there is nothing can compare it in the world of man.

When i mentioned my faith in Jesus is unbreakable, shortly thereafter i was led to Sears at a mall out of town. I rarely go to this store. There was a T-shirt with the Statue of Liberty on it, which was a sign Jesus gave me when he first returned to my life and the captions reads, unbreakable.

I was glad to go to the thrift store and i found a book with King David on the cover slaying Goliath. I instantly knew it was sign of guidance of who i needed to call upon for help with the Goliath's in my life. i just wanted to confirm that in the recent past i had felt that St. Michael the archangel was helping me to defeat one long-time foe and David was helping me with another. I was at a coffee shop on the Toronto waterfront sitting at the spot my Father and i used to sit, and there i prayed that these individuals be removed from my path as well as to stop interfering with my family, and I was invoking King David in my prayer, i swear to God that just then there was a jazzy song playing on there music system and it said, "David was small but mighty..." and it made reference to how he defeated Goliath...i believe this is by Bob Kauflin and Jason Hansen. Even for myself these things almost seem surreal but when you walk with God you are conversing with him constantly and miracles become every day occurrences. I needed to write about this so i picked up a notepad because I didn't want to wait. So i was writing on the subway and when i finished, i literally said to God i want more of this, what next? I looked up and there was an advertisement to sign up for a free session at the Kabbalah centre. I had just picked up a book on this and again i had the sense that this is what God was leading me to. All of this occurred i believe directly because of the prayers i sent to the halocaust victims.

I heard something on the news that it was estimated that approximately 3,000 Native American children died in Catholic schools. I'm not sure if that was just in Canada but this is a perfect example of how obviously these people who removed these children from their homes and families could not have been acting from the will of the Father. Do you think this is that Jesus would have done? It must have been the influence of the enemy and look how much damage he did by dividing people. This is what he does. This type of intolerance and indignation has also pushed people away from church. We all have to understand and recognize how he works so we can more easily reach a place of awareness and then forgiveness so that bridges can begin to be built it is only in coming together that we can defeat our common enemy. We also need to understand that we are all the same and that there is one God.

I went to see a local theatre do Godspell yesterday. I didn't realize the song Day by Day was in it. Also this week, Hair is playing and one of the songs is "Dawning of the Age of Aquarius/Let the Sunshine In", by Fifth Dimension. I know this is no coincidence it reminds me of around 1971, i remember what a beautiful time that was. I feel that that energy is returning both to my personal life and to the world in general. I'm learning that there is a shift. Trudeau was Prime Minister at that time and i just remember what a happy, optimistic time that was in Ontario and Canada and in my life. We need to bring back the light into our country and the world. I remember the 70's as something very special and it stays with my heart. It seemed like a perfect world at that time.

I have nothing against Pope Benedict but i feel the shift has something to do with a change there as well. Maybe just because the new Pope will be more youthful and vibrant and will bring a higher energy. The shift is on and it's an exciting time.

How does it go "... in with you more nearly, loving you more dearly Lord, day by day ..." This was in Godspell but apparently written by St.Richard of Chichester.

I felt guided to contact my old teacher and friend, Many Horses, i was resistant at first but spirit was persistent. It's always good to connect with true friends. There is so much crap sometimes it's just nice to know there are highly evolved people out there that love, appreciate and support you. It was nice to connect and i informed him of some spiritual issues i was dealing with and he confirmed what i thought and gave me some advice.

I had a dream that night where there were many native warriors and i didn't know at the time who the person was they were confronting put they put many arrows into him. As i lay there thinking about it, i recalled a dream i was having previously and there was another person who is often in my dreams that is lumped with the other two that i have had trouble with. The bottom line is don't question. If spirit keeps guiding you to do something. Don't think you're too big or important to call upon a friend for help and be grateful to all people and appreciate all people and do what you can for all people because you don't know who's going to come to your aid one day. It's beautiful how things happen. It also just opens up new or old doors again. I ran into a couple of other old friends today who are very much into the Native American teachings. No such thing as coincidence.

I was just thinking about whether i should go to this Kabbalah seminar on Sunday and immediately on t.v. they showed a commercial that showed a tree growing and then apples appearing. This is almost the same picture that is on the cover of this book 10 minute Kabbalah, Blessings, Wisdom and Guidance from the Tree of Life that i feel recently guided to purchase.(by Shoshanna Cohen).

Today being March 1, 2013 is the world day of prayer. Last night, i saw the play Hair with the song, This is the Dawning of the Age of Aquarius/Let the Sunshine In. I have been seeing a wheel being turned, representing a changing of the power structure, an overthrowing of certain energies and possibly people. It's going to be truly amazing. I know that this will affect my personal life as well as the world.

Just been thinking about understanding and following God's will in terms of Adam and Eve vs. Mary and Joseph. One gave into temptation and ignored God and created original sin, the other by following and accepting God's will created the birth of our savour. To understand and accept his will is no small thing.

I've been thinking about the concept of wanting a permanent love but we can't own anyone's love. We can own his love that is permanent. We share love. When we connect with his love then i am love and share it with everyone i meet without possessing or controlling or needing or expecting anyone in return. Getting too attached in romantic relationships is still a struggle for me.

I had a vision where i was standing in a stream of living water. As i walked up the stream, i saw Jesus was there. As i looked down into the water, i saw a beautiful fish looking up at me. I wanted to pick it out of the water and hold it but if i did that, the fish would die. I think this metaphor also represented someone in my life and a difficult lesson for me on allowing and not possessing, about freedom and letting go of control and expectations of the other person, and living more in the moment and going with the flow. I new the Lord was right in the middle of this situation and teaching me. I'm trying to remember that God brought us together and he alone knows the future. I also feel that when we look at someone and feel love, it's like God recognizing himself in the other person. When i stay in the place of love rather than fear attachment doesn't seem to happen.

I went to Wasaga Beach and the hotel i booked just happened to be right next door to a church. I kept hearing the words "revival meeting" and didn't know what it meant and as i attended the church service, there was a shelf with the wooden letters revival right in front of me. Obviously it was very significant for me to be there today both for prayers that i said and issues that seemed to be helped but especially in giving my burden to God and Jesus and letting them carry it for me and trusting that the outcome of a certain situation is in his hands and i should stop worrying so much. When getting too attached to the physical world, i.e. relationships, it helps to start shifting the focus on heaven. It just brings so much peace and reveals God's blessings at work. It reminds us of how we have to keep things in perspective.

When getting guidance, i often get false guidance from spirit trying to mess with me and provoke my fears. It's my fault for not grounding myself first, surrounding myself in with white light. Also i found reading a page or two of the Bible helps to remove negative energy and spirits and help bring higher guidance in. When reading a passage i tend to just open it and trust that's where i need to read. While in Wasaga i read one part with Moses, and i felt he helped a great deal by washing alot of negative spirits away that were around.

I'm trying to learn to live in the moment more, the present lasts forever. But do it with love and faith, that is what freedom is. I've been experiencing a lot of guidance that has been trying to conjure up things and exploit my fears and push my buttons. It's been a good and challenging experience to learn how to better rely on my connection to Jesus to set me straight and receive his guidance. He keeps saying to me to use discernment, so i have been trying to work on the best method personally to do that and i feel it is a very personal thing that you do to know what you're getting is real. He often has been telling me to stay in the heart. One reason he tells me that is that when i am fearful and can't hear him so well and, i have to realize that i have to be very careful what i hear or see or experience. When i am relaxed i am better able to receive good guidance. I found and was told that writing out what i was getting from Jesus to be much more trustworthy than what i was hearing. Also, i now ask if i am unclean, if this is coming from God or the light. I only accept and fully believe what comes from him. I found that saying prayers while in church or after reading the bible to work really well.

I've found that the energetic attachments that people have made from past relationships can still be there, can be very real and can hold us back, and need to be looked at with spiritual eyes and removed.

These i feel are referred to as psychic cords or other types of energetic attachments can be viewed and can be cut using our own mind or calling upon Michael to use his flaming sword. Sometimes, you can also see chains attached to people's ankles or wrists, or hand and arms holding onto their physical parts and certainly sexual attachments both to their genital area and chakras have to be removed. There is also attachments on a soul level (i heard referred to as ungodly soul ties in the Freedom Series by Peter Horrobin from Ellel Ministries). These attachments can seriously interfere with the person's freedom or forward movement and are also ways that people can maintain some control over the other, often there can be energies or spirits that can be involved as well, also they can stronly affect or control a person's sexual energy. Attachments are also made in the mind making a person feel that they still need the former person in some way or influences over their thoughts and behaviours. The attachments can be made elsewere as well and are very real and can be powerful.

Unimaginable blessings can come from saying Hail Mary's, The Lord's Prayer (Our Father) and the 23rd Psalm.

I had heard from a former girlfriend that she read in a Michael book that often, he would leave a feather to show that he is there. The other day, i was saying some intense prayers and Michael was invoked and sure enough, i found a large white feather right at that moment. A sign that He is near. Bless him. Jesus said to me that, "it's easy to see when the light is on."

You have to stay pure, the temptation is always there to stray. Pure and simple it is the devil trying deceive you and play games with you. We are all tempted but we must resist if we wish to be a child of God. We must stay in the heart and love. If we give into the temptation, we lose ourselves, we lose our soul, we lose our self-worth. It's not worth it. Remember that's what the Garden of

Eden is all about and it's just as real today. Staying in the heart often results in getting hurt in the world; but it is the very fact that you stay in the heart, your self-love, love of and from God, love of God, love of life, goodness and kindness that brings you through and allows you to triumph over everything and face the new day with your head held up high.

In trying to compose an e-mail to someone concerning a very delicate matter (and i had been asking all day for help), i got a phone call from Crossroads Ministry and a woman talked for a bit and then she asked if there was anyone that needed prayers. I told her about the situation and i also asked she pray for me to be guided. I told her that i was trying to compose an e-mail and she told me to pray to the Holy Spirit and ask for his words to be given to me, because they would make an impact on the person. The words seemed to flow when i typed. Thanks be to God and Jesus and the Holy Spirit for answering my prayer in my time of great need.

For a while, i lost the strength of my connection to Jesus. He said, "not so." Okay then, i feel that i lost some clarity because today, i was able to channel him much clearer than i had in a long time and there's no greater and rewarding and reassuring thing then 'knowing' that he's the one talking.

I had heard from spirit, "now you're ready for a course in miracles." I tried to sign up for two of these courses by that name and reached dead ends. At the same time, i was sent an e-mail from the Kabbalah Centre inviting me to a new moon meditation. (i hadn't been there or heard from anyone there in six months.) When i got to the meditation, the first thing he said was this new moon was about making miracles happen. I decided to take the second and third levels of the class to see if this would help get my life working better.

I have been put into a very difficult situation with some other individuals, one day, i found myself reaching upwards and connecting to God and bringing his energy into the place to bring in light to the place and situation.

The next day, i was put into a difficult situation again and i asked God, where are you? Why am i being tormented like this? I heard from spirit that i had a lesson to learn. I realized or was told i had to stop giving my energy away to the negativity and put my focus on the light or God or positive things. I became empowered when i did this. That night at class, our teacher, was teaching about the same thing. On my way home from class, i heard his spirit tell me, "let the light lead you," he also told me that he would help me.

At church, the minister, talked about how God has a way of providing for you what you need on a daily basis. This reminded me of what my teacher said at the Kabbalah Center had said. At home that night, the song that was playing as i was talking to my friend about this stuff was "... Life has a way of helping you out ..." By Alanis Morrisette. Then a little later, the Rolling Stones song Can't always get what you want..."but if you try sometimes, you'll find you get what you need."

In an awkward situation i became aware of the support and energy from one of my friends supporting me and spiritually holding my left hand. Jesus also guided me to avoid some people. When one of the people came close by i heard my Kabbalah teacher's voice say, "The restaurant is closed", which is an expression he used in class, to stop feeding an unpleasant situation, stop giving your energy away to it. God does provide everything we need, including wonderful people who are brought into our lives to support and guide.

I had a situation earlier where I felt the movie, the Jackie Robinson movie, was purposeful for me to see. I even felt his spirit. He was all alone and was encouraged to not fight back but to lift himself above and be better than them. Also, you see how a few bright lights come into his life in a sea of darkness but those bright lights made all the difference to show you are not alone and that God is watching and sending you angels. The Kabbalah teaches that we bring ourselves those situations to overcome so they are actually blessings providing us opportunities for growth.

I was getting ready to leave on vacation felt i was led to heal and release and to get my spirit and desire for life back again. One day on the beach as i wrote about the situation suddenly music from someone in front of me (it was silent before then) sang "Don't worry, be happy", this is by Bobby McFerrin. God's always helping you out!

I remind myself that you have to trust God to bring into your life what you need. It may not always be what you want, though, but it's putting our trust in him. I'm hearing, "please play the cards your dealt." If it doesn't contain love, it's no good. Love means respect and honesty and caring. Without love, there is nothing. Without being selfish, i know i need to put the focus back on myself and my own life. Enjoying my own experiences and feeling good about what i do and who i am. Also you can still love someone but don't give your life to someone who hasn't earned it and doesn't deserve it.

I was reading the book, The Secret, which talks about when you're feeling alone or lost or hurting or selfish or unhappy it's because your connection to the Creator has been lost and you need to strengthen it. I know this and have even written about it but it's easy to forget. Suffering is caused by wanting or needing, an emptiness is inside you that wants to be filled. When you fill yourself with the light, sun, God, Creator, you become fulfilled and don't need anything. You also become a giver or channel of the light and the light seems to lead you and provide you without effort on your part (or minimal). Just paying attention to where you led. When you want or become selfish or needy, you cut yourself off.

When i am missing someone, i think i may have been living vicariously through them and this is why i need to focus more on myself and my experience in life as authentic and valid. I have to enjoy my own experience which is a walk with God and, therefore, i am never alone but blessed and fascinated by the fullness of the experience. The Secret, a book written by Yehuda Berg, talks about being like the Creator. This reminds me of Stalking Wolf (Grandfather from Tom Brown Jr.) telling me in a spiritual development class, "to be like a sunflower, always keeping your face towards the sun...as the sun moves across the sky the sunflower turns to face it," an interesting metaphor I think. I see the sun like God, both figuratively and perhaps literally, radiating his light into the world. By staying connected your strong, independent fulfilled and a giver of the light, a channel, when you keep yourself sustained by His light and love there is no need.

My Kabbalah teacher, also recommended that this was the best way to deal with my situation, to bring the light in which gave me the confirmation that i was on the right path.

I gave a lot of energy in a relationship and feel its loss because of the attachments and expectations i had to the energy and person, i was needing that this expenditure of energy would bring certain results in terms of a return of energy. It's a matter too of knowing when to stop giving your energy away. Stop feeding it. Also remember how to replenish your energy from the source and how to stop expecting a return from another person. But if that person isn't able to return an equal amount of energy, is it a suitable relationship for you. There needs to be a balance of give and take. The old saying it takes two to make a relationship work is true and both have to be willing to surrender certain things of themselves, they can't have it both ways. If a person can't give themselves freely, there's no way to force them. Follow the light. Let the light lead you.

It's been reminded and suggested by the Kabbalah teachings that judgment is something you have to be very careful about. In situations where a person is exhibiting behaviours we don't agree with, we have to be careful not to take on a superior attitude, thinking us better. We have to always be aware of our own ego and what the things we witness in our lives are telling us or showing us about ourselves.

If I am witnessing it, the Kabbalah would say it's being witnessed because it's a correction i have to make on some level within. In any event, that's all i can do is to fix myself and be as an example or to point the way. A friend of mine reminded me that Jesus told his disciples that if you are not respected or your guidance is not welcomed, leave and wipe your feet at the door. Walk away.

Lately, i have had the chance to see Godspell again, the best play i have ever seen, by Michael Tebelak. I saw the movie Son of God and i watched Chariots of Fire again. I've never seen a more inspiring movie. I believe i heard Eric Liddell's voice say to me, "Be as a light in a dark room." I also got a piece of mail that said, "Stand strong, never give up," and i felt it was God directed.

I was at a female friend's place and i had a vision of Mother Mary standing beside the bed giving healing and comfort and i believe i heard her tell me to return to Mass. On the Thursday before Easter, i had a vision of Jesus washing the feet of myself and my friend.

The Kabbalah class talks about the 'blessed and the cursed.' The cursed are the ones that succumb, that give up. The blessed are the ones that find the 'light' and rise above. Focus on the light. Look for the light in a situation. God is always at work.

I've been dealing with a very difficult personal situation. Jesus has said to me, remember who brought you and i will be there with you to the end. There's a lot of negative energy around this situation and Michael told me last week he would be with me as well. I found a feather close to where i was and I knew Michael had left it there.

Jesus always said to me to don't hate the people involved. It's okay to hate the actions and the energy or spirits that reside in dark minds. But forgive and forget and to walk away. Stand strong in your faith it is your shield and your armour. God reminds me "I will give you the strength to overcome all adversaries."

I continually prayed to lift my spirit and raise my energy above the negativity. Time and time again, i also felt and saw signs that God was sending me help. "You never stand alone when you do the Lord's work." Many times people would come to me to help and they didn't even realise they were sent or that there spirit's or energy were helping me. I became involved in alot of spiritual warfare with some individuals that very negative. I felt i was guided to. They all seemed to work together. I knew that Jesus had brought into a situation and it's the second time i have been put somewhere to battle this type of stuff. This is after long and extensive personal battles that i have had on my own. Some of the details i have not talked aboutof what i have experienced. I remember my teacher Jean telling me years ago that people who go through what i have are going through it for a reason. Either it's to teach others about it or to help others who are experiencing it. I was closely guided as to how to proceed. Many times the right person would just appear. One is an old friend of mine who is a strong warrior. When he showed i knew i was being guided to fight. There was another who i barely knew who i saw his spirit bow before me and offer his sword. He is an independent person obviously with a strong sense of right and wrong. There were a few others that helped me in such ways and it just shows the power of God, but also give credit to the high characters of these people. One time someone was sending me negative energy i could feel his hand on my throat, immediately a large friendly fellow stepped in front of me and blocked it. It truly is amazing.

I again am reminded of the healing and cleansing power present in water and sunlight. Also lately, i am astonished by the healing energy i have received from trees. I've also have been recovering with help from the Kabbalah Centre. I feel that it has helped bring a lot of light in and raise the despair. Although when i felt most desperate it was time to more fully embrace my Catholic faith.

Part of my process of healing the wounds of a past relationship entailed visiting those places (a lot of times seemingly by chance) that i had been before with that person. It seemed like it laid a new memory on top of the old one, like paving over a road. Or going some places brought out emotions that i needed to release not just with that person it also helped in the past in dealing with grief with my parents.

I often talk about my most recent past life to explain to people that it must be authentic because it was so unexpected. In my most recent life, i was killed or at least my family was killed, by allied bombers during the Second World War. When i did the reggression, i came down through a midst of bombers and found myself as a child pulling bricks away from the rubble of the building my parents were trapped in. The other day, i was walking towards my car. Suddenly, there was this noise and coming directly over my head flying low was an allied bomber. At the same time, a crow was cawing. So i knew it meant something significant. I have also been this week releasing and reviewing my attachment level to a past partner. I believe this and may be another past life where i died young, explain why i get deeply attached when i shouldn't be. It also explains why i had severe separation anxiety when i was young. I think this occurred about the same age. I have to mediate on that past life and leave that condition there. (As my teacher Jean's guides.) I feel i may use a rattle to summon lost spirit or energy that i had left there as well while releasing the past, we have to bring our spirits or energy back but leave the condition behind. I believe this also has to do with these situations where i am being ganged up on by a number of people, as this is the second time it has occurred. I think this is partly why it was important for me to fight and overcome. There are so many layers to things.

On Father's Day, I had a surprising blessing. While at mass, i had a clear vision of my father all in white, some type of robe and a pious looking hat. I feel that his transformation is complete. OK, i know it's never ending.

I was with a friend in Toronto at a waterfront festival and i told her of a time being there with my parents and i paid to take them on this 1½ hour sail. It was a total rip-off because there were problems with the sails and nothing was done about it in regards to a refund. My Mother was disappointed and i was hurt by that and still bitter as i felt my Mother was often short changed. My friend and i walked along and a girl, within five minutes of being there, asks if we would be interested in going on a free sail. It was just a small boat but it was fun and it was just another reminder of the prizes that accompany a walk with God. i kind of felt my Mother's spirit must have went on board with us there was another time when i was there by myself and i couldn't help recalling that bad experience and believe it or not i had the distinct feeling that Jesus took both of my parents out sailing with him on that day. I remember seeing my Mom with her sunglasses with this band and her hair wind swept and i remember afterwards hearing my Dad saying very clearly and excitedly "what a day."

I've had a long battle trying to get work done at my condo (foundation) and now to get them to come back and complete the patio, but something has been telling me that divine timing is involved and it's all somehow related to events regarding my own path. It seems like on so many levels that a completion is about to take place. Or a solid foundation is being put in place. On a different matter i seem to have some type of connection to the 1812 war. It started when i found an 1812 coin in my Mother's belongings, i was told it meant "my victory." I started finding these commemorative 1812 coins in my change and I only seemed to get one after a significant event. I feel alot of it corresponded to helping a particular person, without getting into personal details. Other things that happened also had to do with places that were significant for that war. I should also mention that a very strong guide of mine was a soldier during that war and i met him at the fort in Niagara On The Lake. I guess it's just that the spirit world is fascinating and is always trying to tell us things in a very unique and personal manner. It's always with us if we but stay alert.

I can often detect the presence of that so called 'noogies' by a sudden feeling of needing to use the bathroom or generally an unsettling feeling in the lower areas. I have been dealing with removing them by a certain method but lately, i recalled how using a drum and calling 'kway' to what the Native American's refer to as the direction keepers, they helped the problem with hydro at my house and i have since found to be helpful in removing them. They can seriously influence people and disrupt their purity by enticing addictive behaviour.

Up north on vacation and my friend wanted to go to mass. We didn't make the local one so had to go a bit of a distance. As we were sitting in the car waiting, six crows came and landed on top of the roof, three of them directly on the cross itself. My friend said, Father, Son and Holy Ghost. She's learning.

Also had a blue jay nearby. On the altar, i had a vision of a buffalo, standing there. Turns out this Catholic Church (St. Joseph's) was on or near an Indian reserve. My friend mentioned the native saint Kateri Tekakwitha on the way back. As she looked her up on her blackberry i had a vision of her behind us in a native dress and her hands holding something at her chest. It resembled the picture my friend was looking at as she was holding a cross to her chest. I just found it very beautiful how these two cultures or faiths had found a way to merge together here.

Another amazing event happened in St. Jacob after vising the Angel store and a few other places where i found spiritual items, we were walking back to the car and there on the path before our feet was a rainbow. We could see both very clearly. There was no water on the ground from rain or sprinklers and not even a hint of rain in the sky. I have never seen that before.

I just find that these two are prime of examples of God and spirit showing signs when we are on the right track. Doing the right things, buying the significant item. I have for many years had a lot of signs from hawks and crows that seem to flank path or fly directly over my head or show a direction or caw to give me a message. These two birds have been my meat and potatoes in terms of signs for many years now. Bless them. I know it all started by reading the Ted Andrews book, Animal Speak. No kidding, it started right afterwards. The gifts that God brings amazes me. Right people at the right time, being at right place. It's awesome, ever fails to capture my sense of wonder and feelings of being blessed and loved.

The other day, i felt i spoke with the Buddha. I feel he has come to me a few times before to help bring peace. He reminds me "that peace is found in the mind." "He says that the age of light is at hand." I asked why he was here and he said "it's simple because you enjoy being free. He says be a slave to no man or woman."

He reminds me that, "The mind creates the physical. He says it's good to enjoy pure and simple things. Do your duty and resist thoughts that are impure." I accept help from all sources of light. God bless.

When i went to the chiropractors office, which was in the same building i used to visit with my first doctor. My old doctor's spirit visited me in the waiting room, a very gentle and compassionate man. He's there to give me help, he's still a doctor on the other side.

The quest for inner perfection is the course to travel. Finding the peace, tranquillity and love within yourself. No one can do it for you. You're not alone. You have help along the way. We're guided to rise above our own faults and feeling at one with the God that created us, our true nature. No one can stop us, only ourselves. It's our path that makes us wise, if we choose to listen to above.

Keeping clean in spite of being uninvolved requires discipline. Bicycling seems to help me use up my reserves of energy that are pent up. It helps to explore new areas and enjoy new things. The excitement of life, joy and creativity are all spun from the same place as sexual energy. Sexual energy wells up inside and needs to be expressed in good things that dont destroy your karma and caring attitude. Doing household chores also frees you; uses your time wisely, not wasting it on wanton ways, filled with desires. Treat yourself to good, wholesome rewards. Keep your reserves full. Don't give it away to just anyone. Choose wisely. It's energy. How you deploy it depends on you.

Went to a spa that i go to occasionally when I need to unwind. I've seen Jesus the time before and this time, wringing a cloth. I felt he was showing me he's releasing those pent up sexual feelings but also releasing memories and energy from the past. I find the steam room especially useful and this is where he seemed to want me to release. Said some prayers which i felt helped. I was shown a gateway to a new beginning. I heard "success"and"leave it to me." I apologized to Jesus if i had trouble keeping pure thoughts and actions and said, "It's easy, just be him."How can I? I said, He said, "Attempt it."

Acting in ways that lessen ourselves, we are giving our powers, our energy away. Being keen to keep what is ours and proud of who we are becoming is key. "Go the way of God and flowers bloom in your footsteps." That is fulfilling. There needs to be fulfilment on the spiritual. The physical needs to be part of God's plan, not man made, heaven sent. If you don't, stay connected to God/spiritual then life feels void of any purpose or meaning.

I went to a wedding up in the Muskokas and i feel it helped bring a profound change. I forgot how beautiful it was but it also brought back very powerful memories of childhood. Both on fishing/cottaging trips with my Father but also a time when i was sent to a Christian camp in the area and first found Jesus. I remember accepting Jesus when i was up there and feel that being there now brought some of that time and the energy of my childhood experiences back into my life. I can't help but think of the power and memory that is stored in these old rocks here.

I also felt the presence of my native guides while there and their blessings. On the way home, i 'accidentally' went through a native reserve. I realize that it probably wasn't an accident and needed to connect with their power as well. The presence of God is felt in those places of supreme beauty. About the Native American reservation again, the day after returning from the trip up north i went for a drive to Port Dover, the highway was closed because of work on the powerlines and i had to detour through the Six Nations reservation. Okay i get it, i need some of their support. During this time i was saying prayers invoking Mother Mary and i felt an umbrella was put above me as protection. I was having a bad night dealing with things from my past and feeling discouraged. In the mail i received a calendar. It said "Always Believe"; and "Good things come to those who believe. Better things come to those who are patient, and the best things come to those who never give up." Author unknown.

These things seem to happen all the time. Messages and support from God and support from the light when you need them most. At the same time, i got a prayer card from St. Thérèse and again, it's a reminder to never stop praying.

I had a dream and a couple of energies were in it that are best described as zombies. When i found two dead baby rabbits trapped in a window well on my property, i remembered a dream i had years ago of these two energies (i won't describe them) eating rabbit after rabbit that were coming out of a hole in the earth. I feel the rabbits represent fertility and obviously they seemed to be taking that from me. Around this time, i decided to get a gold chain out of a safety deposit box. I thought i might sell it but thought again. I was guided to the most frequent thrift store and i heard the word synchronicities. I was walking around and as i went to the jewellery area, two people were inquiring about a gold chain. I stopped next to them, after they left, i had a closer look. I felt Jesus was telling me to move to the right and there was a large gold cross. I felt I was meant to buy it and wear on that gold chain. As I was standing in line, i looked to my right and there was a sign that said, "Zombie containment area." (the store was in the process of getting all decked out for Halloween.) Nevertheless, i felt that this was the key to solving the issue. I also pulled an Angel card that said call upon Michael to help with this situation. Also those detours that took me onto the reservations i felt was definitely a sign for me to call upon the Native American spirits and guides and direction keepers to help me out. As i was getting back on the main road, i was told to ask for a sign and i did so and almost immediately there was a billboard that said "every life counts." I felt very strongly that God was directing me to see that.

I have been having an issue with my left arm and a very good friend of mine, who is a very devout Catholic, was next to me and i heard her spirit commanding that "it get out." I know that she was referring to a negative spirit that was causing this problem. I've had visions of my left arm being held behind my back and my teacher Jean saw this as well. Then later, i have seen it being stretched out like 'elasticman.' Jean said, "I had to go to where it was attached to and cut it." I've also seen a band tied around my arm and someone putting a needle in to draw something out of it. Another time i saw sometype of yellow electronic device on my right arm and i ended up going to physio for problems with my arm. When i battle certain individuals i am guided to i feel energy or light return to my arm and it gets stronger. Praying also helps, especially the Lord's Prayer.

During the course of this trial, i have felt the presence of many evil spirits that try to ruin things like 'noogies', necromancers, i have also seen two demons, and i have frequently had visions of snakes, like ones from the Garden of Eden. I have recently seen a snake that had about seven or eight heads on it and the faces were human. I recently had a vision of another spirit, a man with a black mask and a zipper for a mouth, no shirt and standing with arms crossed, blocking something. This is the type of stuff you need Michael and King David's help with.

I have had frequent visions of Jesus and he's sawing wood. This shows me he is working on it. I feel that we are getting close to conquering this enemy as lately i have seen him using a plane on His project and examining his work carefully. I recently had a dream (one reason we should pay close attention is because it can give us answer). In this dream, these two demons are collaborating. One is green and goes back to an old friend of mine i was having trouble with before. The other is red and i know who he walks with. As far as i know, these two people don't know each other in the physical. I saw what they were planning an attempt to cause harm to me.

I have recently seen things in these two peoples personal life go badly for them. You tell me who wins. Recently, i noticed a bees nest outside of my kitchen window and to me, it's a blessed sign from God that the bees are working on bringing honey and the fertility of life to me.

I have to tell another fascinating story of how spirit works. My friend had been wanting to go visit a certain thrift place in Burlington after i told her about it. I once found a beautiful cedar lined trunk there for $20 that i placed my parents' belongings in and put away, that was in 2008. (About six years ago). So we went and i found a little green steam cleaner that i had been wanting after my last one, which my Mother brought, leaked and caused me to have to get new floors in my condo. But i did it through insurance and it was a blessing in disguise. But lately, i kept thinking about the trunk and what a great find it was. I also found myself over the last week or so wanting to watch Pawn Stars and Storage Wars. It's all about finding hidden treasures.

Anyhow, i decided to take the trunk out and go through their stuff. i can't believe it, i found my Dad's two gold rings which i thought were stolen. I thought they were lost for good back shortly after my parents passed. The really interesting thing is, i found them a few hours before my Father's birthday. I know now that they were dropping hints for me to see so i would find what was misplaced. They say that they come around on anniversaries and I know it's true because i have felt them around for at least a few days prior. They also come around when you need them.

I decided to put stuff back in the cedar lined trunk. I felt i was being told to go buy some good steaks and i found some on sale. I kept hearing, "it's a special day." After a nice b.b.q., i was told to go to Bayfront Park, a favourite place of my Mother's, as i arrived, i went for a walk. A whole bunch of Canadian geese came in honking. I then heard a shot as a park conservation officer set it off to scare away the geese. As they took off, i heard the words "a find send-off." I had a vision of my Mother and Father walking into the late afternoon sun.

As i was going through all their stuff, i felt it was very helpful for me to go into the quiet and peace and to remember. It's helpful to go back to your roots and remember who you are and what's important. I heard my parents say, "It's up to you now to carry on!"

I feel much more positive and things are resolving. I remember my teacher J., saying that it takes a year in order to heal; and i feel this is definitely true in my case. I also feel that Mother

Mary spoke to me and said, "I had fought hard." I feel lately that more power had been given me and my prayers, i began petitioning St. Thérèse, as well as St. John Paul II and i feel that St. Jude had been very important to me as well. I had also found that when enclosing someone's energy inside of a gold cage of light, surrounded with crucifixes facing inward, i also at times put mirrors around them facing inward.

I was reminded about a baseball game I went to with my minister from the Baptist church a few years ago and on the train ride, i remember expressing to him what do you think it would be like if Jesus and the Buddha were sitting together in a coffee shop talking? Do you think they would be arguing? I think it would be wonderful to witness that. I think they would be talking about love, contentment, peace, etc. The very next day, i found a c.d. at the usual store, by Ravi Zacharias, Jesus talks with Krishna.

For me, Jesus is the Saviour, no doubt, but he works with other beings of light on the other side and they help each other to work for the common good of man and the earth. To bring peace and love and undsrstanding into the world. To connect man to the light, to heal, to embrace a Godly life and to be as friends to one another not to do harm. To share. To allow the light to enter into the world.

I would like to share a bit more about some of the other helpers. When Buddha came recently, it wasn't the first time. He brings peace and a few times he seemed to have a cobra with him, which to me was a protection. I have seen King David quite a bit recently and i find that he often has two lions with him. He has a chain for a leash and has one in each hand. Of course he has a slingshot with him as well. When doing prayers for Pope John Paul 11 (now Saint) would come and he often had a stick in which he would knock away things that were attached, like psychic cords, and i am sure other stuff. St. Thérèse often shows up carrying a doctor's bag to do healing. Michael, i frequently call upon him and sometimes i will catch a glint from the silver shaft of his sword, or of him using his spear to stab something on the ground. One i have felt guided to call sometimes and is very powerful but rarely have mentioned him (mostly to keep it secret to protect our connection) is Ganesh, he frequently smiles and has a very benevolent presence, he likes to hug. I have often been led to find his figure or frequently will come across an East-Indian friend when i need to call upon him, so i will take the opportunity to ask for his assistance. I feel he's much like Michael and is good at helping to clear the path for you, he's very strong. He wanted me to share this. When i asked, i could feel his presence and this is all with respect and permission of course of The Lord Jesus Christ.

I have for a while now been aware of a noose spiritually and energetically. My friend also saw this. I believe this was the cause of my neck problems and believe it was kind of a persecution laid out for me by some evil people.

One evening, i was told to kneel and pray. I did so and i felt King David's presence with me very strongly as i left the house. I believe he wasn't the only one. (i have to avoid revealing some information here) As i getting ready to leave the house i noticed a spider on the wall. When i arrived were i was going, there was a newspaper there with a picture of a hangman's noose on it (advertising for a play) called, And Then There Was None, by Agatha Christie. This was later put in my face again to show me the solution to the problem to remove the noose. God knows everything that's going on and guides you through it when you deal with the dark side.

The situation with my arm was so real on a spiritual level that i awoke after some sleep one morning and my left biceps was sore again, this time there was a large bruise on it with fingermarks and no one had touched me there in the physical, nor did i bang into anything. When i later checked the mail, i had an advertisement from the Bradford exchange that had a picture of Jesus with his arms outstretched and said, "Our Lord Triumphant." I feel that i was definitely battling with the devil and winning. I had a visit from Michael, the Archangel, tonight. I was watching a video of the show The Office. When it finished, he said, "good show." He told me that "i have done enough fighting." "To leave it alone and let God work his miracle." "Don't try to fix anything, just smile and point the way." I heard Jesus say, "That the Father wants me to walk away from this mess." I had a vision of me walking forward into the light and leaving behind a bunch of smoke. Today, i had a vision of someone rowing a boat and i heard "Michael rowed the boat ashore." Either way, i feel that i am making a life change that will allow for new and brighter beginnings in my personal and spiritual life. Hallelujah.

The Father wanted me to add one parable, a man is walking down a beach picking up a black stone and throwing it away into the ocean. He says "It's like this when you confess your sins to us." "You give it to me and you are clean." Amen.

Bibliography

Andrews. Animal Speak. The spiritual and magical powers of creatures great and small: Llewellyn publishing, St. Paul, Minnesota,1996

Arrien. The Four-Fold Way. Walking the paths of the warrior, teacher, healer and visionary: Harper-Collins publishing, New York, New York 1993.

Bercholz, Chodzin.Entering The Stream.An introduction to the Buddha and his teachings. Shambhala pub.1993.

Berg, Michael.The Secret: The Kabbalah Cenre.New York, New York.as well Los Angeles, CA., 2002. Bro.Edgar Cayce on Dreams: Warner Books.New York, New York.1968.

Brown, Dufresne. A journal of Love and Healing.Transcending Grief: Hay House Inc., Carlsbad, California, 2001.

Brown. The Quest. New York, New York: The Berkeley Publishing Group.,1991.

Castenada. The Teachings of Don Juan. A Yaqui Way Of Knowledge: University of California Press, Berkeley, California.1968.

Dyer. Your Sacred Self: Harper Collins publishing Inc., New York, New York.1995.

Gratton, Mahatma 1 and11. The I Am Presence: Light Technology publishing, Sedona, Arizona.1994. Horrobin. The Freedom Series.(audio):Ellel Ministies,Lithia,Florida.2011.

Holy Bible. King James Version: Memorial Bibles Inernational Inc.1974. Lee. To Kill A Mockingbird: J.B.Lippincott Company.1960.

Mails. The Hopi Survival Kit: Penguin Books Inc., New York, New York.1997.

Moore. Care Of The Soul: Harper Collins publishing Inc., New York, New York.1995.

Newman, Berkowitz, Owens.How To Be Your Own Best Friend: Random House publishing group. New York, New York,1971.

Piper.Desiring God. (cassettes) 2006 Novel Audio,Inc., Muttnomah publishing, Inc.1986. Destiny God Foundation.

Ravenwolf.Angels, Companions in Magick.Llewellyn publications. St.Paul, Minnesota.1996. Redfield, Adrienne. The Celestine Prophecy. An Experiential Guide: Warner BrothersInc. New York, New York.1995.

Rinpoche. The Tibetan Book Of Living And Dying: Harper Collins publishers. New York, New York.1993.

Sams. Sacred Path Cards.The discovery of self through Native teachings: Harper Collins Publishers, New York,New York.1990.

Sams, Garson. Medicine Cards. Bear and Co.1988.

Schneider, Pieroth.Archangels and Earthangels: Arcana publishing.Twin Lakes, Wisconsin,2000. Sun Bear, Wind, Mulligan. Dancing With The Wheel.The medicine wheel workbook: Simon and Schustet, New York, New York,1991.

Thurston, Fazel.The Edgar Cayce Handbook For Creating Your Future: Ballantine Books Inc., New York, New York,1992.

Virtue. Archangels and Ascended Masters: Hayhouse Inc., Carlsbad,California,2003. Poems Ehrmann, Max.Desiderata.1927.copyright renewed 1954, Ehrmann, Bertha. Shoffstall, Veronica.Comes The Dawn.

Van Dyke, Henry. Standing By A Seashore.

About The Author

When I was about 10 years old my parents sent me to a camp where I met Jesus. He was by my side every night for a few years until I chose to leave based on something that happened in my life. It wasn't that serious what happened but it somehow stopped something inside me from being alive.

In my mid-thirties I began a spiritual search that was precipitated by a difficult relationship. I Began with many readings on books about Buddhism, Native-American teachings, Soul healing books, Carlos Castenada teachings. I Followed many teachers and did many studies and experienced and witnessed many things first hand for approximately 20 years. Then when things got really difficult in my life guess who's helping hand came to me in my time of need, both Jesus and His Mother.

The teachings I had in that time were not a mistake I felt I had to go on a search but also had to learn from personal experiences so I could share this experience with others...During this time I had become a Usui Reiki Master, a Spiritual healer, a dowser, a medium. I Have attended many workshops and Native-american circles. I Have taken spiritual development classes at a spiritualist church, healing classes at three different spiritualist churches taken a course on healing with the Holy Trinity, was involved with a high level meditation class for approximately ten years, have experienced several past-life regressions, I did one to one prayer sessions with a Spiritualist Minister and medium, Rev. Susan Di nsmore, for over a year and I took a mediumship course at Lillydale Spiriyualist Centre. There have been other teachings that include dowsing to adjust frequencies and energies, teachings about prayer ties by Many Horses, not to mention the hours of one to one discussions I had with the one who I consider not only my mentor but my brother. I also was led to take a number of courses at the Kabbalah centre, and this was after I was a devote Christian. Many years back I also had significant learning and experienc in working with what was referred to as the Mahatma energy or higher rays and Angel workshops.

I feel that my varied experiences are significant because it is a path of truth I have sought which needs to be experienced first hand.

Printed in the United States
By Bookmasters